THE WAY IT WAS

THE WAY IT WAS

Ted Wilson

This story is based on the life of the author. The events as related are as
factual as the memory of the author allows. The names, some occupations
and places mentioned have been changed.

This book was printed in the United States of America.

To order additional copies of this book, contact:
Xlibris Corporation
1-888-7-XLIBRIS
www.Xlibris.com
Orders@Xlibris.com

Dedicated to:
My son Craig, daughter Patti, grandson Dominic and granddaughter Jami. I share my past that they might see me other than as a father and grandfather.

ACKNOWLEDGEMENTS

My wife Jean, without her patience and assistance in the many, many hours of research, typing, drafting and computer skills, this story would not have been told and written.

My son Craig and his wife Suzanne for their advice, encouragement and guidance in obtaining resource material.

IN MEMORY

Of Zora, the mother I never knew, who gave birth to eight children, but was denied the right to be a mother to them. She lived in a world known only to her, a wasted life for fifty three years. A travesty of God's justice.

Zora, the child I learned to love, only in death could she find peace of mind she never had in life.

* * *

Of Ziv, the dad I didn't live with, who fathered eight children any man would be proud of. He lived a lifetime of regrets, a lonely man haunted by a mistake he made as a young man.

He died alone, the date unknown. May God forgive him— I did.

* * *

Of Marcus, my brother I only knew a few years as a fun loving young boy. We shared our lives briefly during the Depression of the thirties.

He died for a cause few remember, but how and where?

THE WOMEN IN MY LIFE

It has often been said that females are the weaker sex. Nothing is further from the truth. Throughout my life I have had the good fortune of having several foster mothers. Some of those times were happy, some unhappy. I shared their hardships, laughter, tears, pain, suffering and felt the love they had to offer. It never ceased to amaze me how adaptable they were to the unjust situations that fate chose to give them.

My story tells about those mothers and women in my life who helped me grow up through some difficult times, allowing me to live a happy, productive life.

Mrs. Hardy, Mrs. Gibson, Bessie Cooper, Ella Cooper, Nellie Perry, Hattie Schmidt and. . . . . Zora.

Dora, whose heart I broke.

Cassie, who broke mine.

My wife Annie who mended that broken heart and took me into her life and gave me a home and family. For over fifty years she has been my companion, lover and best friend.

INTRODUCTION

This is a story about a child who grew up in the Depression years of the thirties. It follows him through the war years, as a young man and post war years as a husband, father and grandfather.

It is told as seen through the eyes of a grandfather and comes out of the mind and heart of a young boy.

The events as related are as factual as the memory of myself, family and friends allows.

Now is the time to remember my past and share it with others.

FORWARD

Come, take a trip with me through the memories of my mind, as I retrace the footprints of my past. Laugh at me as I stumble through childhood, cry with me as I experience the trials and tribulations life has to offer, share the love I find in having a family of my own.

The past is for the old to reflect upon, not to dwell on or live in. It's like a dark night, you know what's out there, but can't see it clearly.

The present is for adults to live in, like the early morning sunrise. The promise of a new day. It is now.

The future is for the young, like a bright moon on a starry night full of life and hope to wonder and dream about.

I live in the present, tomorrow never comes—it is always today. Too soon all of those tomorrow's are the past.

Perhaps, reliving the past with me will help us to remember that love and a family are the most important things life has to offer.

Jean, Craig, Suzanne, Patti, Dominic and Jami you are my past, present and future. I LOVE YOU!

PROLOGUE

Ziv Sabitch was born in 1895 in Serbia, a Slavic country in Eastern Europe. His grandfather traveled to America, lived in New York for a short time, then returned to his family in Serbia. After listening to his grandfather talk about the wonders of New York, Ziv decided to go to America to seek his fortune.

He traveled by train from Serbia to Hamburg, Germany, then boarded the SS Graf Waldersee to immigrate to America. It was an uneasy trip for the passengers crowded aboard the ship as it plowed through rough seas. Suddenly a message came over the radio. The unsinkable British luxury liner Titanic, on her maiden voyage from England to New York, struck an iceberg in the Atlantic Ocean off the coast of Newfoundland and sank. More than 1,500 lives were lost.

Ziv was one of more than a million immigrants who arrived annually in the United States during the early 1900's. They looked for work in the booming industries that depended on cheap labor to fatten the pocketbooks of a wealthy few. The passengers and crew cheered loudly when the Statue of Liberty came into view. The SS Graf Waldersee sailed on to dock at Philadelphia, Pennsylvania in April, 1912.

* * *

Seventeen years old, Ziv had no formal schooling. He could not read, write or speak the English language, but was full of hope for the future. Ziv looked forward to finding a job, working a few years, making a lot of money, then returning to Serbia to buy a farm and become a wealthy land owner.

Ziv's first job was driving a team of horses, picking up garbage on the lower East side of New York where most Slavic immigrants were settling. He met Zora, an Albanian girl, at a dance and after a short courtship they were married. The yearly arrival of their children postponed Ziv's dream of making any money quickly and returning to Serbia. He wanted to become a United States Citizen and learn the American ways.

With the added responsibility of the children, he moved his family to Flint, Michigan, a fast growing industrial city. Ziv went to work in an automobile factory. General Motors Corporation, the main employer, had factories scattered throughout the city. The population consisted of many immigrants from Europe. The country's demand for automobiles created an industrial giant out of what used to be a quiet farming community.

*　　*　　*

This story is about a Serbian, Albanian family growing up in the Great Lakes area. It takes place from the stock market crash of 1929, to the year 2001.

The story revolves around one of the boys, Nick, who finds himself in an orphanage, and is told that his father and mother are dead. He runs away to search for his brothers and sisters.

Joseph, Nick's older brother, knows but refuses to talk about the reason for the family breakup, his father's absence or his mother's illness.

Nick's brother Marcus was tragically killed, But how? When? Where? Somehow he had to find out.

Let my story begin. . . . .

ONE

"May-cuss, Wa-yatt, Nee-ek, what are youse boys doing to that gurl? Get your pants on boys and little girl go home! I'll take care of deez hon-yocks so they won't bother you again!" The little girl was bigger and older than we were, and as I watched her running towards the woods, her bloomers in one hand and shoes in the other, Dad grabbed me and Watt each by an ear. Kicking Marcus in the rear he said, "A good whippen' will teach youse boys to re-spec gurls."

Marcus cried out, "But Dad, she asked for it when she held up her dress and pulled down her bloomers and said, "Do you boys wanta fruck?" I protested, "I didn't get a turn." Dad, said, "Your turn will come when you're older Nick." I was three and a half, Watt five and Marcus six and a half years old, the day we got our behinds spanked for looking at the nakedness of a willing girl. It was October, 1929, the stock market crashed and the Great Depression began.

*   *   *

Our family lived in the basement of an unfinished house with a wooden outhouse in the backyard, two blocks from the Fisher Body factory, at 200 Alley Street in Flint, Michigan. Ziv, my dad, a stocky, handsome man, had black curly hair. Zora, my mother, a blue-eyed beauty, was short and small boned with dark brown hair.

Twelve year old Joseph, the oldest child, had a slight build and wavy brown hair. Sonya, ten and a half, looked like mother. Hedy, nine, was tall for her age and had long blond hair and freckles. Marcus, Watt and I were look alike towheads. Younger brother Jay was a sickly two year old.

Mother had a bad time with the birth of Alfred, the last of our family. The midwife had Dad get a doctor to help with the delivery.

The basement was small and crowded for such a large family. We were always bumping into each other. Dad built two wooden-framed beds that fastened against the wall. He and Mother slept in one bed, with Jay and Alfred in a crib nearby. Sonya and Hedy shared a bed. A pile of small, thin mattress pads were stacked in a corner during the day. At night after we shooed the chickens out of the basement, we older boys spread the pads on the floor along one wall to sleep on.

Dad worked at the General Motors Fisher Body Plant hanging doors on car bodies as they went down the assembly line. He made thirty-two cents an hour. Our family owned a big, three-seat 1928 Buick that was used for special outings to Belle Lake for a swim and picnic. As we drove away, the neighbors muttered to each other, "That foreign hunky family has a big new car, but live like animals in a basement house."

The strain of raising the family and trying to make ends meet in such trying times caught up with Mother. The following spring she became ill and had to go to the hospital. It was May 30, 1930.

*   *   *

After the stock market crashed, living got mighty rough for us Sabitchs'. Dad's factory job was reduced to part-time, working only one to two days a week. With Jay, two and a half, Alfred a year younger, six other children, Mother in the hospital, Dad, thirty-five years old, was carrying a big, big load. A burden he had to shoulder alone. His American dream had turned into a nightmare.

Joseph worked part-time with Dad for our neighbors, the

Porters. They had an orchard and a fruit market, and Dad used their old Model T truck to peddle fruit around Flint. I liked riding in the back of the truck, smelling the fruity aroma of apples, peaches and pears. I couldn't understand why it was so hard to sell the fruit. Everybody was hungry and stood in long lines to get some food to eat.

My big brother Joseph, worldly at age thirteen, told me, "Nick, times are tough, but they are going to get a lot tougher."

To me, a boy of four, the economics of the times didn't mean a thing.

* * *

A neighbor woman occasionally helped with the washing, cooking, cleaning and taking care of the babies. Dad would pay her a quarter and sometimes fifty cents for helping around the house. With Sonya and Hedy helping, Dad managed somehow to keep the family together.

My older brothers and sisters attended the Flint City school. I attended the neighborhood Greenway school. Dad went to school nights, where he struggled to learn English and to become an American citizen. He had a hard time communicating with people.

* * *

One night after class Dad stayed to meet with a group of men who had been laid off from the Fisher Body Factory.

He said, "Nick, you go outside and sit on the porch. This meeting shouldn't last too long."

It was quite dark out, so I sat on the porch in the light shining through the window. The men argued and talked in loud voices.

One man told dad, "The only reason you haven't been laid

off is you do the work of two men. You're keeping one of us from having a job."

Dad protested, "I've got to work. My wife's in the hospital and I have eight children to feed. Working one or two days a week is better than none. I don't want to cause trouble and get fired."

* * *

The men were unhappy with the low pay and working conditions in the factory. It was time to organize and form a union so all workers received fair treatment from the Fisher Body Management.

The men planned to stage a strike outside the factory and keep the scab workers from entering until the Fisher management agreed to recognize a workers union. Dad didn't know what to do. He didn't want to be a scab, but couldn't afford to support any strike at this time.

Dad decided not to work the day of the strike or help in the union organization; instead he took me for a ride on the streetcar to downtown Flint. I got sick from the swaying motion so we walked back. It was a long, long walk for a little boy. As we strolled along the length of the Fisher Body factory, I noticed police cars in front of the plant. Dad told me the workers were trying to form a union to represent them. I couldn't understand why the workers wanted to strike when there was so little work available.

"Someday, Nick, when you're older, you will understand," my father told me.

The workers attempt to organize a union was short lived. One of the men who attended the meeting told the plant management about the proposed strike. The management hired a squad of "goons," to beat up the union leaders. The police were called to the Fisher Body plant to stop the riots and the strike leaders were arrested. The men vowed to continue to fight Fisher Body management's unfair treatment. Someday they would have an organized union representing them.

*   *   *

Dad told me, "Nick, my foreman found out I attended the union organization meeting. I've lost my job. The car is going to be sold and we can't have our neighbor help with the cooking and cleaning."

*   *   *

Times were getting tougher. It had been three and a half years since the stock market crashed. One out of every four workers was unemployed.

*   *   *

The Flint Journal barely mentioned, on the back page, the workers attempt to form a union. The story of Charles Lindbergh, Jr., the two year old son of the world famous aviator, kidnapped and murdered by Bruno Hauptmann, appeared on the second page. The front page news: Franklin D. Roosevelt, the new President of the United States and his promise of a "New Deal," gave hope to a country deep in trouble. It was the spring of 1933, the depth of the Great Depression.

TWO

"I'll race you down to the gate and back." I motioned for Pat to get on a tricycle as I hopped on one. Pat had a head start and beat me back. When I caught up with him, he pointed to the sky. I said, "Yeah, it's time for the Sunday afternoon parachute jump."

Most of the boys and girls were already on the lawn waiting for the jump. I was living at the Whaley Orphanage in Flint, a facility founded for children without parents or families.

I couldn't remember how or why I had arrived at the orphanage. Somewhere in the back of my mind I remembered my father, mother, brothers and sisters. It all seemed so long ago. To a little boy of seven a lot of things aren't too clear. I sat down on the lawn and let my mind drift back to the events I remembered about my family.

I went everywhere with my father, Ziv, but Zora, my mother, I couldn't remember at all. Big brother Joseph worked after school and weekends at the Porter Orchard. Sonya and Hedy, my older sisters, spent all their time doing housework and taking care of the younger boys, Jay and Alfred. Mostly I recalled playing with and getting in trouble with Marcus and Watt.

Why was I alone at the orphanage, without my family? I had to keep the memory of my family alive. If it took the rest of my life, I vowed to find them. It was June 23, 1933.

*   *   *

The orphanage, a large red brick building, had two dormitories on the second floor, one for boys and one for girls. Everyone ate in the central dining room. There was a big garden and orchard in the back with several acres of lawn, surrounded by a high chain link fence. The orphanage was located near Hurley Hospital and Stevenson school.

Mrs. Hardy, the director of the orphanage, was a soft-spoken, dignified looking, middle-aged woman, tall and slender with short wavy brown hair. Her eyes, a light brown, twinkled when she smiled. Her responsibility was seeing that the boys and girls were well taken care of.

Mrs. Gibson, the resident nurse, a short, plump and stern disciplinarian, supervised the boys. She also set up and monitored the children's daily activities.

Mrs. Gibson explained to me that each morning when she woke us boys up I was to wash, brush my teeth, get dressed and be ready to eat when the bell sounded. She told me where I would sit and that I would not be allowed to leave the table until I ate everything set before me. She gave me my work assignment; after breakfast I was to clean the wash basins, toilets, urinals and shower stalls, then sweep and mop the floors. The work assignment lasted one hour, then I could play until dinner. After dinner I would work outside for one hour, pulling weeds out of the lawn, earning a penny for every twenty five weeds I pulled.

Next came a nap; no talking, no reading for one hour. An hour after supper was set aside for activities, both boys and girls participating. Then to bed after saying the Lord's Prayer.

"Do you have any questions, Nick?"

I thought a minute and asked, "When will I see Dad, Mother and my brothers and sisters?"

Mrs. Gibson replied, "Your dad and mother are dead, gone out of your life. You are fortunate that the Whaley Orphanage has taken you in, providing you with a place to live."

I cried out, "But, how, why? What about my brothers and sisters?"

"You are too young to understand, Nick. Most of the children here don't have any parents. When you are older you might get to see your brothers and sisters."

I started to cry. "I don't like you and I don't want to live here."

Mrs. Gibson turned red and reached for a thick, wide leather belt hanging on the wall. "I've got too many boys to take care of and haven't got time for any nonsense from you." She whacked me across my bare legs with the belt. "Quit your crying and go to bed. You are very young and soon will forget your family."

As she left, Mrs. Gibson said, "The schedule and rules are posted, the older boys will read them to you."

* * *

My bed and locker were next to Pat Dugan's. Pat was a little older than I. A happy kid and always smiling, he couldn't speak or hear. Pat looked at me, made a sour face and stuck the middle finger on his right hand into the air, then pointed down the hall to Mrs. Gibson's office. I quit crying and started to laugh. I knew what Pat thought of Mrs. Gibson. He held his finger to his lips to tell me to be quiet. We weren't allowed to talk at bedtime.

I laid awake long into the night crying. Mother and Dad both dead! Why wouldn't Mrs. Gibson tell me how they died? Why couldn't I remember how I arrived at the orphanage?

It was difficult to get used to the regimentation that all of us were forced to follow. With great difficulty I learned to eat everything put on my plate. After sitting by myself when all the other kids had finished eating and gone out to play, I could, by drinking a lot of water, eat all the food put before me. Learning how to live at the Whaley Orphanage, I had little time to think about my family. Try as hard as I could, I didn't escape the discipline Mrs. Gibson handed out. When I didn't get my work assignment finished on time, she was quick to use the belt. She made me hold out my hands, face up, and smacked them with a thick leather belt until I cried.

*   *   *

I liked playtime with Pat. The playroom was downstairs in one corner of the orphanage. Two sides were all windows, making the room nice and bright. In one corner was a trunk full of Lincoln Logs. Pat and I made houses and buildings by the hour.

In the months that followed I became friends with most of the children in the orphanage. I especially liked the twins, Janet and Annet Flowers, pretty, older girls. They had long black, curly hair and green eyes. They teased me about my bright blue eyes.

During my free time, I went to the garden and orchard to help the gardener pull weeds. He liked to make things grow, supplying the kitchen with vegetables and fruit all summer. The gardener gave me fruit and vegetables that I hid in my locker for Pat and me to eat when we got hungry between meals. He had a big pen in the garage, and raised rabbits as a hobby.

At night I had a bad time in the big dorm. When the nights were hot and humid, I rolled from side to side trying to get cool. I eventually would fall asleep, thinking of living with my family, lots of toys to play with, good things to eat and the Flowers twins.

*   *   *

Sunday mornings were a real treat. We got to dress up and go to church, a chance to escape the confines of the orphanage. The younger kids were assigned to the older boys and girls, and allowed to walk the fifteen blocks to the Episcopal church in downtown Flint. The walk took us past the dairy where we stopped to look at the horses stabled there, and hollered at the milkmen driving the horse drawn wagons, making deliveries. The walk also took us past a neighborhood corner grocery store and most always the penny for the church collection was spent at the store.

Once at the church we were assigned to a Sunday school teacher by age group. One Sunday my teacher took me out of class to the main part of the church, to the altar. The minister sprinkled water on my head and everybody said "Amen." The Episcopal church sponsored the orphanage and the church board members helped manage the activities.

Sunday afternoon the boys and girls got together in the central living room to play games. Some days family members would come for a visit and take kids out of the orphanage for a few hours.

Most always, weather permitting, Sunday afternoons in the summer an airplane flew overhead and a man jumped out and parachuted to the ground, landing near the Flint Park Amusement Center. Sometimes a big cigar shaped dirigible drifted by, high in the sky, like a silver cloud.

*   *   *

One day Mrs. Gibson called me to her office. "Nick, you start school next week, in the second grade. If you get in trouble for any reason, and get a whipping, I'll give you another one when you get home."

"I'll try to be good Mrs. Gibson." I didn't want to be punished. I had enough of that.

The Stevenson school was only two blocks from the orphanage. I stopped at the neighborhood grocery store to buy candy with the pennies I earned pulling weeds.

At Halloween time, the teacher told the class that we were going to have a party. We could dress up in any kind of costume we wanted. It would be a fun day and maybe at night our parents could take us trick or treating. When I got back to the orphanage, I told Mrs. Gibson about the party. I asked her if I could go trick or treating around the neighborhood.

Mrs. Gibson replied, "Nick, none of you boys or girls are allowed outside the orphanage, except to go to church or school. Don't get any ideas about trying to go trick or treating or I'll give you a whipping you won't forget! We are going to have a party tonight. There will be popcorn, candy and apples to bob for."

* * *

An older boy told me that he would be leaving the Whaley Orphanage soon to join the CCC. The Civilian Conservation Corps was a project that President Roosevelt created to give unemployed young men a chance to learn a trade, earn some money and have a place to live.

He said, "When you are as old as I am, you can join too. It's a good way to get out of this orphanage."

I told him, "I don't want to stay here until I'm old enough to join the CCC. I want to live with my family."

"Don't worry about it, Nick, most of the kids are adopted or go to live with foster families."

* * *

During the winter there was lots of snow and it was quite cold. On the first clear day, we kids shoveled snow off the pond near the orchard so we could slide and go sledding. The younger kids rode down the toboggan run with the older kids. I had fun until I got cold and wet, and then I went inside the basement to dry out my clothes and warm up by the big furnace.

The janitor told me that the coal bin was getting low. He

hoped there would be enough to last the winter. John L. Lewis organized the coal mine workers in the south, and was threatening to strike if they didn't get better working conditions, and higher pay. I remembered the strike at the Fisher Body factory. I told the janitor about the police beating up and arresting the strikers, and my dad getting fired.

*   *   *

Just before Christmas a young man came to the orphanage to see me. "I'm going to be your big brother."

I said, "My big brother is Joseph, where is Joseph?"

"I don't know, but we can pretend I'm your brother."

On Saturdays we went for long walks and played together. He asked me what I wanted for Christmas.

I thought a minute and said, "A big jackknife and a flashlight."

Christmas morning, under the tree, there was a gift for me; a flashlight.

*   *   *

Later that spring, Mrs. Gibson asked me to come to her office. She told me Mrs. Hardy would like me to have dinner with her.

"You get cleaned up, Nick. Mind your manners, and eat all your food. If she asks how you like it here, be sure and tell her you do, and that I am kind to you boys and treat you well."

All the kids liked Mrs. Hardy; she didn't yell or whip the children like Mrs. Gibson did. The next day I got ready and waited in the hall by her private dining room.

Mrs. Hardy said, "It's all right, Nick, come in and sit down at the table with me."

She was quiet during the meal. After dinner she started to talk.

"I asked you to have dinner with me because it is your birthday. Happy Birthday, Nick! Are you happy here?"

I said, "No, Mrs. Gibson is mean to us kids."

Mrs. Hardy said, "She is a stern woman and has a big responsibility taking care of you children."

"Mrs. Gibson told me that my father and mother are dead. How did they die?"

"Nick, you are too young to understand, it's best that you forget about your parents. Maybe I can find you a new family."

I couldn't, and didn't want to forget about my parents. It was my eighth birthday, March 25, 1934.

*   *   *

The next morning Mrs. Gibson confronted me. I was bending down, scrubbing out the toilet.

She glared at me. "Nick, you got me in trouble with Mrs. Hardy when you told her I was mean to you. I have the authority to punish you if you are disruptive and disobey my orders."

She closed the door behind her and grabbed me by my arm. She whacked me across my legs with the belt. I gritted my teeth, then cried out loudly as Mrs. Gibson continued to beat me across my back and legs.

"That's for disobeying my orders. Maybe now you've learned a lesson, and won't cause me any more trouble."

She stalked out of the bathroom, leaving me curled up, and crying on the bathroom floor.

*   *   *

A few days later Mrs. Gibson told me to get cleaned up, that I would be going for a ride with Mr. and Mrs. Lewis to visit them in their home.

"Be sure to mind your manners and just maybe if they like you enough you could live with them."

31

Mr. Lewis, a big man with gray hair, had long, shaggy eyebrows and a thick, black mustache. He seldom smiled, and talked in a loud booming voice. Mrs. Lewis, a short, stocky woman with blond hair, had big brown eyes. She obviously was the boss of the family, and when she talked, Mr. Lewis would say, "Yes dear, that's right, dear."

The ride was long, and soon the motion of the car made me dizzy and sick to my stomach.

"Stop the car," I said. Too late, I threw up all over the back seat. I rode the rest of the trip to the Lewis home in the front seat. Mr. Lewis wasn't happy about cleaning up the mess in the car.

Their home, located in a neighborhood with big houses, had three stories, with a big tree shaded, fenced backyard.

Mrs. Lewis needed a child in her life. "Nick, I want you to come and live with us."

I replied, "I have my own family, Mrs. Lewis. Someday I'll find them and we will live together." I didn't want a new family.

Going back to the orphanage, I rode in the front seat and didn't get sick. Mrs. Lewis told me if I changed my mind and wanted to live with them, to let Mrs. Hardy know. I related my weekend trip to Pat. He thought living with the Lewis family would be better than staying at the orphanage and having Mrs. Gibson beat me all the time.

*   *   *

The next week I was told that a Mr. and Mrs. Donovan were going to pick me up and take me for a visit to their home for the weekend. Mr. Donovan, a short, fat, nervous man, had a bald head. Mrs. Donovan was a tall, skinny woman with long, braided hair hanging down her back. Mrs. Hardy suggested that I sit in the front seat so I could look out and enjoy the ride better. The Donovans lived about twenty miles south of Flint. They owned a grocery store at the crossroads, near a mill pond.

I had fun playing in the water and eating all the candy and fruit I wanted.

Mrs. Donovan asked, "Nick, how would you like to live with us?"

I liked the Donovans. The mill pond was a great place to swim and go fishing, and the grocery store had all that fruit and candy, but they weren't my mother and father.

On the ride back to the Whaley Orphanage, I told Mrs. Donovan, "I have to find my brothers and sisters. I don't want to be adopted. I'm going to live with my own family."

*   *   *

I woke up the following morning and couldn't open my eyes; I thought I was going blind. Mrs. Gibson told me my eyes probably got infected from pulling weeds in the lawn. Pat's eyes were infected, too. Mrs. Gibson put some ointment in our eyes and said in a few days the infection would go away. Meanwhile, we must stay in bed. She moved Pat and me to a double bedroom away from the other kids.

"You boys can keep each other company, I'm going to let you talk all you want to." Mrs. Gibson laughed and said, "It will be a one way conversation. That deaf dummy, Pat, won't keep you awake talking."

As she left the room, we both gave her the one finger salute, then, smiling, reached over and shook hands.

I enjoyed being alone with Pat. We had no trouble communicating. By gesturing, pointing, finger signs and facial expressions, we could understand each other quite well. Pat felt frustration in not being able to talk, he could just grunt and squeak. It bothered me when the other kids called him a dummy. He was really a very smart boy.

I told Pat, "As soon as my eyes are better I am going to run away and try to find my brothers and sisters."

Pat wanted to go, but I knew he would have trouble if we

got separated, communicating with people, so I told him I was going alone.

Mrs. Gibson put ointment in our eyes, then left us alone most of the day. I made plans to run away. I would take my flashlight, four pennies and Pat's jackknife. I had discovered a small hole in the fence at the far end of the garden while helping the gardener. I could squeeze through it and be on my way.

I was excited. I gestured to Pat, soon I would be free of Mrs. Gibson and the orphanage, and searching for my brothers and sisters.

THREE

My work assignments completed, during playtime I went down to the garden, through the orchard. The sun shone brightly as I slipped through the hole in the fence. I had hopes of being with my brothers and sisters by nightfall.

I walked a long way that day, hiding in woods and backyards, stopping at a store to buy some candy. Toward evening when it started to get cold, I wondered where I could sleep that night. Suddenly I recognized the road and some of the houses, where I walked with my pretend big brother. I decided to go back to the orphanage. I was glad that I had my flashlight. After dark I slipped back through the hole in the fence and headed for the garage. The door was open and I found some carrots and apples to eat that the gardener kept to feed the rabbits. I climbed into a box of hay and covered up just as a car pulled into the garage. Mrs. Hardy and Mrs. Gibson got out. Mrs. Hardy was crying.

Mrs. Gibson said, "Don't cry, the police will find him in the morning."

"I know, but he's such a little boy, and I have to go away for a few days. Mrs. Gibson, you will have to take care of things until I get back."

I woke up early and slipped through the fence again, heading for the countryside. I walked a long ways, and in the afternoon a woman stopped me and asked who I was and where I lived. I told her just up the road. She said she would give me a nickel and something to eat if I would go to her house. I was hungry and thirsty, so I went along. While in the kitchen eating, I heard the woman talking on the phone in the other room.

"Did you hear the news? Clyde Barrow and Bonnie Parker, the notorious Bonnie and Clyde bank robbers, have been shot and killed near a little town in Louisiana." Then she whispered, "I think I've found that boy the police are looking for."

I ran out of the house, into the woods as fast as I could go. That night I went back to the orphanage and slept in the hay box in the garage again.

Early the next morning I again slipped through the hole in the fence and headed for the country. It soon started to rain, and by noon I was cold, wet, hungry and tired. I decided to go back to the orphanage, I couldn't find my family this way. Mrs. Gibson's punishment would only hurt a short time anyway.

Reluctantly I headed back. Late in the afternoon I crawled through the hole in the fence and while I was walking in the orchard, the gardener spied me and said, "Where have you been, the police have been looking for you for three days."

I told him about walking around the country all day and sleeping in the garage at night.

He said, "I'm taking you to see Mrs. Gibson, Mrs. Hardy is away on business."

Mrs. Gibson smiled sweetly when I was brought to her office. After the gardener left, she reached for her leather belt and said, "I'm going to give you a whipping. I'll make an example of you, so the other boys and girls won't try to run away."

Mrs. Gibson grabbed me by the arm and proceeded to beat me across my back. I cried out and kicked Mrs. Gibson in the shins. The gardener had heard me screaming and came back to the office.

"What's going on, Mrs. Gibson? Mrs. Hardy wouldn't approve of what you're doing. Go to your room, Nick."

When Mrs. Hardy returned, she called me to her office. I didn't know what to expect. She asked me why I had run away. I told her about Mrs. Gibson being mean and whipping us boys, and that I wasn't going to stay at the orphanage.

Mrs. Hardy was quiet for awhile, then said, "I guess I

haven't been paying enough attention to what's going on around here. I've given Mrs. Gibson too free a hand. That's all going to change, I can't have any of my boys and girls being mistreated."

Then she said, "Nick, I think it's time for you to see your brothers."

*   *   *

She said very little as she drove south of Flint near the town of Fenton. We left the pavement and drove about two miles on a dusty gravel road to a small farm. As I got out of the car, Marcus and Watt ran out of the house to meet me. They wore shorts, no shirt, and were barefoot. The sun had bleached their hair to a light brown, and their skin deeply tanned. Both boys looked very healthy.

After I talked to Marcus and Watt a few minutes, Mrs. Hardy introduced me to Mrs. Bessie Cooper and her son Clark. Mrs. Cooper was a plump, pleasant looking woman with gray hair. Clark, a tall, good looking young man, was in his late teens. Bessie's husband had died the year before. Mrs. Hardy told me I would be staying with my brothers for awhile. Then she left to drive back to Flint.

The first thing we did was to go to the barn to see the animals. Marcus told me, "Be careful around the horses, always talk to and pet them. Don't scare them or they will bite and kick at you."

He showed me two scars on his chest where a colt had kicked him and knocked him against the back of a stall. He was sore for a long time.

Watt asked me if I wanted to go for a horseback ride. I had never been on a horse and was quite frightened. Watt and Marcus put halters on King and Queen to ride and brought out Molly for me. She was a big work horse. I had to climb up on a fence to jump on Molly's back. King and Queen headed for the apple orchard, with Molly trotting behind. I grabbed Molly's mane with both hands and held on tight. As she was going under an apple tree, a big branch caught me and knocked me off Molly onto the ground. Marcus and Watt rode back laughing and told me I would soon learn to steer Molly.

* * *

I was glad to be with Marcus and Watt again. They asked me how I liked the Whaley Orphanage, what I did there and how I got along. I told them about Mrs. Gibson, the time I ran away, and how she beat me.

Marcus declared, "That bitch wouldn't of whipped you if I'd been there."

They didn't know where our brothers and sisters were living. The three of us vowed someday the family would be together again.

Marcus and Watt liked living on the farm, playing in the big fields and woods nearby. They helped with the farm chores and the Cooper family treated them well. Clark's cousin lived in Fenton, but drove out to the farm to help with the haying and grain harvest.

The house had a second floor and a basement, no electricity, running water or inside toilet. Kerosene lamps supplied light at night. Marcus, Watt and I toted the water from the hand pump in the yard to the house and barn. We split wood into kindling for the cook stove in the kitchen. The toilet, a two-hole outhouse by the barn, smelled pretty bad. After living in the orphanage, the farm seemed a wonderful place to live.

Mrs. Cooper kept us boys busy working in the garden and helping her around the house. She cooked and canned all the time. Her pantry in the basement held many jars of fruit, vegetables and meat, neatly placed in rows on the shelves.

During the week we climbed in the horse tank to cool off and clean up, but Saturday night Mrs. Cooper heated water on the cook stove and we took baths in a galvanized tub in the kitchen.

Mrs. Cooper had been a teacher and knew education was important. She enrolled us boys in summer school. We had to walk about a mile and a half down the road to a one room schoolhouse. The teacher said that summer school should not be all work. We would put on a play for the adults. It was called Rumplestilskin. Marcus and Watt said it was sissy stuff, but I had fun playing the part of an elf.

*   *   *

Bennett Lake was a mile from the farm, and occasionally Clark and his cousin would take us swimming. Marcus and Watt could dog paddle a little. I couldn't swim, so Watt put me on his shoulders and took me out in the deep water. He soon was over his head. Struggling to keep me on his shoulders, he managed to find his way back to shallow water. Watt swallowed a lot of water and threw up when we got back to shore.

When our hair got long and hung in our eyes, Mrs. Cooper gave us each a dime to get a haircut, and a penny to spend on candy. We walked two miles from the Cooper farm, where there was a general store, barbershop, gas station and grainery, servicing the surrounding country. By now the bottom of my feet were tough, and walking two miles on the gravel road didn't make them sore.

When we returned to the farm, Clark asked me if I wanted to go with him. A bunch of pigeons roosted in the barn across the road. He was going to shoot squab for supper. He had a big double barrel shotgun and when it went off it made a terrifying noise and the pigeons scattered and flew in every direction. Clark managed to kill a few. I helped him clean them. What a mess, blood, guts and feathers everywhere. Mrs. Cooper fried the pigeons to a golden brown, then made a gravy by adding flour to the hot grease. We had biscuits, mashed potatoes, sweet corn and cherry pie for dessert. I didn't need any water to wash down that meal.

While we were in the barn helping Clark with the chores, a neighboring farmer stopped by all excited.

"Clark, did you hear the news? John Dillinger, public enemy Number One, has been shot and killed outside a theater in Chicago." It was midsummer, 1934.

FOUR

The vacation with my brothers soon ended. Mrs. Hardy showed up and told me I would have to go back to the Whaley Orphanage with her.

I protested, "I'm not going back to that orphanage, I want to stay here and live with my brothers. I don't want that mean Mrs. Gibson beating me anymore."

Mrs. Hardy said, "I'm sorry, Nick, but you can't stay here with Mrs. Cooper. She has to sell the farm and move. Mrs. Gibson is gone. I discharged her and a younger lady is taking care of the boys now."

Mrs. Cooper had tears in her eyes. "Nick, someday maybe you can live with me and your brothers."

She cried as she bid me goodbye. Marcus and Watt stood quietly by. Reluctantly, rubbing my eyes, I got in the car for the drive back to the orphanage. I gave a faint wave to my brothers as the car slowly drove away.

*   *   *

Most of the same kids were still at the orphanage. I missed Pat Dugan. Mrs. Hardy told me that he was living at the Flint School for the Deaf, learning to talk sign language with his hands. A pleasant young nurse had taken Mrs. Gibson's place.

I got reacquainted with the Flowers twins, Janet and Annet. I played with them during the free period. Janet told me to meet them after supper in the garage near the rabbit pen. The twins had something for me.

I wondered what it would be. I remembered the time in the

woods with Marcus and Watt and what the neighbor girl showed us boys. I hurried out to the garage after supper. Janet and Annet were standing near the pen, petting the rabbits.

I said, "Hi girls, what do you have for me?"

The twins blushed, then each gave me a kiss. I was somewhat taken back by the boldness of the girls, but was happy to realize they had a crush on me. I liked both of the girls. I didn't know which one I liked the most.

Living at the orphanage wasn't half bad.

*   *   *

The following week, Mrs. Hardy told me I had been picked to go to Camp Arrowhead for two weeks.

The camp was situated on a small lake off Fenton Road, half way between Flint and Fenton. All the boys slept in tents with wood floors, and ate in a big dining room. I didn't know anyone, but I soon became acquainted. We were kept busy with swimming lessons, hiking, nature and craft classes. I spent most of my free time in the water practicing the dog paddle. I didn't want to be caught in deep water again and not know how to swim, like the time at Bennett Lake on Watt's shoulders.

Sunday, visiting day, most of the boys went up to the big Pow Wow building to meet with their families and show them around the camp. I was practicing swimming at the lake when I heard a voice say, "Hi, Nick, how about showing me around the camp?"

What a surprise, there stood big brother Joseph! Boy, was I glad to see him! We walked around to the edge of the campgrounds and found a big windmill.

Joseph said, "Let's climb to that platform near the top. We can look for animals through my binoculars."

We talked most of the afternoon. I told Joseph about living at the Whaley Orphanage and my visit with Marcus and Watt at the cooper farm. Joseph said Mrs. Hardy told him I was at the camp and he could visit with me. He was seventeen years old now, small for his age, with thin, curly brown hair, and a slightly crossed right eye.

Joseph bragged about traveling around the country. He jumped rides on freight trains and rode to whatever town the trains stopped at. When he could, he stayed at the local YMCA, but quite often he hung out with the hobos who camped outside of town. Joseph told me Mrs. Hardy was going to get him a job at one of the GM auto plants in Flint, and then we would see more of each other.

He was quiet and thoughtful when I mentioned that Mrs. Gibson told me our mother and dad were dead.

"Yes, they are gone out of our lives. I don't want to talk about them!"

I asked about our brothers and sisters. Joseph told me that Sonya and Hedy were living with relatives in New York. Alfred and Jay had been adopted, and he didn't know where they were living. I hardly remembered my younger brothers.

"Joseph, does that mean I will never get to see them again?"

"Yes, Nick, I don't think we will ever see them again."

I wondered why Joseph hadn't tried to keep the family together. I guessed he was too busy traveling around the country and taking care of himself.

*   *   *

The cold weather set in early and I spent a lot of time in the warm basement. While helping the janitor shovel coal in the furnace a few days after Thanksgiving, a special news bulletin came over the radio. The vicious killer and gangster, Baby Face Nelson, public enemy Number One, had been shot and killed by the FBI near Fox River, Illinois. Baby Face Nelson had at one time been a henchman for Al Capone and John Dillinger.

*   *   *

For Christmas I received a jackknife. My pretend big brother told me that Santa Claus had left it under the tree for me. I had lost all faith in Santa Claus. The present I wanted and asked for each year was to be with my family, but I still lived at the orphanage.

I decided I would run away again. It was February, with snowy, biting winds and bitter cold. I knew that I should wait until spring when the weather warmed up, but the confinement at the orphanage was too much for me. I thought about last summer on the farm when I stayed with Marcus and Watt and knew I had to be with them.

My plans were soon forgotten when Mrs. Hardy called me to her office and said, "I have good news for you, Nick, you are going to Fenton to live with Marcus, Watt and Mrs. Cooper." It was Valentine's day, 1935.

FIVE

The village of Fenton nestled at the foot of a wooded range of hills, surrounded by many small lakes. North, east and west of the town, there were several large dairy farms. To the south, small, run down hillbilly farms and orchards occupied the area. The people of Fenton enjoyed the friendly easygoing atmosphere of a small town. Many of them commuted to work at the General Motors automobile factories in Flint.

I was glad to be back with Marcus and Watt again, away from the Whaley Orphanage.

Marcus told me that since the time I vacationed with him and Watt, Bessie sold the farm and they helped move furniture from the farm to Fenton. Marcus and Clark's cousin drove one team of horses with a wagon load of furniture and Watt helped Clark drive another. It was about a ten mile trip from the farm to Fenton on Bennett Lake Road.

Clark went to work for room and board on a farm in the country. We three Sabitch brothers would be living with Mrs. Cooper and going to school in Fenton.

* * *

The Cooper house was a small, wood framed two story structure, with a basement. The house was painted yellow. A red pitcher pump supplied water for the sink. A kerosene oil stove, and a wood burning cook stove heated the kitchen. Water often dripped from the wooden ice box to the linoleum covered floor. The dark, damp basement held a coal furnace, wringer washer with tubs, shelves of canned food, potato storage and a black, sooty coal bin.

Outside behind the garage stood a wooden outhouse. Sears, Roebuck and Montgomery Ward catalogs, to be used for reading and wiping, lay between the two seat holes. A small sack of lime, stuck in the corner on the floor, occasionally had to be dumped in the holes to cut the smell and sight of what was in the bottom.

The house, located at the edge of town, had been built next to a cemetery and gravel pit. A block away, on Shiawassee Avenue, the wealthy lived in the biggest homes in Fenton.

Mrs. Cooper, a woman in her early fifties, was a gentle, caring person. Widowed, we boys filled a void in her life, but sometimes more than she bargained for. As our foster mother, she received twelve dollars a month for each of us from the State. The money was for food, clothing, shelter and our school needs.

Mrs. Cooper, Bessie as she preferred us boys to call her, had taken on a big responsibility in agreeing to keep us. We still had a family resemblance, but no longer looked alike. Marcus, twelve, had a stocky build, with big ears that stuck straight out the side of his head. Watt, ten, always cautious, had a shock of curly brown hair. I was nine, hyperactive, with my top two front teeth far apart, and bright blue piercing eyes.

Being active boys we often got on Bessie's nerves. She tried to be patient, but the loss of her husband, the move from the farm, and the noise and confusion of taking care of three boys would get to her. One day when I was being extra bad, Bessie scolded and spanked me. I had to sit in a corner for half an hour.

At bedtime Bessie said, "Nick, when you get cleaned up, come and sleep with me."

Her bedroom, much cleaner and better smelling than our room, was light and pleasant. She tucked me comfortably in her bed.

"I'm sorry, Nick, that I had to spank you. It's easy to keep out of trouble if only you will listen to your good conscience. When you want to do something and feel guilty about it, don't do it. When you listen to the devil and do something wrong, you will be punished. We all must be responsible for our actions."

After Bessie said her prayers she told me it had been hard to believe in the Lord after losing her husband and leaving the farm. She cried herself to sleep.

*　　*　　*

Bessie, a neat and organized person, prepared three meals a day. She insisted we do our share and told us what work had to be done. I had to set the table and wash the dishes for breakfast, Watt did the same for dinner and Marcus supper.

The house had to be cleaned every Saturday morning. Watt dusted, swept and straightened up the upstairs bedroom. Marcus mopped the kitchen and pantry and I cleaned the living room and parlor. Monday morning, wash day, Marcus heated water and filled the washer and rinse tubs. I cut the Fels Naptha bar soap into shavings to put in the washer. Watt emptied the washer and tubs.

Every morning Marcus tended the coal furnace in the basement, then I took over during the day and Watt checked it at bedtime. We took turns emptying the ashes as needed.

I had learned how to do my share at the Whaley Orphanage and I thought doing the work with my brothers would be fun. Somehow we argued a lot about who should do what. Marcus told Watt and me what to do more than he helped us.

We spent most of our playtime in the gravel pit pretending to drive the old steam shovel or looking for bird nests in the holes on the side of the hill. Marcus and Watt teamed up to pull me around in an old wagon. At first Marcus and Watt liked me around, and we played together a lot.

Bessie always told Marcus when we went somewhere, "Be sure and take good care of your brother Nick."

When we returned home I always told Bessie where we had been and what we had done. Pretty soon Marcus and Watt started to tease me and call me the 'tell-all-tag-along kid'. I got angry at Marcus and called him 'mule ears.' Marcus hit me a couple of times and I started to cry, then he called me a cry baby. I ran into the kitchen and picked up two big butcher knives and started for Marcus. Watt was scared and grabbed my arms and shoved me against the wall. Marcus hit me in the muscle of each arm until I dropped the knives.

Things got better with us after that. I learned to keep my mouth shut to Bessie about our activities.

Marcus told me, "Nick, you are okay, for a little kid you sure are scrappy."

*　　*　　*

On weekends Bessie took us for a drive in the country in her old '32 Chevrolet to visit her sister, who lived on a farm in the rolling hills, a short distance south of Fenton. The Hermans were middle-aged hillbilly dirt farmers. Clara was plump and short like her sister Bessie. She chewed tobacco and swore frequently. Webb, her husband, a tall, skinny Kentuckian, spoke with a southern drawl.

Bessie let us stay a few days with the Hermans. We helped Webb and the hired man feed the livestock, but mostly we played in the hayloft.

Upstairs in the attic I found a trunk full of Horatio Alger books. I read all those books and vowed someday I would be rich like Horatio Alger's characters.

Juno, the Hermans hired man, was tall with long black hair and a shaggy beard. He had coal black eyes and his right eye turned out from the side of his face. Juno liked to tell dirty stories.

He told me, "The sharpest thing in the world is a fart. It can go through your pants without making a hole in them. The lightest thing in the world is your pecker, it will raise at a thought."

Marcus said, "Juno isn't playing with a full deck."

Watt thought he was real weird. Juno had only been with the Hermans a few months.

*   *   *

Webb had a big stud horse named Hugo. The neighbors brought their mares to the Herman's for Hugo to breed. Mr. Herman didn't want us boys to watch the breeding.

Mrs. Herman said, "Those Sabitch boys have got to learn about life. The barnyard is as good a place as any to see how babies are made."

Marcus had found a place in the barn loft, near an open window, overlooking the barnyard. I was glad to be in a safe place to watch the breeding. Hugo, a frightening sight to behold, reared up when Webb brought the mare to the barnyard. He pranced up to the mare, stuck his nose under her tail, gave a loud snort, whinnied, then jumped straddle of her.

Marcus said, "Look at the size of Hugo's dong."

It was two foot long, and nearly touched the ground. Webb quickly reached down under and helped him enter the mare. When Hugo lunged into the mare, I thought for sure he would split her in two. I feared Webb and the mare would both be killed. Slowly Hugo slid off the mare. She kicked him in the ribs, then turned around and bit his rump. Hugo stood meek as a lamb, with his head down.

Webb led the mare out of the barnyard and said, "Okay, boys, Hugo's all frigged out, you can come down and pet him."

We liked playing in the hayloft and straw stacks, catching sparrows for the cats to eat.

On Saturday night after chores we piled into the Herman's

Ford and drove to Foxton's country store to do the weekly shopping and later to sit on the hill by the store where free movies were shown on the side of a building painted white.

When we got back to the farm we took a quick dip in the horse tank to cool off before going to sleep in the hot, muggy upstairs bedroom.

After a few days at the farm, Webb drove us back to Fenton in his old Ford.

* * *

Bessie reminded us that the grass was getting long and had to be mowed before supper. After dark we boys climbed to the top of the steep hill across the street from the Cooper house. I couldn't get the sight of Hugo breeding the young mare out of my mind until a hound dog howled in the distance. Marcus had been practicing imitating and answering the howling hound. He stood up, tilted his head back, looked at the moon and started to howl. Soon other dogs in the neighborhood began to bark and howl. Marcus kept howling back.

Below the hill, the grumpy next door neighbor came outside and shouted, "I know you Sabitch bohunks are up there making that commotion. If you don't be quiet, I'll get my shotgun and shut you up!"

We hid on top of the hill until he went back in the house.

When we got back home Bessie asked, "What was all the barking and shouting going on outside?"

Marcus said, "Just a hound dog howling at the moon."

* * *

Bessie always managed to get us to church. Sunday morning she gave us each a nickel for the collection, and off we went for Sunday School lessons at the Presbyterian Church. The class teacher was dedicated to teaching us all about Jesus.

When the collection plate was passed, Watt would drop his nickel in, and Marcus and I kept ours to buy candy on the way home. When we were away visiting at the Hermans, we either went to the Lutheran Church in Parshalville or the Presbyterian Church around the corner on Old U.S. 23. I didn't care for Sunday School very much. What I really liked was when the congregation would sing, "The Old Rugged Cross," "Onward Christian Soldiers," "Rock of Ages," "Amazing Grace" and "How Great Thou Art."

*   *   *

I overheard Bessie talking to Clark about the depressed economy. She thought things were going to get better.

"Maybe, Clark, you can get a job with the WPA."

The Works Project Administration was one of President Roosevelt's New Deal programs for spending Federal money throughout the country, creating work for the unemployed.

Bessie became excited about the recently passed Social Security Act.

"Just think, Clark, an old age pension program where a small amount of money would be withheld from your paycheck throughout your working life and then you would retire on a monthly pension from the government until you die."

Clark was too young to think about retiring and dying.

He said, "I don't even have a job with a steady paycheck, Mother, but I'll look into the WPA jobs program."

It was the end of summer, 1935.

51

SIX

That fall Marcus and Watt went to the Fenton High School and I went to the South Ward School, about ten blocks away. Watt was not happy starting school. Most of his class had been held back a full year by the school superintendent. Watt was taking the fourth grade again, the same grade I was in, only in a different school.

When the ground froze up, Marcus said, "I know how to make some money. Let's run a trap line. We can use those old traps in the garage that Clark brought from the farm."

We set traps in ditches and along streams out in the country inside the triangle, Owen Road to Jennings Road, Jennings Road to Silver Lake Road and back to Fenton. We checked the traps before and after school every day. We soon found out that the earlier the traps were checked the more animals we caught. Other boys had traps in the same area and whoever got there first took all the animals.

The anticipation of finding animals caught in the traps, made the cold, wet feet we got tramping through the woods and ditches worthwhile.

The animal hides sold for fifty cents for a muskrat up to two dollars for a prime skunk pelt. A fur buyer in town bought everything we trapped; possum, coon, rabbits, muskrat and skunk.

*   *   *

The weather turned warm early that spring. Marcus packed some sandwiches in a sack and we headed for the countryside.

We hiked down Owen Road to where the old wooden, hump back bridge crossed the river that ran into Silver Lake.

By midday the temperature was almost seventy degrees. Marcus was anxious to start the swimming season. He took off his clothes and dove off the bridge into the water.

He hollered, "Kerist, the water's ice cold."

He scrambled up the bank, his lips turning blue. Shivering he said, "You guys are next."

Reluctantly Watt and I took off our clothes and jumped in the shallow water near the shore. With teeth chattering we climbed the river bank. Watt's and my peckers had shriveled up. We looked like we had two belly buttons.

"Let's build a fire to warm up and dry out," Marcus said.

He took a newspaper sticking out of a mailbox and started to crumble it up.

"Look here at the headline, boys. That guy who kidnapped and murdered the Lindbergh baby four years ago finally got what he deserved."

The headline read, "BRUNO RICHARD HAUPTMANN—EXECUTED."

It was April 3, 1936.

*   *   *

Times were tough in the Depression years. Bessie knew about hard work and how to make ends meet.

She told us, "If we want to eat next winter, we have to put in a garden this summer."

Clark borrowed a team of horses to plow and work up the garden. I walked in the furrow behind him as he struggled to keep the single bottom plow upright. I picked up a lot of worms and grubs to sell later for fish bait. Bessie showed us how to plant potatoes, corn, tomatoes, beans, melons, cucumbers, peppers, carrots, onions, cabbage, lettuce and squash.

The seeds and plants grew fast in the hot, wet, humid Michigan summer weather. I had the unpleasant job of ridding the potato and tomato plants of bugs and worms. I found an old can in the junk pile and poured some kerosene into it. The potato bugs were many and easy to find. I picked them off the potato plants and dropped them in the kerosene. They spun frantically around, then died. The tomato worms were more difficult to locate. They were light green, the same color as the tomato leaves. They were about two inches long, with a big horn sticking up on one end of them. I had to put on an old pair of gloves to pick them up and drop them in the kerosene can. They twisted and turned a long time before they died.

Marcus and Watt pulled weeds and hoed between the rows. After working in the garden all morning, we decided to go to Silver Lake in the afternoon to cool off in the clear spring fed water. It was a four mile walk. The pavement was hot, but our feet were tough, as we never wore shoes during the warm weather. It was fun to stick our toes in the hot tar between the pavement cracks. No cars came by so we had to walk all the way to the lake.

The lake was quite deep in spots, where a barge dredge sucked marl from the bottom to make cement at a plant on the north end of the lake. There were no houses around the shore. We had the lake to ourselves. We walked to the east side where an old building from the cement plant was left standing. Marcus and Watt were pretty good swimmers. They swam and played in the deep water. I stayed in the shallow water and dog paddled back and forth to an island about 150 feet from the main shore.

*   *   *

During the growing season we walked to the Denton Hill Berry Farm. We paid ten cents a quart to pick the fruit. We brought strawberries, raspberries and cherries for Bessie to cook, can and store in the fruit cellar.

We harvested the vegetables as they ripened. Bessie showed

us what to do. We put the tomatoes in boiling water in a big tub, peeled them with a knife and then made juice, sauce and catsup. The corn, boiled in a tub, the kernels sliced off with a knife, then canned and some made into corn relish. The rest of the garden vegetables were also cooked and canned in a similar manner. The potatoes were dug out with a pitchfork and put in a big bin in the corner of the cellar. The popcorn ears were picked and shucked together to get the kernels off the cob and put in glass jars. Nothing was wasted.

Autumn is the prettiest time of the year in Michigan. The hardwood leaves all turn brilliant colors.

Bessie drove us along the back country roads where we picked up hickory and walnuts. The hickory nuts were shucked and stored in the attic in old flour sacks. The walnuts required more work. We used the corn sheller to shuck the dry walnuts, and spread the green ones in the driveway. After the car had driven over them a few times the shells loosened enough to be shucked. We sacked and stored them in the attic.

*   *   *

Bessie's sister, Clara, stopped by for a visit. Her husband, Webb, had just finished the butchering. Their car was loaded down with a quarter of beef, half a hog and a dozen chickens.

When she left she smiled and said, "Boys, that meat will help keep your bellies full this winter."

It took a week for us boys to help Bessie cut up, cook and can the meat in quart mason jars.

Bessie bought sacks of flour, sugar and salt from the Fenton Mill, to be stored in the attic.

Friday evenings I walked two miles to a farm on Owen Road to get milk, fresh from the cows, for five cents a quart. Bessie baked every Saturday; cookies, pies, cake and bread. By the end of the harvest season, the fruit cellar, attic and pantry were stocked with enough food to last through the winter and well into the next growing season. The need to buy anything in the grocery store rarely arose.

*   *   *

Summer faded into fall and the Presidential Campaign heated up.

Bessie told me, "'Alf' Landon doesn't stand a chance. I'm going to vote for Roosevelt. His New Deal programs are starting to put the country back to work."

F.D.R. was reelected President. It was November 3, 1936.

SEVEN

I was glad when school started. This year I would be in the same school as Marcus and Watt. The large brick building housed a gym, workshop, cafeteria and classrooms. Children from kindergarten through the twelfth grades attended classes in the same building.

Watt's class, retained the previous year, was in a different homeroom. I didn't see much of him at school, except during gym class, when the fifth grade boys got together and played soccer and basketball. School was beginning to be fun. My classmates from the Ward School attended, and I became acquainted with several new kids who enrolled.

*   *   *

Before Christmas Marcus suggested we surprise Bessie and go to the country and find a Christmas tree. Marcus told her we planned to play in the gravel pit and would be back soon. It took us two hours to walk to Cooper's old farm in the country. Marcus found a small pine tree in the woods and cut it down. We started back the middle of the afternoon, taking turns carrying the tree, one on each end. About halfway between the farm and Fenton, a man driving a truck stopped and gave us a ride home. The tree was in sad shape, with branches gone from the top where we had held onto it.

*   *   *

Mrs. Hardy stopped by the next day to talk to Bessie and see how she was getting along with us.

Bessie said, "They're good boys."

Then she took Mrs. Hardy to the garage and showed her the sad excuse for a Christmas tree.

"You know the boys walked all the way from my old farm and carried that tree back here just for me." Bessie's eyes watered. "It's not much to look at, but the thought is what counts."

Mrs. Hardy left three big packages for us to open on Christmas morning.

*   *   *

When we came in for dinner, Bessie told us she had to go downtown for a little while.

"Don't get into any mischief while I'm gone. Santa Claus is coming soon."

Marcus didn't believe in Santa Claus. "If the grownups need an excuse to give kids presents, I'll pretend to believe in him."

I didn't know what to believe. Many things in my life I didn't understand.

Watt told me, "If there was a Santa Claus we would be living with our own family."

Marcus said, "Let's go see what we are getting for Christmas."

He opened the closet door in Bessie's bedroom and on the floor we saw three big packages. He took the top one and started to unwrap it.

Watt cautioned, "Be careful, don't tear the paper."

The box held corduroy knickers and a pair of high-top leather shoes with a jackknife in a pocket at the top. I thought the knickers were pretty neat.

Marcus said, "They're for sissies, Nick, but these high-tops will be great for stomping in the snow."

Marcus carefully re-wrapped the package and put it in the closet.

When Bessie came home she asked us to help make decorations for Christmas. Marcus popped a big kettle of corn. Watt and I made popcorn balls, and used a needle and thread to make long chains of popcorn. Then we threaded strings of cranberries.

Bessie sent us to bed early saying, "Boys, Santa Claus is on his way from the North Pole."

We got up early Christmas morning. In a corner of the living room the Christmas tree stood, all decorated with strings of popcorn, cranberries, and popcorn balls hanging from the branches. Under the tree we found three big presents and a few small ones. I did my best to look surprised when the gifts were opened.

Marcus commented, "These knickers don't fit, but the high-tops will do fine."

Christmas vacation was more fun than ever that year with the leather high top shoes. I could keep my feet much warmer and walk in deep snow. At night, after wading in the snow, slush and water all day, I stuffed newspaper in the shoes to soak up the moisture, then set them on the register to dry. Bessie showed me how to soften tallow in tins on the stove and then rub the tallow in the leather. It did a good job of waterproofing the high tops.

Across the street from the Cooper house was a steep hill. It was a good place for the whole neighborhood to go sliding. We used cardboard or barrel staves and when it was icy enough we just slid on the seat of our pants. After the snow became real deep we borrowed the neighbor's toboggan and went to the steep hills outside Fenton near Herman's farm. It was fun going down, hard work pulling the toboggan back uphill.

*   *   *

There was no heat in the upstairs bedroom. We endured the long, cold winter nights by piling on lots of blankets. Marcus slept in one bed, and Watt and I in another. In the closet we kept a porcelain pot, for emergencies. If we used it, it would smell all night, and had to be emptied in the morning, washed out and brought back upstairs, or we could take a flashlight and walk outside in the snow to sit on a frosty wood seat in the cold, smelly outhouse.

There were two low double hung windows in the bedroom, one facing the cemetery, and the other in front facing the gravel pit. Marcus told Watt and me how to avoid using both the potty and the outhouse.

"When you have to go, open the window, stick your pecker out and pee outdoors."

Bessie remarked, "You boys must have good bladders, I never see you empty the potty in the morning or hear you come downstairs at night to use the john."

Marcus, the first up in the morning, would stoke up the coal furnace. Watt and I came down later and stood on the register in the living room. We didn't move until it got so hot we almost burned our feet. Then Watt and I fired up the wood cook stove to heat the kitchen for breakfast. Bessie made a hot breakfast for us; oatmeal, hot Ovaltine and homemade bread toasted on the top of the wood stove.

When we left for school we walked around the side of the house and kicked snow over the yellow pee holes in the snow.

*   *   *

Clark stopped by for one of his frequent visits with his mother.

Bessie was reading the Flint Journal and muttering to herself, "I can't believe it, with so many people unemployed, the workers in that automobile plant in Flint are striking and refuse to work."

Clark said, "I've been hearing about that strike. The workers say they aren't getting paid enough and are not being treated fairly. They're trying to organize a workers union."

Bessie handed Clark the paper. The headlines read, AUTOMOBILE WORKERS AT FISHER BODY, GENERAL MOTORS, FLINT, MICHIGAN STAGE A SIT DOWN STRIKE. It was the end of December, 1936.

EIGHT

Late in the winter when the snow started to melt during the day and would freeze at night, Bessie told us about tapping the maple trees and making maple syrup. She said if we tapped the trees and brought the sap home she would show us how to boil the sap into maple syrup.

There were many maple trees in the neighborhood, as well as in the cemetery. Marcus used an old wood auger and a drill to make the holes in the trees. He then pounded a short metal pipe in the hole and hung a gallon pail on the pipe. The sun and moon did the rest. Once a day we gathered the sap and took it home. Bessie poured the sap in a three gallon pail on the wood stove. Most of the sap boiled away, but she managed to get enough maple syrup to put on our pancakes for breakfast.

*　　*　　*

Marcus asked Bessie if it was okay for us boys to go to Parker's orchard and camp out for the weekend. It was early spring and the days were quite warm.

She said, "All right, but take enough bedding to keep warm and something to eat. Just stay out of trouble."

We took some blankets, cooking utensils and Marcus' Daisy BB gun and walked through the hills. The camping site was near a small pond by the old barn in the orchard, across the road from the Davis farm.

Marcus tied a rope between two trees. Watt and I threw an old blanket over the rope. It made a tent for us to sleep in.

We played cops and robbers in the woods, shot frogs and birds with the BB gun and jumped in the pond to wash off. For supper we built a fire and had bird breasts and frog legs. By evening the air was very cool, so we decided to take our blankets and sleep on the hay in the old barn.

The next day Watt said, "We better go back home and check in with Bessie, let her know we're okay, then we can come back and spend the rest of the weekend at our campsite."

Marcus agreed, "Let's just leave the camping stuff here, then we won't have to carry it home and bring it back."

* * *

On the way home I had to take a poop. As I was bending over, Marcus shot me in the ass with the BB gun. I screamed loudly and called him a no good bastard, then picked up a rotten tomato and hit him in the face with it. Watt picked some up and the tomato fight started; Watt and me against Marcus. Soon we were covered with rotten tomatoes. We had a good laugh, but knew we would be in trouble when we got home.

Sure enough, Bessie was furious. She asked us what happened.

Marcus said, "It all started when Nick swore at me and hit me in the face with a rotten tomato."

I was angry, but I couldn't tell Bessie that Marcus started the fight. She would find out about the BB gun.

Bessie said, "In the house, Nick. I'm going to wash your mouth out with soap, and when Clark gets home he is going to whip you."

I gagged on the soap, and Bessie said, "Your mouth should be clean now, I don't want to hear about you swearing again."

When Clark got home, Bessie told him about the tomato fight and me swearing. "Don't let me down, I told Nick you were going to give him a whipping."

Clark didn't like the idea anymore than I did, but he had to

enforce Bessie's discipline. He took me down into the basement and got out the razor strap.

He looked at me and said, "I believe everyone should have
a second chance; if you promise not to swear again, I'll just
pretend to whip you. Nick, when I slap this strap against the
wall you yell loud enough so they can hear you upstairs."

Clark slapped the wall and I cried out until Bessie called
down, "That's enough, Clark, I think Nick has learned a good
lesson."

When we got upstairs Bessie had tears in her eyes and
said, "I guess Marcus and Watt have learned a lesson, too."

Later Marcus asked me if the whipping hurt much. I didn't
tell him I faked it. "Yup, it hurt a lot and it's all your fault."

*   *   *

Marcus told Bessie we had to go back in the hills to get our
blankets and camping stuff.

She said, "Don't you boys get into anymore trouble."

When we arrived at the campsite, nothing had been disturbed. We built a fire and Marcus fried bacon strips on the hot
rocks around the fire pit. For supper we ate bacon sandwiches
and had marshmallows for dessert.

Marcus said, "Boys, this is really living."

I commented how lucky we were living with the Coopers,
having lots of friends and being healthy.

Watt said, "If we are so lucky, how come we're not living
with our family?"

Watt, a pessimist, quiet and conservative, always saw the
serious side of things. Marcus, a fun loving, happy optimist
saw things through rose colored glasses. I, a realist, looked at
things and situations and saw them as they really were.

Marcus said, "Boys, we are having such a good time, let's
stay here a couple of more days."

I went along with anything Marcus did. Watt knew for

sure we would get whipped by Clark when we got home, but decided to stay with us.

What a time we had, climbing trees in the woods, roaming the hills and fields and playing in the barn. After dark we went out under the maple trees and shone the flashlight up into the leaves, spotting the sparrows roosting for the night. We shot them with the BB gun and took the dead, bloody sparrows back to camp. In the morning we would feed the birds to the cats that hung around the old barn.

*   *   *

It was warm enough to sleep outside under the bright, starry sky. We settled down and soon fell asleep. Something woke me up, did someone scream? I lay awake for a long time, then told myself I must have been dreaming. Finally I went back to sleep. I told Marcus the next morning about hearing screams and waking up.

"You're always having nightmares about something, Nick. Let's take those sparrows over to the barn and feed the cats."

The smell of musty hay and horse manure was strong when I opened the squeaky barn door. Marcus threw the sparrows on the barn floor. The cats came from everywhere and fought each other for the birds.

I walked to the back of the barn into the dimly lit grainery. A shadowy figure carrying a gunny sack ran out of the back of the barn. I looked through the cracks in the siding, it looked like Juno, Herman's hired man. What was he doing here? I went to the front of the barn and told Marcus what I had just seen.

He said, "It's probably one of the hobos who hang around town."

We nervously broke camp and headed back home, staying hidden in the woods and along the fence rows. It was mid-afternoon when we got back home. Bessie and Clark arrived later.

I heard Clark talking excitedly to Bessie.

"Mother, I've just heard that Mr. Davis, his wife and sister were murdered on their farm across from Parker's orchard. They were found this morning, dismembered and stuffed in a grain box in the barn. The sheriff is out there investigating.

Bessie sobbed, "What a terrible thing to happen to anyone. Clark, you better talk to the boys. They were camped out near there over the weekend."

Marcus had heard about the murders.

I said, "We better tell the police about seeing Juno in the barn. Do you suppose he might be the killer?"

"No, Nick, the Davis' car and hired man are missing. He's the suspect. About those screams you heard the other night, I don't think you were dreaming."

When Clark questioned us about our camping trip, Marcus said, "No, we didn't hear or see anything."

*   *   *

The Fenton Independent front page news read: DISMEM-BERED BODIES OF JEHIEL AND ELEANOR DAVIS, AND LYDIA HILDEBRANT FOUND IN A GRAIN BOX. The news article went on to say the farmer's car and the hired man were nowhere to be found. It was April 14, 1937.

NINE

The Comstock family lived behind the Cooper house. Jock, a year older than me, had blonde hair, blue eyes, a big nose and a loud boisterous laugh. He lived with his widower father. Addie, his cousin, lived with grandpa and grandma Comstock on a farm west of Fenton. She spent a lot of time in town with Jock. Addie had light brown hair, brown eyes, a full bloomed figure and was in my class at school. The Comstocks were devout Catholics.

Marcus wasn't too sure about the Comstocks. "Nick, Catholics are sinister, mysterious, and can condemn you to hell!"

Marcus became acquainted with Jock when he invited him over one day to help dig for gold out by the barn. Jock had marked off a spot on the ground about four feet by six feet. Marcus asked Watt and I to help dig. It took us a week to dig down about five feet.

Jock finally said, "Forget it boys, if there was any gold in the ground you would have found it by now. Don't worry about putting the dirt back in, my dad and I will cover the hole with the privy."

Marcus said, "It will be a cold day in hell when I dig for gold again." He knew he had been tricked.

*   *   *

Jock made it up to us when he invited us over to play basketball. He had knocked out the bottom of a bushel basket and nailed it to the side of their barn. Jock gave us an old softball to shoot baskets with. He told us we could play basketball at his place anytime we wanted to. Mr. Comstock was an active church member. He had a workshop behind the house and was always making gambling games for the Church Festival held each fall. Jock and I helped Mr. Comstock make a big round mouse house, to be used during the Festival. We caught a lot of field mice and put them in a live cage. At the Festival people would put money in front of a mouse hole, then a mouse was put in the center of the game. If the mouse ran into the hole where your money was you won. The church made a lot of money on the mouse game.

*   *   *

Bessie was listening to the radio when I got home. I asked her what a Catholic was. She told me they were people like us, with a different religious belief.

Suddenly the radio program was interrupted by a news bulletin. The German airship Hindenburg, the largest dirigible ever built, had crashed in flames near Lakehurst, New Jersey. Thirty-six people were killed.

Bessie moaned, "Oh, what a tragedy."

It was May 6, 1937.

*   *   *

Addie liked to play church. She had a corner in the barn loft fixed up with some chairs and an old couch. One rainy day she asked us boys to come over and play church with her. Addie's girlfriend, Patsy Martin, was there. Patsy was older than us boys. She had budding breasts, small waist and a plump rear end. Patsy was a freckle faced imp with a boys short haircut.

Patsy soon became tired of church. She said, "Let's play mom and dad."

Marcus' ears perked up. "Do you know how to play that?"

Patsy replied, "Sure."

Addie said, "I'm going in the house to run the clothes through the washer wringer and hang them up to dry. It's not nice to play mom and dad."

After Addie left there was an awkward silence.

Finally Patsy said, "I suppose I better go help Addie."

Suddenly we heard a yell for help. I looked out the window and saw Addie crying and yelling. She was on the back porch. Her arm was caught in the wringer of the washer. Marcus ran out of the barn and stopped the washer and released the pressure on the rollers. Addie's arm wasn't broken, but it was very painful. Patsy stayed to finish washing the clothes and running them through the wringer. On the way home I wondered what Patsy had in mind when she wanted to play mom and dad.

*   *   *

Jock invited me over that night to listen to the heavyweight boxing match. Addie sat across the room from me. I was so taken up with her I couldn't concentrate on the fight.

I hardly heard the announcer when he said, "Ladies and gentlemen we have a new heavyweight champion of the world."

Joe Louis, the 'Brown Bomber' had knocked out and defeated James Braddock in the eighth round of the match. It was June, 1937.

*   *   *

Joseph showed up at the Cooper house one day as nonchalant as if it was yesterday when he visited me at Camp Arrowhead. I hadn't seen him for three years.

He had been in the CCC's in northern Michigan and now worked at the Chevrolet plant in Flint. He owned a 1934 Chevy and lived alone in an apartment near the Chevrolet plant.

He surprised us by saying he had located Hedy through Mrs. Hardy. She was living with the Brook family on the north side of Flint.

Joseph took us to see her. Hedy missed her family and cried as she hugged and kissed us.

She sobbed, "It's not right that Jay and Alfred have been adopted, and we can't live together as a family. I've cried so much since our family broke up."

Joseph spoke up, "Hedy, we can't change what's happened to our family. Let's enjoy what time we have to visit together today."

The breakup of the Sabitch family occurred four years ago. Hedy, seventeen, chubby with blonde hair, had a dry sense of humor. She had moved around quite a bit. First with an aunt in New York, then with a family in Detroit and now with the Brook family in Flint.

Hedy told us that Sonya lived with relatives in New York, then married and settled in Racine, Wisconsin. She was glad that we were getting along with Bessie in Fenton.

As we left, Hedy tearfully promised to keep in touch. Now five of the Sabitch family could visit and be together occasionally.

Bessie had tears in her eyes when I told her about our visit with Hedy.

"It's a real tragedy what's happened to your family."

*   *   *

Bessie had received a letter from a friend of hers in California, inviting her to spend two weeks with her. She asked Marcus if he could take care of his younger brothers for two weeks while she was gone. Clark would check on us to see if we needed anything. Marcus told her he would take care of us and promised to be good.

Bessie left the next week with tears in her eyes, saying, "I hope I'm doing the right thing."

We got along fine, did as we pleased and stayed up late at night. The last part of the second week we decided to use the BB gun to shoot sparrows nesting in the maple tree.

Watt said, "If Grumpy hears us he will yell and chase us away."

Grumpy was the name all the kids called our neighbor. He was a real grouch and didn't like kids.

We shot about a dozen birds, then a shot went wild and broke Grumpy's window. We hid in the bushes when he came out of the house.

He hollered, "I know you hunkies are out there and you better come over tomorrow and pay me for that broken window."

When Grumpy went back in the house, Marcus said, "He didn't see me break that window and can't prove I did, but I'll give him something to holler about."

Marcus shot out the corner street light, then shot and broke another window. We ran like hell to our house, went upstairs and hid under the bed.

Soon we heard someone pounding on the front door, yelling, "I know you Skabs are in there, I'm going to call the police and they will take you to jail."

We stayed upstairs and soon we heard Grumpy talking to the police outside.

He said, "I want you to arrest those boys, they shot out the street light and broke two of my windows."

The policeman asked, "Did you see them do that?"

"No, but I know they did."

Soon they both left the front yard.

Watt said, "We'll catch hell when Bessie gets home."

The police talked to Clark the next day and told him about the windows.

Clark said, "I'll talk to the boys and see what I can find out."

Clark told us, "I don't want to know what happened, but if

I were you I'd have this house and yard in tip top shape when Mother gets home this weekend."

We worked the next two days and had everything spic and span when Bessie arrived home. She said that the trip was the most fun she had in a long time. Bessie even went to a Night Club and saw Can-Can dancers and a stage show. We never heard anymore about Grumpy's broken windows.

* * *

We decided to go swimming at the mill pond, not far from Foxton's Country Store. Jock Comstock had been there a few times with a friend and said it was a lot better place to swim than Silver Lake. There was a diving board, a raft and a lot more kids. We took the shortcut, walking the railroad tracks from Fenton to Silver Lake, by the old cement plant to the mill pond. It had a nice sandy beach. We had fun swimming and playing around the dam and waterwheel by the grist mill.

It was getting late, but if we hurried we could still get to Foxton's in time for the free show, outside the general store.

Many farmers came into town on Saturday night to shop, and then watch the show. We ran into Webb Herman after the show. He took us home, and asked Bessie if we boys could stay at his farm and drive the teams during the haying season. She said we could stay for three days, then we had to get back home to keep the garden and lawn up.

* * *

Webb had fixed up a platform seat on the front rack of two wagons. We could sit on the seat and drive the team without getting in the way when the hay came up the loader onto the wagon. Watt drove for Webb, I for Juno the hired man.

I kept wondering if it really was Juno I saw in the barn the night of the Davis' murders.

What started out as fun became hot, hard work trying to hang onto the wagon seat, bumping along in the field.

Juno acted like he was possessed by the devil. He hopped about on top of the hay yelling, "Nick, you son-of-a-bitch, keep those horses pulling steady. Don't cut the corners too quick. Keep the wagon over the center of the hay row."

It soon became a contest as to who could load up first and get to the barn, where Marcus set the hay forks and drove the team, pulling the hay up to the loft.

Webb's wife kept us supplied with cool lemonade, sandwiches and pie for snacks. She commented, "You Sabitches are good workers."

Webb and Watt put up more hay than Juno and I did, which made him unhappy with my driving.

"The next goddamn haying season, Watt is going to drive the team for me."

The hay was put up in three days, and Webb took us home. Bessie later told us that Mr. Herman thanked her for our help, and that we could come out to his farm anytime we wanted to.

* * *

That winter Marcus got a temporary job delivering the Fenton Independent, a weekly newspaper, in the morning before school. It was such a big route that he gave part of it to Watt and me. My customers were in and around the downtown area close to school. I got up real early during the trapping season to check and see if any animals had been caught in the traps. One cold snowy morning after tromping through the deep snow in the fields and wet drainage ditches, then peddling the Fenton Independent, I was late for school.

The teacher said, "Nick you must get to school on time," then quickly added, "You better take your wet high tops off and stand near the hot water register to get warm and dry off."

The teacher was a matronly woman and was partial to me

because I was an orphan. She tried to be mother and teacher to me without being too obvious. Jock Comstock called me teacher's pet and said he sure would like a paper route so he could be late for school and get special privileges.

At school we were assigned desks in alphabetical order. My desk was in the last row. I used to daydream a lot about how it would be to do it with Addie Comstock. She always wore the shortest dresses and sat with her legs spread apart, but not far enough to see her panties.

One morning when I came to school late, the teacher told me I would have to stay in during recess and write a hundred times on the blackboard, 'I will not be late for class.' When everyone was out of the classroom and I had the blackboard filled, I wrote real big, I climbed up on the teacher's desk and set the clock ahead a half hour. At the end of the day while the class was being dismissed, the Principal came down the hall and asked the teacher why she was letting the class out early.

I was just going down the hall when I heard, "Nick you come back here, I want to talk to you."

I confessed to the teacher that I had set the clock ahead. The Principal took me to his office and gave me a good spanking. He must have called Bessie and told her about the clock, because I received another spanking when I arrived home.

The next day the kids all thought I was really something. At recess they all wanted to play with me. Even Addie thought I was some kind of hero.

*　　*　　*

With school out for the summer, whenever we could we headed out to Silver Lake for a cool swim. By now I could dog paddle real good.

Marcus said, "Let's swim across the lake to the island on the other side and see what's over there."

It didn't take long to get to the island. We didn't find a

sandy beach, just lots of gooey, mucky marl. We stood in the shallow water and worked our feet in the muck until we could hardly get out. After awhile we decided to swim to the bridge on Owen Road. We stopped along the way at a boathouse dock near the bridge to look at a Chris Craft mahogany wood boat.

Marcus said, "I'm going to have one just like that someday, boys."

He would give anything to drive around the lake in that speedboat. It took most of the afternoon to get back to the swimming beach.

*   *   *

Addie Comstock and her girlfriend, Patsy Martin, were there.

She waved at Marcus, "Let's go swimming."

Marcus commented, "Wow, look at Patsy, she sure is getting to be a big girl."

Suddenly we heard a man yelling for help. We ran along the road and spied a canoe overturned and a man clinging to the side of it, offshore in deep water. Marcus started to swim to him, but before he got very far, the man disappeared in the water, so Marcus headed back to shore. We were pretty scared, but managed to flag down a car, and told the driver to go to Fenton and tell the police. We stayed around until the police showed up. It was too dark to do anything. The police said they would provide a diver first thing the next morning.

Bessie wasn't angry with us for getting home late when we told her about the drowning.

We went back to Silver Lake the next day to watch the diver look for the body. He wore a metal helmet with an air hose to breath from, attached to a tank in the boat.

A Flint Journal news reporter stood on shore taking pictures. Harry McElya, a one armed lifeguard from Flint, dove in the water trying to locate the body. I watched from the shore.

Finally on the third try he came to the surface carrying a body, which was bloated, with the skin black and blue. I got sick and threw up. The man wasn't anybody we knew. He lived in Flint and had come out to go fishing and didn't know how to swim.

*   *   *

The front page of the Flint Journal the following day showed a picture of the one armed lifeguard bringing the drowned man to shore. The headline news stated that Amelia Earhart, the world's most celebrated woman aviator, on her flight around the world, had disappeared at sea somewhere near the Island of Howland in the Central Pacific. It was July, 1937.

TEN

Marcus and Watt had gone swimming at Silver Lake without me. I decided to go and play in the gravel pit near the cemetery. As I approached the old rusty steam shovel, smoke drifted out the open door. A boy looked at me as I climbed up into the cab of the shovel.

He said, "I'll bet you're one of the hunky brothers I've been hearing about. Which one of the Skab-bitches are you? Cab Bitch, Scab Bitch or Son-of-a-bitch?"

I didn't say anything, then the boy said, "I'm just kidding, my name is Bert Wilton, I like to smoke, swear and fuck. Don't you?"

I stammered a minute and then said, "Yes, I do. My name is Nick Sabitch."

Bert, cocky and very sure of himself, was a handsome boy about my age, with sparkly brown eyes and curly brown hair.

"Have a smoke on me," Bert said, handing his cigarette to me. I puffed on it, then coughed as the smoke went down my throat.

"That's no way to smoke, you don't puff it, you suck on it." Bert took a long drag on the cigarette, and exhaling he blew smoke rings in the air. "Damn this tastes good! Sometime I'll let you smoke one of my dad's cigars, they're even better. Want another drag, Nick?"

I coughed and said, "I've got a sore throat, I'll try it again when my throat's better."

Bert dropped the butt on the floor of the steel cab and crushed it out with the heel of his bare foot.

He glanced at me and said, "I've fucked three different girls, how many have you?"

I thought back to the time in the woods with Marcus, Watt and the neighbor girl. "I guess maybe one."

Bert snickered, "You don't know if you fucked a girl or not? I'll bet you're still cherry!"

"Where do you live, Bert?"

"Around the corner from here. Come on, Nick, I'll show you."

We walked about a block to Shiawassee Avenue to a big house with a car barn and a horse barn. Bert showed me his spotted horse and his mother's black horse. Also in the barn was a new four door Buick.

Bert said, "That's our family car, my dad has a company car he drives back and forth to work."

Outside the kitchen door, a big black chow, in a fenced pen, growled as we started to go into the house.

Mr. and Mrs. Wilton were not home, so Bert took me through the house to the tower above the third floor. Looking out the windows we could see the steam shovel in the gravel pit, the school behind the house, and most of the other big houses on Shiawassee Avenue.

"Bert, your dad sure must have a lot of money to live here."

"He's a big shot at the Buick automobile factory in Flint."

"I've got to go, thanks for showing me your house."

I told Marcus and Watt about meeting Bert.

Marcus said, "Wow, he must be a rich kid. I've walked by those houses many times and always wondered what kind of people live in them. Let's get better acquainted with Bert; maybe he will let us ride his horse."

I asked Bessie what a hunky was.

"Why do you want to know, Nick?"

I told her I had been called that a few times.

She thought a minute, then said, "Your father came from Serbia and your mother from Albania. Sometimes thoughtless people refer to Slavic immigrants as hunkys. You can be proud of your heritage."

*   *   *

I couldn't quite remember when the Acme cement plant at Silver Lake closed down. The dredge stayed moored to the north shore for a long time. When the dredge quit working more kids came to the lake to swim.

Bert told me what a great swimmer he was, so I took him with us one day. Being new friends we wanted to show off.

Marcus said, "Let's swim over to the dredge dock and back."

It was half a mile from the island to the dredge. We all started dog paddling out in the lake.

Bert said, "I think I better go back to the shore, I would get a cramp if I swam that far. I'll walk along the road and meet you at the dredge."

We kept on swimming and Marcus remarked, "I think your friend Bert is chicken."

We made it to the dredge. Bert was there waiting for us. We played on the dredge for awhile then decided to swim back.

Bert said, "I'm going to walk back, then I better get home."

*   *   *

Whenever we had some money to spend we went downtown to the Rowena Theater. On the way to the theater we played and waded in the Shiawassee River that flowed through town. Next we stopped and checked out Wolcott's mill to look for birds nesting in the eaves, then across the street to Mickey's Dairy. For five cents we could buy a dip of ice cream and for a penny more a double dip.

We climbed up the back stairs and got on the roof of the Variety Store, where nothing cost over twenty five cents. Marcus threw cherry bombs in the street and watched the horses jump about. Eventually we arrived at the theater and for ten cents we watched the afternoon feature with Judy Garland and Mickey Rooney.

*   *   *

The latest comic book character was "Superman." With a dime burning a hole in my pocket, I walked downtown to buy one. As I was passing the bank, a masked man ran out of the bank with a gun in his hand. He pushed me aside yelling, "Get out of my way kid!" He jumped in a car parked along the curb.

I ran across the street to the corner drug store, shouting to Mr. Otis, "The Bank's been robbed!"

He grabbed a rifle from behind the counter, ran out of the store and started firing at the robber's car, speeding down the dusty road. The car careened around a corner and sped out of sight, and range of Mr. Otis' rifle.

The police questioned me about the bank robber. I was of no help. Everything happened so fast and the robber had a bandana tied over his face.

Marcus asked me when I got home if I was scared.

"Not until Mr. Otis started shooting at the car. I was afraid the robber would shoot back."

Marcus said, "I probably would have pissed in my pants if I'd been in your place."

*   *   *

Every Wednesday night during the summer the town had a concert at the bandstand on Shiawassee Avenue, across from Wiltons. The adults gathered around to listen to the music while the kids played hide and seek behind the trees. When we tired of the game we settled down and listened to the music.

Addie Comstock was sitting next to me. I said, "I wish they would play some good music."

Addie replied, "Why don't you ask some boys to come to Jock's Saturday night, and I'll play some good music on my record player. I'll ask some girls to come and teach you boys how to dance."

Saturday night we Sabitch and neighborhood boys went to Comstocks. Addie had asked some other girls to come to the dance. The boys stood in a corner, not knowing what to do until Addie said, "Okay you can't learn standing in the corner, come on get a girl and I'll show you what to do."

We started with the two step, two steps ahead, two steps back. What a boring dance, but it was fun holding the girls close and we changed partners after each record.

Before the evening was over I had danced with all the girls, even Addie. She was the best. I had trouble two stepping. My feet wanted to spin, twirl and dance to the beat of the music. The girls liked fast dancing best.

Before we went home, Addie said, "You guys need a lot of practice, I'll have the dance again next week."

The girls took turns having dance practice and after awhile we could circle two step, polka and fast dance.

*   *   *

Throughout the time we had been living with Bessie, many homeless people stopped by asking for something to eat. Bessie never turned anyone away, she always fixed them a hot meal, and some food to take with them.

Once in awhile the "Gypsies" would come to town. Bessie never liked them. She told us they steal and sometimes kidnap kids. One day a wagon load of Gypsies stopped at the house. Bessie wasn't home. We remembered what she had told us about them stealing, so we didn't let them in the house, but gave them food. They seemed friendly enough, and invited us to come downtown to see the Medicine Show they were putting on.

That night we went to see the show. Marcus said, "Let's stay together, remember what we heard about kids being kidnapped."

The wagon was parked in the street by the Drug Store. A big crowd of people were standing in front of the wagon. A Gypsy girl was doing a belly dance, while a man was talking to the crowd, and selling bottles of "medicine" for a dollar. He said the contents of the bottle would cure everything. Another man got up on the wagon with him, and was holding a big lizard up for the people to see.

He said, "This poisonous lizard bit my hand, if I hadn't drank this potion, I would have died."

The crowd must have believed him, a lot of them bought the bottles of medicine.

After the show, Marcus told the Gypsy he would buy a bottle of potion if we could see the lizard. We couldn't touch it, but got a close look. It was about eighteen inches long, kind of pink and black. He told us it was a gila monster that lives in the west.

A man stayed in the background following us when we left to go home. Marcus stopped and took a drink of the potion.

"I'll take a swig of that stuff, boys."

It was Juno, Herman's hired man. He smelled bad and looked worse.

Marcus started to say no, then thought better of it. "This stuff tastes like panther piss, you can have it."

Juno grabbed the bottle, and as he shuffled away, I commented, "I'm sure he was in the barn at Parker's orchard. What's he doing in town?"

Watt spoke up, "I heard Clark tell Bessie that Hermans let Juno go. Let's tell Clark about Juno taking our medicine potion."

Marcus said, "No, we'll catch hell for buying and drinking that stuff."

*　　*　　*

Clark, a tall, handsome, young man with black hair, worked at a feed store, delivering coal around Fenton. Twenty years old, he had a friendly smile and an easy going disposition. He had an old, black two door Ford, smoked, and drank beer. Bessie didn't approve. We thought he was a neat guy. To help pay for his room and board, he painted the house during the summer.

Clark generally stopped by the house to have lunch. He came in looking like a black man, with coal soot all over him. After he washed up, Clark turned the radio on to listen to Kate Smith sing "When the Moon Comes Over the Mountain" and "God Bless America." He sure liked to hear her sing.

Clark said, "You boys better go downtown to Wolcott's Mill and take a good look, because they're starting to tear it down to make way for a new Community Building."

After lunch we walked downtown, and sure enough a big wrecking crane was knocking down the mill. We felt pretty bad. We had a lot of fun playing there and would miss it.

Jock Comstock joined us and said, "This isn't any fun watching the mill get destroyed. Let's go to the gravel pit and play king of the hill."

We played until dark, then laid at the top of the hill watching the stars come out. We saw a lot of bright lights in the north sky. What a beautiful sight, the northern lights lit up the sky like searchlights.

Suddenly a voice said, "Can I watch with you boys?"

It was Patsy Martin. Somehow she always showed up when a bunch of us guys were playing together and having fun.

Marcus said, "Come over here by me, Patsy."

In silence we watched the bright spectacle in the sky. I heard Patsy's muffled voice, "Do you want to, Marcus?"

"Sure, Patsy, I want to, but not with these other guys here."

"They can take a turn Marcus, then they won't be able to tell on us."

Had my turn finally come?

Suddenly a loud voice said, "You boys come off that hill. It's your bedtime Jock."

I lay awake long into the night wondering what I would have done when my turn came with Patsy.

ELEVEN

The Flint Journal representative told us that a daily paper route had opened up and it was big enough to split three ways. He explained the route process, and collection procedure. Each one of us would have fifty customers to peddle papers to seven days a week. The paper cost each customer eighteen cents a week, of which we would receive three cents.

The papers would be delivered to a shed behind the Otis Drug Store in downtown Fenton. The delivery man would stop every other week to collect fifteen cents per week, per customer for the Flint Journal. Anything left over was our profit.

We didn't realize that the Journal got their pay whether we collected from all the customers or not, and getting eighteen cents a week from some people, was like pulling teeth. The delivery man warned us not to let anyone get too far behind on paying for their papers.

He said, "The Lend Spend program that President Roosevelt recently announced might help to perk up the economy, but there are over 10 million people still out of work, and some of them are your customers."

My route started from the corner of Leroy Street and Shiawassee Avenue all the way out to Owen and Silver Lake Roads. It took two hours to pick up the papers at Otis', walking the whole route and back home.

Because of delinquent customers, it took us a month before we had any profit. We somehow managed to collect enough money to pay the Journal. Bessie always let us spend our share any way we chose.

*   *   *

We had just figured out the paper routes and making spending money when Jock Comstock asked us if we wanted to go to Shore Acres Golf Club and make some money caddying for the golfers. Bessie said we could as long as we were back to peddle papers on time.

The golf club was about five miles north of town near Lake Fenton. We walked all the way. When we arrived at the club, the owner explained to us that the caddies who arrived early were first up unless a golfer asked for a certain caddie.

The green fees were forty-five cents for nine holes or eighty cents for eighteen. On weekends the fees were fifty cents and a dollar. The caddie fees were twenty-five cents for nine and fifty cents for eighteen holes. Any tips we received we could keep. It was hard work, at least two hours to walk nine holes. Sometimes we caddied double if the bags were light. On slow days we hunted for golf balls in the ponds and woods. We cleaned them up to sell.

Between caddying, selling golf balls and the paper route, we always had spending money.

It wasn't long before we bought bikes to use peddling papers and riding to the golf course and back. Watt was a better saver than Marcus and I. He had enough money to buy a brand new bike with a basket in front to carry papers, a built in headlight, kick stand and a metal carrier behind the seat. It was from Montgomery Ward and cost nineteen dollars. A real beauty. Marcus bought a used balloon tired bike and I bought a skinny tired used bike.

*   *   *

Marcus and I had another leisurely talk in the john. He told me I had better take a last look at the girls wearing underwear in the catalogs, because he heard Clark and Bessie talking about having a bathroom installed in the house.

Marcus said, "It will be nice not to have to tramp through

snow and mud to go to the shit house. No more catalogs, just soft rolled paper."

I thought to myself, it will be nice, but I am going to miss sitting, thinking, daydreaming, and being by myself.

I told Marcus, "It won't be as private and the house will always stink."

It took two men a week to dig a ditch from the road to the corner of the house for the sewer line, and another week to build a small bathroom at the end of the pantry, complete with bathtub, stool and washstand. We helped Clark shovel the dirt back in the ditch. The outhouse was left standing, and when I felt the need for peace and quiet, I still enjoyed looking through the catalogs and daydreaming the time away.

*   *   *

During the winter the workload slowed down, and so did the spending money. We started running the trap lines again. Early in January, one morning before school, Watt and I checked the traps outside the cemetery, and we noticed where a trap had been pulled deep into the hole and a lot of blood spattered on the snow. We couldn't see into the hole, so Watt reached down and grabbed the chain to pull the trap out. He let out a yell and started rubbing his face. A big skunk had shot Watt in the eye. We finally got the skunk out, killed and carried it home. It was cold enough to keep the carcass frozen.

I arrived late for class. Everybody knew when I entered the room and walked back to my desk. The smell was over-powering.

Jock Comstock whispered, "Jesus Christ, Sabitch, you smell like a dead skunk."

The teacher said, "Nick, you go to the Principal's office right now."

The kids all snickered, and held their noses as I walked out of the room. I thought, I am going to catch it for being late for class.

Watt was sitting in the office, and when I walked in the Principal said, "I'm going to excuse you boys from school today; go home and get aired out. Tomorrow be in school without the skunk odor."

*   *   *

The big striped skunk we trapped had started to thaw out. Marcus had watched some older boys skin a coon. He allowed he knew what to do. He nailed the skunk by its' back feet to the outhouse wall. Using a razor, he cut around the back feet, down the inside of the legs and around the ass hole. The skinning was going according to plan until he started to pull the hide down over the body. The pee sack and stomach burst, squirting blood, guts and skunk juice all over. What a stinking, putrid mess! Marcus finished pulling the hide down to the head and cut it free of the body.

He commented, "Nothing to it, huh boys?"

I stretched the hide over a cedar shingle, sprinkled some salt on it, then tied it to a nail to dry and cure in the outside air and sun. Watt took the carcass and threw it down into the bottom of the outhouse. We went into the house to wash up. Bessie caught our scent, and ordered us outside.

She said, "Hose down in the garage and burn those stinking clothes in the trash can, and pour a sack of lime down to the bottom of the outhouse to cover the skunk's carcass!"

Marcus didn't understand why Bessie was so upset with the rank odor. "Shit houses always smell, what difference does it make if it comes from a skunk or people?"

*   *   *

In the spring when the weather warmed up, Jock suggested we skip school, and he would teach me how to whistle. Marcus could howl real loud, like a hound dog, and I wanted to sur-

5-WILS

prise him by whistling when he howled; like calling a dog home.

I met Jock in the playground, and we headed for the fields and woods to the back of Jock's grandfather's farm off Owen Road. It was a warm spring day, just right for skipping school. Jock whistled by putting a finger on each side of his mouth and blowing through his teeth. After many tries, I could whistle almost as loud as Jock.

Jock helped me peddle papers that night. As he was going home he said, "My dad will write an excuse for both of us so we won't get in trouble tomorrow."

*   *   *

Jock came over and asked me if I wanted to help him haul ashes. His dad had built a doodle bug and trailer. The doodle bug was made from an old jalopy car. The frame, wheels and motor were exposed. An old horsehide seat with the springs sticking out was used for a seat behind the steering wheel.

Most of the townspeople had coal stoves or furnaces and all winter dumped the ashes out back somewhere in a big pile. Jock and I shoveled four or five loads a day and made two to three dollars each on the weekend. It was hard work, but we made spending money and I learned how to drive the doodle bug.

*   *   *

Jock's grandpa kept an old 38 revolver in the farmhouse. Jock invited me out to go in the woods and shoot the gun. I had never shot anything bigger than a BB gun.

I said, "Jock, let's take turns, you shoot it first."

"No, I shot it once Nick. If you're chicken I'll take it back in the house."

The gun was so big it took both of my hands to hold it. I

knew it would break my wrist when I fired it. We played in the woods most of the morning before I got up the nerve to pull the trigger. The noise hurt my ears more than the kick hurt my hands.

Jock said, "There are five more shells left to fire in the chamber, blast away."

"That's enough for me, want to take a turn Jock?"

"No, let's go back and play in the barn."

In the back end of the barn was an old buggy. The shafts were broken off near the front axle.

I said, "Wouldn't it be fun to ride the buggy down Denton hill into town, Jock?"

"Sure, but it's three miles to the hill and another mile to the top."

"Let's get Watt and Marcus to help. Four of us can do it easy," I said.

Jock tied a rope to each side of the front axle so we could steer the buggy. We pushed the buggy all the way to the Cooper house. Marcus and Watt helped push it to the top of Denton hill. Watt and I jumped in the back and Marcus and Jock in the front. The buggy lurched from side to side, bouncing from pothole to pothole down the steep road at breath taking speed. Marcus and Jock were each holding a rope to steer with.

It was a good thing no cars were on the road. We rode the buggy over a mile, then Jock's rope broke and he lost control of the steering. The front wheel dropped in a big pothole and the buggy crashed and overturned in the ditch. None of us boys were hurt other than a few cuts and bruises. The buggy was a wreck.

Marcus said, "You'll catch hell from your grandpa, Jock."

"No," he said, "It was just taking up space in the barn. It wasn't any good anyway."

*   *   *

Bessie was sitting at the kitchen table crying when I got home. I thought, I'm going to catch it now.

Finally Bessie said, "Mr. Comstock's mother died and I will be helping them make funeral arrangements."

Jock's grandmother was a good friend of Bessie's. We went to Comstocks that evening. Grandma lay in the casket, peaceful in death. Her hands were clasped across her chest, her eyes closed, as in a deep sleep.

Addie said, "Doesn't she look peaceful in her sleep?"

I couldn't say anything.

After the funeral, Bessie told us she would be working part-time at the Comstocks, and that we had to be more helpful around the house. I had trouble sleeping that night. In my mind I kept seeing Jock's grandmother in the casket. I shuddered as I visualized the closed casket, buried deep in the ground. No way could she get out. How could she get to heaven.

I decided to ask Marcus. He would know. Marcus told me that peoples bodies didn't go to heaven, just their souls did. I asked him what a soul was.

"Jesus Christ, Nick, why worry about something you don't understand. Let's go up to the bedroom. I have something to show you that you can understand."

Marcus opened the attic door and reached behind it. He brought out a 22 Browning pump rifle. He had bought it from an older friend for ten dollars. The rifle was kept in the upstairs closet, and when we wanted to take it out of the house, one of us put on a pair of bib overalls, slid the gun down inside along our pant leg, and walked stiff legged out of the house. A box of 22 long rifle shells cost twenty cents.

Clark found out about the gun, and said, "You boys be careful when you're shooting. Better not let Mother know you have a rifle."

TWELVE

The day after Grandma Comstock's funeral, Jock and I played in the old steam shovel in the gravel pit until dark. When I arrived home, Marcus and Watt sat in the living room listening to the radio.

Bessie, sitting quietly in her rocker, said "Boys, I've got some news for you. Your dad, Ziv, is coming for a visit."

I said, "Who? Dad's dead!"

"No, you might have been told that, but it's not true. Your dad had to go away, and couldn't keep the family together. I'll let him tell you about it tomorrow when he gets here, but now it's time for you boys to go upstairs to bed. You have a big day ahead of you, and need your rest."

It had been over five years since we had seen Dad. Would he recognize us?

Marcus had grown into a big, stocky kid, always smiling and laughing. His ears stuck out from the sides of his head. The devil stuck out in almost everything Marcus did. He had no hang up about listening to his good conscience.

Watt, still of small stature, had a big chest with a full head of curly, dark hair. Life was serious to Watt. He reluctantly went along with what Marcus did.

I was an imp with boundless nervous energy. I had small facial features and small ears tight against my head. I took life as it came, the good and the bad, adjusted to what had to be.

*   *   *

Later when we were upstairs in bed, Marcus said, "I thought

Dad was alive, but I wasn't sure so I didn't say anything to you guys. Tomorrow will be some kind of a day for us won't it?"

I lay awake a long time, unable to sleep. Why did Mrs. Gibson tell me that Dad was dead? The time I asked Joseph about our parents why wouldn't he talk about them? Did he know Dad was alive? I couldn't remember the last time I saw my dad or how I came to be at the orphanage. What did he look like? Where had he been? I finally fell asleep dreaming of the time our family would all be together again.

*   *   *

Noon the next day a shiny black 1936 Chevy pulled in the driveway. A short man with a barrel chest and dark, curly hair got out. Yes, I did remember him! We ran out to greet him.

With tears in his eyes, Dad gave each of us a hug and said, "I chure missed youse boys."

Bessie introduced herself. She had prepared a big dinner. "I'll be gone for awhile, you boys have a good visit with your dad."

We all started talking at once. Marcus told about living on the farm, and then moving to Fenton. I talked about living at the Whaley Orphanage, and mean Mrs. Gibson. Watt told about the visit with Joseph and Hedy.

Dad didn't mention where he had been or what he had been doing. He did say that he found work on a dairy farm quite a distance from Flint.

Suddenly it dawned on me, if Dad was alive, what about Mother? I told him about Mrs. Gibson telling me that my parents were dead. "Why did she say that?"

Dad didn't know. "Your mother is alive, and is in the insane asylum at Pontiac and can't be a mother to you boys."

I asked when he would take us to see Mother.

"Boys, I've been to visit her. She doesn't know who I am. Her mind is bad, and she is very violent. I don't want you boys to see her now. Maybe if she gets better, then I will take you to visit her."

I asked, "When are you going to get the family back together?"

Dad thought a minute, then said, "I'm going to talk to Mrs. Hardy and see what I can do. Right now I can hardly afford the one room house where I'm living. It's such a small place, I've just barely got room for myself."

Dad hadn't seen any of the other brothers and sisters. When he got time off again he would look them up. He was quite upset when he talked about Germany invading and conquering Czechoslovakia.

He said, "If Hitler continues his conquest of Europe, the whole world will soon be at war."

Dad left with tears in his eyes. "I'll keep in touch with youse boys."

*   *   *

That night we talked over our visit. We had a dad and mother again, even if we couldn't live together as a family. I was deeply troubled to think Dad had let the family break up, and I had to go live at the Whaley Orphanage. Where had he been the last five years? He didn't want to talk about it. I wondered why?

When I asked Marcus, he replied, "Jesus Christ, Nick, don't worry about something you can't do anything about. Just be happy that Dad's back and is okay."

Marcus knew things would be all right now. The family would soon be reunited.

Watt said, "I don't think so. How could the adopted brothers ever be family again?"

I said, "Maybe part of the family could be together."

I fell asleep crying softly to myself. Poor Mother in an asylum in Pontiac. I knew about institutions from living at the orphanage in Flint. It was July, 1938.

*   *   *

The next day we were waiting behind the Drug Store for the Flint Journal truck to bring the newspapers. Mr. Otis came out to the shack and told us the paper truck had broke down and would be quite late. We might as well go home, have supper and come back later. Mr. Otis owned the Otis Drug Store. He was a big fat man, bald, with a black fringe of hair all around the bottom of his head. He wore spectacles that perched on the end of his nose. He was always jolly and joked with us.

We decided to stay. We went next door to the meat market. In the back room lard was rendered in a big cast iron kettle. The butcher always let us have all the pig rind we wanted. We each filled a sack with fried pig rinds and walked back to the paper shack. While we were eating the rinds a voice outside said, "Can I have some boys?" It was Patsy Martin. What was she doing here?

Marcus said, "Come in Patsy, have some of mine."

We ate the pig rinds in silence. The roar of the paper delivery truck coming down the back alley broke the silence.

Patsy said, "I better go home boys."

It was late when we finished delivering the newspapers. I asked Marcus what Patsy wanted back at the paper shack. He told me she is a 'Tom boy' who likes to play with boys.

*   *   *

Saturday morning early we walked to Shore Acres Golf Club. In back of the club house was an old barn. In the winter ice was cut out of Lake Fenton, put in the barn and covered up with sawdust. The ice would be used in the summer for cooling beer and pop. When the bartender needed ice, one of us caddies would dig out a block, hose it off and put it in the cooler. We received a Coke for our effort.

A nickel slot machine was kept near the bar for customers to play. It was illegal to have the slot. The club owner received a tip that the Sheriff was going to visit his club. We took the slot machine and hid it in the caddie shack. Marcus decided to play the slot. He put in five nickels and bang, he hit the jackpot. Each of us bought a Big Ben pocket watch with a belt strap for a dollar, some candy and then went to the restaurant next to the Rowena Theater for a ten cent foot long hot dog.

*　　*　　*

An older high school girl, who worked at a restaurant after school, asked Marcus what he thought of the new Community Building? She said square dancing would be starting Saturday night, anybody could go.

"Will they be doing modern dancing, too?" Marcus liked to dance close with the girls.

The waitress said, "No, but anybody can rent a small room downstairs for a buck and a quarter, and hold their own dance. If you boys get enough kids together, and pay the money, I'll chaperone the dance."

Marcus collected enough nickels and dimes from the neighborhood boys and girls to rent a room. Saturday night they all showed up for the dance. Addie Comstock brought her record player. What a time we had! I danced with all the girls. I especially liked Addie. I walked her home after the dance, and she kissed me goodnight. I was in love!

*　　*　　*

Clark was in love, too. Bessie told us that Clark would be marrying Ella Phipps, a girl he had been going with for a long time. Ella, a tall pretty girl, with long blonde hair and twinkling blue eyes, had a great sense of humor. She came from a poor family who lived in the country on a farm.

Clark and Ella were married in October. They came to live in Bessie's house to take care of us boys. Bessie was going to Arizona to live with and work for a friend of hers.

Bessie cried when she left. "You boys behave yourselves and help Ella around the house. I'll be back."

Clark, twenty one, and Ella only eighteen, had taken on a lot of responsibility. Marcus, fifteen, Watt fourteen and me twelve, were more than a handful for Bessie. How could Clark and Ella, newlyweds, manage?

The odds evened out shortly after Bessie left. Dad had contacted Mrs. Hardy, and Marcus was going to live with him.

Marcus, in a cheerful mood, said, "I'm going to be able to do what I want to, not what I'm told to do."

Dad was not so cheerful. If America got involved in the war, his boys would soon be old enough to go.

Marcus said, "When I'm old enough, I'll join the Army and go fight those Nazis and help free our relatives in the old country."

As they drove away, Watt said, "We'll probably never see Marcus again."

I had tears in my eyes and a big lump in my throat. It was Christmas Eve, 1939.

THIRTEEN

Ella had no trouble adjusting to married life and substituting as mother to Watt and me. She came from a large family. Her father died when she was a young girl and Ella had learned how to work and do her share.

After Marcus left, Watt and I each had our own bed to sleep in, and more inside and outside chores to do. We both missed Marcus. Patsy Martin didn't show up, out of nowhere, like she did when Marcus was around. I wondered who would teach me about sex now.

Clark and Ella weren't much more than kids themselves and were fun to live with. Life wasn't too serious to them yet. They could still remember how they behaved at our ages. If I wasn't feeling well or missed school for any reason, Ella always wrote an excuse for me.

*   *   *

Saturday after I finished peddling papers, Bert came running into the house shouting, "Watt's been shot, Nick, he's at the Doctor's office."

I said, "What happened Bert? How bad is it? Where did Watt get shot?"

Bert said, "Slow down, Nick, Watt's okay."

Watt, Jock and Bert had gone shooting. They were in Comstock's old barn. Jock had an old single shot, bolt action 22 rifle. Somehow it discharged while he was loading it. The bullet went into Watt's foot. Watt was taken to St. Joseph's hospital in Flint. The 22 bullet shattered when it hit bone. The

Doctor couldn't get all the pieces out. Watt came home a few days later, wearing a foot cast.

Jock told me he caught hell from his dad. "I'll be more careful where I point that gun the next time I load it."

* * *

Jock was going to wash his dad's car, a new black 1939 Chevrolet, and asked me to help him.

After we washed the car, he said, "Let's take it for a ride."

Jock had driven a little, but needed to practice. He drove the back way out beyond Denton hill. Even sitting on a pillow, he could barely see over the dash. Before we went home, Jock let me take a turn. Sitting on Jock's lap, I had trouble shifting and clutching at the same time, but managed to keep the car going down the road.

I told Bert Wilton about my driving experience.

He said, "Come over to my place tonight, and we'll drive our car."

After supper Watt and I went over to Bert's. His folks were home. Bert told his mom that he would be outside playing with us for awhile. He took us out back to the car barn to the big four door Buick family car.

Bert said, "Be real quiet, we have to push the car out of the barn and down the driveway, past the house to the road. Then we can get in it, and go for a ride."

It took all three of us to push the big Buick far enough from the house so Mr. Wilton wouldn't hear it start up. Bert was just learning to drive, the same as Watt and me. We took turns driving. I had to sit on Watt's lap so I could see over the dash. Bert knew an older boy who worked at a gas station out of town. A gallon of gas cost ten cents. Watt and I gladly paid the dime for a gallon of gas, just to drive Wilton's car. Going back, Bert stopped the car before we got near their house, and we pushed it back to the barn. As we left to go home, I asked

Bert if he wanted to go shooting with us in the morning, but he had to clean out the horse barn.

*　　*　　*

Marcus had left his 22 pump rifle in the upstairs attic for us to use.

I had fired the rifle a few times, and was anxious to become a better shot. Watt suggested we hike out to the barn near the Davis' farm and shoot pigeons. "If we get enough we can build a fire and have a pigeon roast."

The Davis farm had not been worked since the murders. The fields around the house had grown up into weeds. I had an eerie feeling as we walked through the barnyard to cross the road to the old barn. A flock of pigeons circled overhead.

Watt stopped to take a pee. "Be quiet when you go into the barn, Nick, or you'll scare the pigeons away. I'll be in shortly."

The side door creaked as I opened it. I heard a rustling sound in the back of the barn. The pigeons must be settling down on the roof, I thought. It took a few minutes for my eyes to get adjusted to the dim light filtering through the cracks in the wall.

As I walked by the open grain room door, someone grabbed me by the arm, and a hand clamped over my mouth. I tried to scream, but couldn't. Turning my head and looking up, I saw a face leering at me. It was Juno!

I struggled to get away, as tears ran down my cheeks.

"You little bastard, What are you doing here?"

I couldn't answer. He shoved me down on the grainery floor, forcing my face into a stale, musty pile of oats. I managed to force my face up, and let out a loud scream. The oats got into my eyes, nose and mouth as Juno shoved my head back into the grain pile. I started to blackout, when a shot rang out, and his grip slackened. I managed to pull my head up.

"Christ, what the hell, it's Juno," Watt said.

I struggled free, blowing snot and oats out of my nose. "Juno tried to smother me, Watt. Shoot the son-of-a-bitch."

He started moving toward the door, saying, "Take it easy with that rifle, I wasn't going to hurt him."

"Don't come any closer, or I'll shoot you." Watt trembled as he kept the rifle pointed at him.

"Let's take him to the police, Watt." I wiped more oats off my face.

Juno said, "I don't know where you got that rifle, boys, but if the police find out they will take it away, and put you in jail." Juno laughed, "I'll just walk out of here, and you boys will never see me again."

Watt followed his movements as he slowly walked out of the barn, and disappeared into the woods.

"What was Juno doing here? Let's go to the police, Watt."

He didn't answer for awhile, then said, "No, Juno might be right about the rifle. Besides, by the time we get back to Fenton, he will be long gone."

We walked back home through the open fields, avoiding the woods.

I lay awake long into the night, wondering if Juno would ever show up again. Did he have anything to do with the Davis' murders? The police had never found Davis' hired man, who was suspected of murdering them. I wished Marcus was back with us. Pulling the covers over my head, still smelling the rank odor of rotten oats, I fell asleep.

*   *   *

My wish soon came true, Marcus didn't stay with Dad very long. He told me, "Dad has been alone so long he was kind of hard to live with."

I told him about finding Juno in the old barn, and Watt scaring him off with the rifle.

"Watt should have shot the bastard, Nick."

Clark made arrangements for Marcus to stay on the White farm where he once worked. They needed someone to do the chores and help with the farming. Marcus could earn his keep, and still go to school.

When Marcus left he said, "I'm giving my rifle to you guys. I'll get a new one as soon as I earn enough money."

*   *   *

I told Jock about Marcus leaving, as we walked home after school. He offered no comment and was unusually quiet.

Finally he said, "My father is getting married, and we are moving to a farm in the country, several miles from Fenton. We have had lots of fun together, Nick. I hope you get to live with your own family someday. Goodbye." He turned and walked sadly away.

Ella knew Jock's dad was getting married, and that the Comstocks were moving away from Fenton.

"Jock is your best friend, and you will always remember the fun times you had together. To help cheer you up, why don't you stay home from school tomorrow?"

Ella had some cooking and baking to do, and wanted help. She was good to me, and real easy to do things with. I liked to color the oleo. It came in a clear sack with a red color spot in one corner. I dumped it all in a bowl and mixed it until it turned yellow, and looked like butter. Ella made cookies, and a big chocolate cake, my favorite.

After supper Clark, Ella, Watt and I were listening to the radio. The news was mostly bad. The Germans had captured Denmark, Norway, and were parading through Paris. President Roosevelt warned the nation against "unpreparedness" in case of war. Clark, who never talked much, seemed especially quiet.

Finally he said, "Boys, I've got some bad news for you. As soon as school is out you will be leaving us. The Wiltons have agreed to have Watt live with them. Nick, you are going to live on a farm with Judd and Nellie Perry."

Clark said he was sorry, but they were going to have a family of their own.

I had a lot of friends in Fenton, and didn't like the idea of living with a new family, and going to a different school. Watt seemed quite happy with the arrangements. A good friend of Bert's, he would still be living in Fenton, but didn't like the idea of us splitting up.

Watt and I talked a long time before going to sleep. He knew the Wiltons, and would be moving a block down the street, but I was going to live with a whole different family. I cried myself to sleep.

*   *   *

The last day of school, the grumpy neighbor yelled at me when I walked by his house.

"I've heard the good news. You Skab Bitches are leaving. Good riddance! You little bastards won't be around to give me any more trouble."

I gave him the middle finger salute, then ran home.

When Mrs. Hardy picked us up, Ella cried, and Clark had tears in his eyes. Both of us boys waved as the car drove off, taking Watt to the Wiltons, and me to the Perrys. It was the beginning of summer, 1940.

FOURTEEN

On the way to Perrys, Mrs. Hardy told me she was sorry that Watt and I were being separated.

"Things don't always work out the way they are planned, Nick. Clark and Ella Cooper are young, and want their own family, and have their own lives to live. Mrs. Wilton considered taking both of you boys, but decided it would be too much. You're close to Bert's age, and would be more competition than a companion for him. Watt is older, more serious, and will be a good example for Bert."

"Mrs. Hardy, why can't I live with Dad, like Marcus did?"

"It didn't work out with Marcus and wouldn't with you. Maybe when you're older."

"My dad said that my mother is still alive. Why did Mrs. Gibson tell me they were both dead?"

"I don't know."

"You told me that I should forget about my parents. Why?"

"I thought it was in your best interest, at the time, that you didn't know your parents were alive."

"Can you take me to see my mother sometime?"

"I can, but I won't, Nick. It is better that you remember her as she was before she became ill."

I didn't have any memory of my mother.

*   *   *

The Perrys had a small farm a mile and a half west of Byron, a small town southwest of Flint. Byron consisted of a grain elevator, saloon, gas station, red brick schoolhouse, a grocery store, post office and telephone switchboard. The Shiawassee river flowed over a dam that powered a cider mill located there.

Mrs. Hardy said, "You will be treated well. The Perrys are good Christian people."

When we arrived at the farm, she introduced me to the Perrys. Judd, a tall, thin man in his middle forties, had a soft, gentle voice. Nellie, a young woman in her early thirties, was heavyset, with black, braided hair, a loud hearty laugh, and the shadow of a mustache under her nose.

I would be sleeping at the top of the stairs in the hallway on a small day bed. Judd and Nellie had a bedroom downstairs.

The Perrys were poor, subsistence dirt farmers. The barn, sheds and outbuildings all needed repairing.

Life on the farm was a lot different than in town. No way to earn spending money, no paper route or golf course, and nobody to play with. My companion and friend was Judd. I learned all about farm chores, up early in the morning to feed the chickens, geese, pigs, sheep and horses, milk the six to eight cows, depending if they were calving or not. I had to turn the separator by hand to separate the cream from the milk, clean the cow barn, hitch up the team of horses and out to the fields for the day.

Judd, a quiet, patient man soon taught me how to do all the farm work. He owned an old W-30 McCormick Deering steel lugged tractor. I would drive the team of horses or the tractor. Because of the daily outside farm work, I didn't have to work in the house. Farming, I found out, was a seven day a week operation, no days off from doing chores.

*   *   *

Saturday afternoon all the nearby farmers went to Byron to shop at the local grocery store. After doing their shopping, they settled down in the vacant lot between the barber shop and the town hall to watch free shows on an outdoor screen.

Nellie introduced me to Dora Simpson. Her dad managed the grocery store. Her mother operated the switchboard in the back of the store. Fourteen year old Dora, a full figured girl with long, curly brown hair, helped in the store.

She was my first contact with any kids my age since I left Fenton. We sat on a blanket to watch the free show, and held hands.

I overheard Mr. Simpson tell Judd, "Nick is big enough to be a lot of help on the farm and you get paid to keep him."

Judd and I worked well together, chores in the morning and chores at night. During the day we worked the fields. I got to drive the old tractor a lot. As long as it was in the soft dirt it rode okay, but on hard ground and on the gravel road those steel wheeled lugs shook the pee out of me.

*   *   *

On Sundays the Perrys took me to the Nazarene Church in Flint. After church we stopped at Nellie's folks for Sunday dinner, and a visit. I often wondered how the Bible could be interpreted in so many different ways by the churches I had attended. What bothered me the most was how nice people acted in church on Sunday, but during the week they smoked, drank, swore and weren't always friendly.

Every summer a Revival group came to Byron, pitched some big tents in a field outside of town, and held Church, Sunday School and Prayer Meetings. The Perrys took me every night, Saturday afternoon and all day Sunday. When the congregation sang, Nellie's voice could be heard above everyone else. She went down to the altar to be saved every time we went to Revival. Nellie tried to have me saved. I told her I had been baptized in a church in Flint.

She said, "Getting saved is something you need to do all the time."

*   *   *

A month after I went to live at Perrys, Bert and Watt pulled up in a new red Buick convertible. They wanted me to spend the weekend in Fenton with them.

Judd said, "Okay, have a good time, Nick, but be back Sunday night. I'll need you to start haying Monday morning."

Bert and Watt had become wild, both smoked and drank beer. That night we drove around Fenton hollering and yelling at other kids, who were doing the same thing. I didn't really want to see a lot of the kids. Living on the farm took me away from the city life.

I couldn't get over the size of Wilton's house. It had three stories and five bedrooms. I had one guest room to myself, with a big four-poster bed, walk-in closet and a bathroom with a large white bathtub. Up to now, I had little contact with Bert's parents. Mrs. Wilton, a nice looking, big boned, middle-aged woman, had a caustic tongue and foul mouth, but a big heart. Mr. Wilton's job kept him on the road most of the time. He was a small man, with a square jaw and penetrating eyes, and always the perfect gentleman.

*　　*　　*

Later that night Mrs. Wilton heard me crying. She came in the bedroom and asked, "What's the matter, Nick?"

"I'm just tired. I'll be all right in a little while."

She sat on the bed and said, "I know what the matter is. Watt must have told you about the plans we are making to adopt him into our family. I feel really bad that we can't adopt you, too. Mrs. Hardy wouldn't let you go. I had a little argument with her, and told her to keep the monthly money the state pays for Watt. I don't need it, or any interference from her."

Mrs. Wilton gave me a kiss goodnight, and told me I could come to visit Watt anytime I wanted to.

I lay in the darkness, dumbfounded and shocked at what I

had just heard. Watt never said anything to me about the adoption plans. I would talk to him in the morning. I had trouble sleeping that night.

The next morning I confronted Watt while he was cleaning out the horse barn. "Mrs. Wilton told me about your adoption plans last night. Watt, how can you even consider it?"

"Nick, I'm sorry, I've been wanting to tell you. Things won't be any different with us, we'll still be brothers. Mr. and Mrs. Wilton have been good to me. I owe them a lot."

I didn't go over to stay with Watt for a long time after that weekend. I knew now that my plans for the family ever living together was just a dream. My brothers and sisters were scattered all over the country.

FIFTEEN

Joseph and Marcus stopped by for a short visit soon after my weekend in Fenton with Watt. Marcus had left the farm, and was on his way to join the CCC. Joseph, still working at the Chevrolet factory, rented an apartment in Flint. He visited with Hedy once in awhile. I asked Joseph about mother.

"I visited her once, Nick, and I don't want to see her again. She's still very ill."

Joseph and Marcus weren't surprised about Watt being adopted by the Wiltons.

Marcus said, "I wish they'd adopt me. I'd like to be rich, and live like they do."

Joseph didn't seem to care. I felt disappointed to think Watt had abandoned the family.

* * *

After Joseph and Marcus left, I went for a walk down the road. A lot had happened lately, and I missed Cooper's old outhouse to sit in, and Marcus to talk to. I felt something strike me on the arm. I continued walking, again something hit me on the chest. It was a green walnut. Then I heard a laugh coming from behind a big walnut tree.

I said, "Hey, if you want a walnut fight, come out from behind that tree."

To my surprise, Jock Comstock stepped out in the opening. "Christ, Jock, is that really you?"

Laughing, Jock said, "In the flesh, Nick. My aunt lives on the farm across from Perrys. She told me Judd had taken in a boy named Nick Sabitch, from the orphanage, to help him on the farm. I had to come over and welcome you to the country. I live with my dad and stepmother on the farm a mile down the road. My dad drives to Flint to work in the Chevy plant. He works the farm in his spare time."

"Where is Addie, Jock?"

"She went back to live with her mother in Detroit. I'm sure glad you are my neighbor. The Perrys are quite religious. Judd's okay, Nellie's a big fat Jesus nut. If you ever get any free time from chores and church, I'll take you for a ride in my dad's Chevy, and his flat bed truck. Gotta go now, see ya."

Jock took off on a dead run, heading for home.

I told Judd about my best friend, Jock, living just a mile down the road.

Judd commented, "I've heard about our new neighbors, the Comstocks. They moved here this spring. I'm glad you have someone your age living close by. Watch out, and don't get into trouble when you're with Jock."

*　*　*

Later that night Nellie received a phone call. Her father was ill. Early the next morning Judd and Nellie left to drive to her folks. I stayed home to do chores. I had finished milking, and was running the milk through the cream separator, when Jock drove in the yard with his dad's Chevy.

He said, "Let's go for a ride, Nick."

"Okay, but I can't be away very long. Judd and Nellie are gone for the day, I'm looking after the place."

Jock took me for a wild ride in the country. He soon tired of driving the back roads, and headed for Byron.

"We should be going back to the farm, Jock."

"Christ, Nick, you don't have anything to do until milking time tonight. Let's see if we can pick up some girls." Jock wanted to show off his driving skills.

We stopped in Byron for a soda. Dora Simpson and her cousin Ginger were in the drug store. Ginger, an older girl with big breasts, had a flirtatious smile. Jock asked her if she wanted to go for a ride.

She said, "Why not, not much is going on in Byron." Ginger hopped in the front seat with Jock.

Dora said, "I want to go, too, but I can't be gone long." She climbed into the back seat with me.

Squealing the tires, Jock drove out of Byron at high speed.

"Let's go to Flint." Jock wanted to impress Ginger.

"You don't have a driver's license. We better stay on the back roads." I wanted to have some fun, but I didn't want to get into trouble.

"Nobody will know, Nick," Jock said as he kept the car headed for Flint.

The girls enjoyed the drive as much as we did. I put my arm around Dora. I was beginning to like her a lot. On the drive back from Flint, Ginger put her arm around Jock. She didn't know him well enough to like him. She just wanted to make sure he kept both his hands on the steering wheel.

Jock dropped the girls off in Byron, then took me to Perrys. I thanked him for a fun afternoon.

"We'll do it again. I'd like to get to know Ginger better. She sure has a big set of tits. I better get home, my dad doesn't know I took the car."

Jock drove off in a cloud of dust.

*   *   *

Joseph stopped by again for a short visit. He told me Marcus was in a CCC camp near Lake Superior. Joseph had visited Watt.

"It's a big change for him from Coopers to Wiltons lifestyle. He'll settle down after awhile. I've got some real big news to tell you. I petitioned the court, and had my name legally changed to Mason. I never did like Sabitch. Mason is more American. You should think about changing your name, too, Nick."

After Joseph left, I wondered why he changed his name. After all Sabitch was the family name. I couldn't understand Joseph's attitude. He seemed to be ashamed of his Slavic background, and being a Sabitch.

*　　*　　*

Jock stopped by again, driving his father's old flat rack Chevy truck. I told him about Joseph changing his name and telling me I should, too.

"Christ, Nick, you wouldn't be the same person with a different name. Don't change it. I haven't got much time, let's go for a quick ride."

He took me for a fast ride down the back roads.

"How come your dad lets you drive without a license?"

"He's not home, he won't even know I drove it."

I took a turn at the wheel. I had trouble seeing over the dash.

Jock said, "I better get home before my dad does, or I'll catch hell."

*　　*　　*

In late August, Nellie took me to Byron to enroll me in school for my freshman year. I met the Superintendent, a little man, with graying hair, styled in a crew cut. He wore large horn-rimmed glasses. His daughter, Lois Bath, a wide-eyed, dishwater blonde, seventh grader, helped out in the office.

Byron high school was large for such a small community in the middle of nowhere. Buses traveled forty miles around the countryside picking up kids to attend school. The students were assigned desks by class in the assembly hall, and moved from classroom to classroom. Fifty students were in my class, the largest freshman enrollment ever at Byron.

*   *   *

School would be starting after Labor Day. I hadn't earned any money to buy school clothes with. Nellie told me to pick up hickory nuts, and she could sell all I picked up for two dollars a bushel. I managed to pick up five bushel. I didn't get ten dollars, only five. Nellie told me because the nuts were on her farm she was entitled to half the money.

Judd said I could make some money working with him. A coal car was on the siding in Byron by the grainery. The car was loaded with big chunked soft coal. The coal had to be picked up by hand and tossed over the side. It took us two days to unload it. It was a dirty, backbreaking job. Judd received twenty dollars from the Coal Company. He gave me five dollars for helping.

Judd was taking a veal calf to market. He told me I would get the money from the sale for helping him all summer. The calf sold for sixteen dollars. With the nut, coal and calf money I had twenty six dollars. I figured my summer's labor amounted to twenty-five cents a day. I ordered pants, shirts, shoes, a jacket and belt from the Sears catalog. I was all set to start school. I had to walk a half mile to the corner to ride the school bus.

*   *   *

After school on Friday was the traditional tug-of-war between the sophomore and freshman boys. Finn Rider, a sophomore, told me their class as freshmen pulled the sophomore class across the river. This year they would pull the freshman class across.

The entire student body gathered at the river for the tug-of-war. Upper grades on one side, lower grades on the other. A rope was thrown across the river, with each side having twenty kids pulling. I was the lead off and Jock was the anchor man for the freshman class. It didn't take long for us to pull the sophomores into the cold water and across the river. The sophomores jumped all over us freshman boys, trying to get us wet.

Sometimes during the noon hour Jock and I would go down to the river. We stripped down to our shorts, dove off the bridge and swam around the old cider mill. I was glad I learned to swim at a young age. Most of the boys in my class were rough and tough farm kids and didn't know how to swim.

*   *   *

The fall Presidential Campaign finally ended. Judd voted for Wendell Willkie. "Roosevelt's been in office long enough. No person should serve three terms as President."

Willkie's campaign fizzled, and Franklin Roosevelt was re-elected.

Judd wondered how long before the United States would be dragged into the European conflict. In Great Britain, Winston Churchill became Prime Minister. The Germans continued their conquest of Europe. Rumors abounded that they were building a concentration camp at Auschwitz. It was the fall of 1940.

SIXTEEN

Dora Simpson called and asked me to go roller skating on Friday night. "Ginger's going. We'll teach you some dance steps."

Nellie didn't think I should go, but Judd said it was okay as long as the Simpsons were taking us.

The girls knew all the dance numbers, and were the best skaters at the rink. Joseph had taught me a few steps, but I had a lot to learn to be as good as Dora and Ginger.

The sky was bright and the moon full when we got back to Byron. I stayed and talked to Dora awhile. It was such a beautiful night, I decided to walk home. Full moons always made me moody. I enjoyed walking alone, looking at the stars and bright sky. I never could get into religion like Nellie did, but looking up above, I knew God was out there somewhere. If not, of all the millions of people in the world, why was I Nick instead of Marcus or Watt? I wondered what other people thought about on full moon nights.

As I walked down the back country moonlit road, a hound howled in the distance. I thought of Marcus, and let loose a long, loud whistle. Then I laughed to myself, thinking of the time I skipped school with Jock Comstock to learn to whistle like that.

*   *   *

Sunday at church, when the preacher called his flock to the altar, as Nellie went down to be saved for the umpteenth time, she said, "Nick, won't you come with me?"

I surprised her by going. She must have been the happiest person alive. After the preacher prayed all over me, I didn't feel a bit different, but Nellie was happy.

My sister Hedy lived a few blocks from the church, and after Sunday school, instead of going to church, Nellie let me visit with Hedy. A young lady of twenty, Hedy had lost weight, and was tall and thin, with long flowing blonde hair. She lived by herself in a small furnished apartment, and worked on the assembly line in the Chevrolet factory in Flint.

Hedy was disappointed to hear that Watt was going to be adopted by the Wiltons. She regularly corresponded with Sonya, who lived in Racine, and hoped to take some time off to go visit her.

*   *   *

I didn't go out for fall football as there was still farm work to do. I tried out and made the Junior Varsity basketball team later in the winter. There was practice two nights a week and league games on Friday night. Most of the time I walked home. Once in awhile I got a ride with a passing car.

I liked going to school and attending the activities. It was the only chance I had to be around other kids. On the farm it was only chores and no kids. That winter I ran a trap line back through the woods and fields. There weren't as many animals to catch as in Fenton along the ditches and ponds, but I managed to trap a few and made a little spending money.

*   *   *

Marcus dropped by to see me. He served a year in the CCC, learning plastics and the tinsmith trade. Marcus told me Joseph quit the Chevrolet plant. Another guy received a promotion that Joseph thought he was entitled to. He didn't see any future at General Motors, so he made arrangements for

Marcus and himself to drive to California, sell the car, and enlist in the U.S. Army.

I was disappointed, and I didn't see how the family could ever be together again. Marcus stayed quite late that night. When the moon came up, we walked down the road. Marcus played a jew's-harp and sang "Red River Valley" and "Blueberry Hill."

"Remember, Nick, when I was younger I wanted to join the Army and fight the Nazis in Europe? Now I'm enlisting, and I'll be stationed in the South Pacific. The buddy deal Japan made with Hitler and Mussolini makes the Japanese a greater threat to the United States than Germany is."

Marcus tilted his head back and gave a long loud hound dog howl at the moon. "See ya, Nick," and jumped into the car. I gave a loud, shrill whistle as he drove away.

I asked Judd about the buddy deal. "Why did Marcus say Japan is a threat to the United States? We're not at war with the Japanese are we?"

"No, we're not. The deal Marcus mentioned is an agreement made between Germany, Italy and Japan last September, called the Tripartite Pact. It spells out the conditions under which these countries would cooperate in the event of war."

"Thanks, I sure hope Marcus and Joseph don't have to fight in a war." It was June, 1941.

*   *   *

I had quite a crush on Dora. Whenever I made a trip to Byron, I stopped to see her. Occasionally we went skating, and she was teaching me dance steps. One night after roller skating, Dora and I talked on the front porch for a long time. Then there was an awkward silence.

"I guess I better be going, Dora."

"It's not very late, Nick." Dora edged closer. "Well, if you have to go, how about a kiss goodnight?"

I gulped and puckered up my lips. Dora put her arms around me. "I like you a lot, Nick." Her kiss was warm and wet.

*   *   *

On Sunday the Simpsons stopped by to take Judd and Nellie to church. I stayed home to clean out the cow and horse barns. It would be late when the Perrys returned. I had started working when Jock drove in the yard with his dad's flat bed truck. He wanted to go for a ride. I said I would after my chores were finished.

"I'll help you, Nick, if you take me for a ride when we're done."

With both of us working, we soon got the chores done.

"Okay, Jock, let's go for a ride." I started to get in the truck.

"Just a minute, not the truck," Jock laughed, "Let's go in Judd's Ford. You said you would take me for a ride."

"I don't know." My good conscience was saying no.

"What's the matter? Don't you know how to drive the Ford?"

The devil won out, I said, "Okay, let's do it."

I managed to back the Ford out of the garage, and drove some distance on the back roads. Jock soon tired of the ride. He told me it wasn't any fun just poking along. Jock wanted to go wide open. When he got in his truck to go home he said he would teach me to drive fast, it was more fun.

*   *   *

With Marcus gone and without Patsy, my sex lessons ceased. I daydreamed and fantasized a lot about what and how I would do it with Dora. No opportunities came my way. We were both very shy. I had a dream one night. Suddenly I woke up all wet and messy. The dream left me with an empty feeling in my stomach. I lay awake a long time thinking about the lost opportunities with Patsy. Could there be something wrong with me? Jock had told me a good fuckin' would straighten me out. How could I find a girl willing to give me one?

*   *   *

Mrs. Hardy came out for a visit before school started. She brought some school clothes for me. I thanked her.

"Stay in school, Nick, someday you'll be glad you did."

In my second year at Byron as a sophomore, I knew most of the kids in high school. Our class was smaller than last year. Jock had a hard time going back to school. He wanted to work in one of the General Motors plants in Flint, where they manufactured machine guns. Manpower became scarce, and General Motors hired anybody who could work. Jock's dad persuaded him to stay in school for one more year.

*   *   *

I continued to see Dora and double dated with Jock and Ginger when Jock could get the family car for an evening. Mostly we went to the roller rink. I had learned all of the dance steps and skated the special numbers.

When I had money, I helped buy gas for Jock's car. We didn't have any money for gas one Saturday night when we were going out.

Jock said, "Why don't I just back up to the tractor gas tank and fill up? Judd will never know the difference. I do it at my place all the time."

I didn't feel real good about it, but the devil won over my good conscience. I said, "Okay, we'll have to do it after Judd and Nellie go to church."

Sunday morning Judd mentioned that the gas tank seemed to empty fast lately. He suspected what was going on. I told myself I would stay home rather than steal any more gas from Judd.

*   *   *

On Sunday I went with Nellie and Judd to Flint. Judd said it was all right if I visited with Hedy while he and Nellie attended church services.

Hedy and I were listening to a radio program, when a garbled emergency broadcast came on the air. The broadcast came from Pearl Harbor, Hawaii. The Japanese were bombing the Army and Navy bases and ships in the bay. It was December 7, 1941, the start of World War II.

*   *   *

Joseph and Marcus were stationed at Corregidor in the Philippines. Judd told me not to worry about my brothers, Corregidor was a long way from Pearl Harbor. They would be safe.

That winter a lot of boys quit school to join the Armed Services. Our daily life became grim; gas rationing, scrap metal drives, War Bond drives, and General Motors, along with many other large companies, changed over to war production. The country, still recovering from the Depression, was now at war with Japan, Italy and Germany. It would be awhile before I realized how devastating the war would be.

*   *   *

A new girl, Cassie Cole, enrolled in our class. A pretty girl, with deep brown eyes and short brown hair, she talked out of the side of her mouth. Cassie had a slender, mature figure. Her family had moved to a farm on the outskirts of Byron.

Cassie's father and mother worked in Flint at the Buick Motor plant. Cassie and I dated, and went to school activities together.

*   *   *

On April 9th, the Japanese overran the Western Peninsula of Luzon in the Philippines and Bataan fell. Seventy thousand Filipinos and American troops were captured, and forced to walk 60 miles to a Japanese prison camp. Sixteen thousand died during the "death march" of Bataan.

The following month the Japanese captured Corregidor. On May 6th, the American Army surrendered. Judd was wrong, Marcus and Joseph were not okay.

I received a postcard from the Imperial Japanese Army, via the American Red Cross. Marcus was in a Japanese Military prison camp.

The postcard stated: I am well, say hello to the family, friends and Bessie. Stay in school, Nick, take care and once in awhile give me a loud whistle. Marcus Sabitch.

I could not even begin to imagine what Marcus was going through. I had heard on the radio, and read in the newspaper about the atrocities and death march of Bataan. I asked God that night to watch over Marcus, my brother, only eighteen, who had so much to live for. In my heart I knew Marcus would gladly give his life for his country, but I prayed that wouldn't happen.

Hedy called me to tell me that she received information from the Red Cross. Joseph had also been captured by the Japanese, and sent to a prison camp somewhere in the Philippines.

*   *   *

At the end of the school year, Nellie told me that she and Judd were going to have their own family. Mrs. Hardy knew of a farmer who lived south of Byron, and needed a helper. I told Jock that I soon would be leaving Perrys.

"I seem to have a hard time finding any place to live very long Jock." I felt very sad.

"Look at the bright side, you're going to get away from Nellie's preaching, and you still attend school in Byron."

Nellie's strong religious beliefs were too restrictive for a sixteen year old, fun loving boy. Mrs. Hardy moved me to the Schmidt farm at the end of the school year. It was the beginning of summer, 1942.

SEVENTEEN

A large new house had been built on the Schmidt farm, located five miles south of Byron. The old one had burned down. A huge faded red barn, and several small buildings surrounded the house. Farm equipment lay scattered in the barnyard.

Hattie, a large, tall woman in her late forties, had graying hair tied in a tight bun with a bright ribbon. A quiet person who seldom talked, spoke as rapid as machine gun fire when she did. Dave, a short bull of a man, in his late fifties, had huge hands, coarse facial features and a bald head. Dave talked endlessly; he never quit.

Ely, their son, lived at home. He was in his middle twenties, a real big, dark, hulk of a man, with curly hair. Their daughter, Cindy, lived in Byron with her husband.

The house had never been completely finished inside. My bedroom was upstairs next to Ely's. The toilet and bathtub were in the back room, neither plumbed for water or sewer. When I wanted to take a bath, I heated water on the wood cook stove and poured it in the tub. The water drained outside in the back yard. The outside privy was still used.

I would receive one dollar a day, room and board in the summer and one dollar a week when school started. Dave's dad must have been an active farmer on a large scale in his day. There was a lot of old equipment. A thresher, beaner, binder, trucks, tractors and other implements were scattered around the barnyard. They were all in need of repair. The livestock was about the same as Perrys had, four horses, ten milking cows, chickens, pigs and sheep. I had a lot more freedom to come and go than I did at Perrys. The Schmidts were not religious like Nellic.

*　　*　　*

I became a worker and companion with Dave. Chores in the morning, work the fields all day, chores at night. We spent more time repairing equipment than running it. Dave had an old flat rack Chevrolet truck, like the one that Jock drove. Dave took me to the county seat, about ten miles from Byron, to get a driver's license. When we went to Byron for supplies or parts for repairs, I drove the truck or Dave's '34 Ford. He was content just to ride along and talk.

Ely worked as a mechanic at the tractor dealership in Byron. He wanted no part of farm chores or working in the fields, which disappointed Dave. The farm had been in the family for years, with Ely the only son to carry on the tradition.

When Ely bought a used 1939 Chevy, he parked his old 1929 Model "A" Ford in the back of the barn. It had been there about two years. The tires, battery and radiator were shot, the body rusted, and the top peeled back and leaked. I wanted to fix it up so I could have a car to drive.

Ely said, "Go ahead, Nick, when you get everything else fixed, I'll help overhaul the engine."

Working on the car in my spare time was a new experience. I hand painted the body black, tarred and painted the roof. Dave took me to the junkyard, and I bought four 1935 Ford wire wheels for two dollars each, a used battery for five dollars, and a radiator for ten dollars. Ely found four old tires and inner tubes at the shop. I patched the tubes, and put boots in the tires. The wheels fit the "A" just fine. Only one job was left, to rig up a hoist in the barn, and pull the engine for Ely to overhaul. It would be a while before I had the time and money to do that.

*　　*　　*

Ely, because he didn't help out on the farm, paid his mother a little room and board money. He liked to tinker with farm equipment and engines and was very good at it.

Ely and I became good friends. On Saturday nights we went to Bennett Lake to spend the evening at Persyks Tavern. A pitcher of beer cost twenty-five cents. Ely liked to drink beer and play the harmonica. He liked country and western songs. When he had enough to drink, he played his favorite, The Wabash Cannon Ball.

I didn't drink, but always had a good time watching people and listening to the music. The boys who farmed across the woods joined us at Persyks. They were rough young men who usually ended up in a fight with someone. Ely was a heavy smoker and so was most everyone in the bar. Before the evening was over, I would have a headache and my eyes burned. I always ended up driving Ely home.

* * *

Tub, the Schmidt's farm dog, about the size of an Irish setter, with yellowish brown short hair, was my constant companion. On full moon nights I walked down the lane, Tub at my side, to think about life and Marcus and Joseph in the Japanese prison camps. I knew Marcus would be looking at the moon. In the distant woods I heard a hound dawg howl. Thinking of Marcus, I gave a long, loud whistle, hoping he would hear it.

* * *

Dave Schmidt was not the farmer his dad must have been. With the grain and bean separator equipment, his dad had gone all over the country threshing grain and beans with a crew of men, until the harvest was over. Dave and I did it the hard way. The grain was cut with a horse drawn binder and shocked by hand. The grain separator was set up in the barnyard. The flat rack truck was driven in the field, hand loaded with shocked grain, then driven back to the threshing machine. I unloaded the shocks in the thresher and Dave bagged the grain. Next we stacked and shaped the straw.

We followed a similar process using the bean separator. It took us days to harvest the crops. Most farmers got together to trade labor and would get the threshing done in a day.

*   *   *

The farm house had a huge living room with an oak floor. We spent most of the time in the kitchen. It was warmer and had better lighting to play cards and checkers in the evenings. Sunday afternoons Ely and I cleaned out the living room and put on our roller skates and skated to music from the wind up Victrola. The living room made a great roller rink. It was the only time it was used.

Hattie was a moody person. When she became angry at Dave, which was quite frequently, she would clam up and not speak a word to anyone. Sometimes it was days before she broke her silence. Then she was just as cheerful as if nothing had happened. Dave, on the other hand, never quit talking, except when he went to Byron to play cards. Pedro was a serious game to him and he never said a word unless he had beat his opponent, then he would hoop and holler.

*   *   *

Dave let me take his Ford to go see Hedy. I hadn't seen her since the last time I went to church in Flint with the Perrys. Hedy married a young man, now in the Army, who had worked at the Chevy plant with her. She continued to work, and maintain the apartment while her husband was in the Army.

At this point I gave up any possibility of the family ever

being together again. Sonya and Hedy were married, Joseph and Marcus in Japanese prison camps, Jay and Alfred legally adopted, and Watt living with his adopted family, the Wiltons. With no hope for Zora to recover, and Ziv living a lonely life by himself, realistically the best I could hope for was keeping in touch with the family. I looked forward to someday getting married and having children; a family of my own.

*   *   *

The war was not going well for the United States. Germany had conquered most of Europe, the Japanese the South Pacific. Every able bodied man, eighteen years and older, had been drafted or enlisted in the service. Ely had flat feet and a punctured ear drum, classified 4-F, so he would not be called to duty.

Schmidt's daughter Cindy's husband was drafted into the Army. She came back to the farm to live, and moved into the big downstairs bedroom. Cindy, two years younger than Ely, had long, curly dark hair, sparkling brown eyes, and a nice slender figure. A gutsy gal, with a short explosive temper, Cindy drove back and forth to Byron to work. Hattie worked endlessly cooking, cleaning, canning and washing. She never complained.

*   *   *

I didn't see Dora Simpson at all during the summer. Ely was my main source of transportation and we went to Bennett Lake or to the county seat roller rink.

*   *   *

I looked forward to going back to school. I hadn't seen Jock Comstock or any of my classmates all summer. Most of my friends were busy working on farms, and seldom got to town.

The school enrollment dropped that fall. Our junior class totaled twenty students. The older boys left to join the service, some worked full time on their farm, or labored on war production in Flint. Jock talked about enlisting, but decided as an upper class man, and with most of the young men in the service, school would be fun this year, with more girls than boys. Next year would be soon enough to join up.

*　　*　　*

Watt turned eighteen in September, and quit school to enlist in the Army Air Corps. He had grown into a handsome, curly headed young man. Since living with the Wiltons, he had become more outgoing, like Bert, and sure of himself. Bert threw a party, and Jock and I went to say goodbye to Watt.

The Wiltons were in the process of selling the big house on Shiawassee Avenue, and buying a farm outside of Fenton. Bert asked a bunch of his friends to attend the party. I met Dag Scully, an older guy, the butcher at the Fenton grocery store. He brought the beer. Dag, a heavy set young man in his middle twenties, liked to party. The boys got pretty wild, most of them hadn't been drinking very long, and a few bottles of beer made them drunk.

Dag, with 4-F draft status, felt bad that he wasn't going into the service. He invited Jock and me to come see him. Bert and Watt got loaded. Jock and I managed to get them to bed, then he left to go home. I stayed the night with Watt.

Mrs. Wilton told me, "For what's ahead of them, I guess they deserve to get drunk."

Watt got sick. He kept saying, "Stop this bed from spinning around, I have to get off."

The next morning he felt pretty bad. He talked about Joseph and Marcus.

"Nick, I'm going over to fight for them."

Watt enlisted in the Air Force. It was the fall of 1942.

127

EIGHTEEN

October was the time for butchering to fill the basement with canned food and meat for the long cold winter ahead. First was a young steer. Dave shot it between the eyes with a 22 rifle. He fastened a short stout pole to the back legs and we hoisted the steer in the air with a rope on a pulley. Dave slit the throat to drain out the blood. I gutted the stomach and we skinned the hide off. We then sawed the body into quarters and hung it in the basement from the ceiling beams.

A hog was next. I cleaned out the big black iron kettle used to cook beans for the pigs and filled it with water. I built a fire around the kettle and brought the water to a boil. Dave shot the hog between the eyes, then slit its throat. I gutted out the stomach, then we hoisted the pig in the air on a tripod over the kettle and lowered it into the boiling water, then pulled it out. We used round metal scrapers with wooden handles to scrape off the bristly hair. We quartered the hog and hung it in the cellar with the beef. We cut up part of the pork and put it in a thirty gallon crock full of salt water, along side the crocks of sauerkraut.

Hattie cooked and canned some of the beef and pork. What was left hanging, Dave cut a piece off whenever Hattie wanted to cook some for supper. Sometimes mold had to be scraped off first.

I helped Hattie butcher the chickens. Dave didn't like that job. I boiled water in the kettle, chopped the chickens heads off with an ax, then dipped them in the boiling water and pulled the feathers out and gutted them. Hattie cut up the chicken, then canned and stored them in the cellar with the vegetables, fruits and berries. Having a lot of good food to eat during the winter would not be a problem.

Once the butchering was done, wood had to be buzzed up for heating and cooking. The past winter we had cut down oak and hickory trees and sawed them into ten foot lengths. We then split them into rails and stacked them in a big pile in the backyard. Dave fastened a big three foot diameter saw blade in a fixture on the front end of the tractor. A belt from the tractor pulley ran the saw. We lifted the split rails on the fixture and ran them through the saw, cutting them in short lengths. The rails were heavy, but the saw was sharp. It only took one Saturday to buzz up the winter's supply. Every day I split wood into kindling to use in the wood cook stove. I never lacked for something to do.

Hay in the barn, grain in the bins, the corn crop was last to be harvested. I drove the team in front of a corn cutter binder. Once the corn was cut and bound, I shocked it by hand. The corn was left in the field most of the winter. When feed was needed for the livestock, I drove the flat bed truck out, loaded it with corn, took it to the barn and shucked the ears for feed. The corn stalks were used for bedding for the cattle.

*   *   *

The harvesting, butchering, buzzing and late field plowing done, we were ready for winter. Daily chores, and Saturday work was left. I went back to working on the Model "A." I rigged a hoist around a beam in the barn, pulled the motor, and took it on the flat bed truck to the tractor shop in Byron. I worked evenings taking the motor apart. I brushed and cleaned every piece in gasoline to get the grease and dirt off.

What a mess. I had no idea how to put it together, but Ely did. He ground the valves, and put new rings in the pistons. I helped him reassemble the engine, and install the clean motor back in the car. Ely signed the title over to me. I bought license plates, and finally had my own transportation.

Gas, being rationed, it was necessary to go to the county seat for a gas stamp. I used the car for non-essential travel, so I was issued an "A" stamp. I could buy five gallons of gas a week, at a cost of fifteen cents a gallon. Getting gas stamps from other kids would come easier than the money it took to buy five gallons.

I drove to school and took Jock for a ride around town.

"You still drive like an old man, Nick, but at least you have your own wheels."

I made a date with Cassie for Saturday night. We went roller skating. Dora was there with Ginger. Cassie was just learning and couldn't skate the specials, so I skated with Dora. She was dating some other boys. Dora was glad I had my own car. We were just good friends now.

*   *   *

I had the Model "A" to drive back and forth to basketball practice and Friday night games. Byron had a winning season going. The practice I received a few years back, with the soft ball and bushel basket Jock rigged up for us boys, paid off. An excellent shot on the basketball court, I was the team's high scorer. The Friday before Christmas vacation Byron held the number one spot in the league.

When I got home from school I had a letter from Sonya, my older sister. Just a short note with a twelve dollar check enclosed. Train fare to get me to Racine, Wisconsin to visit her for a weekend during Christmas vacation.

Dave said he could manage the chores by himself. Hattie cried when I told her I hadn't seen Sonya since our family broke up. Ely took me to the train depot. Cassie went with me. She was sad when I left to board the train, and said she would miss me.

The train ride took eight hours. I thought back to nine years ago, the last time I remembered seeing Sonya. I was sixteen now, and Sonya twenty-two or twenty-three. She would be the fifth of my brothers and sisters I made contact with since we broke up. I wondered if I would ever get to see my adopted brothers, Jay and Alfred.

Sonya met me in Racine. I hardly recognized her. She was petite, with a nice figure, long dark hair, teasing blue eyes, and a contagious laugh. Sonya cried most of the way to her apartment. We talked long into the night about our family.

Her husband had gone away. They were not getting along. He drank heavily, and did not treat Sonya very well.

Sonya liked a good time. We took a train to Chicago, ending up downtown. I gawked at the tall skyscrapers and big department stores, as we walked all through the Loop. We had dinner at a fancy restaurant and then Sonya took me to the Rialto to see a Burlesque Show. There were scantily clad dancing girls, lewd scenes and strippers walked out on a runway from the stage and stripped in front of the audience. It was Christmas, 1942.

*   *   *

January and February are the coldest months in Michigan, with bitter winds, blowing and drifting snow. This year was no exception.

With no heat in my upstairs bedroom, I slept with Ely. He had a small kerosene stove in his room, which we would light, jump into bed, covered with so many blankets we could hardly turn over. The kerosene smelled bad, and the stove had no pipe for ventilation.

During the night a big snowstorm blew in, dumping ten inches of snow on the countryside. The next morning drifting snow blocked the roads. After doing the morning chores, I saddled up the old white work horse, and rode into Byron.

A lot of the farmers were in town, arriving in horse drawn sleighs, drays and logging sleds. They sat around the potbellied wood stove in the American Legion Lodge playing Euchre.

Jock had skied into town, and soon I was pulling him around behind my horse. When we got tired and cold, we went into the pool hall to watch the players. As Jock left to go home, he reminded me of Dag Scully's offer for us to visit him.

"Let's go this weekend, Nick, and see what fun he has in store for us."

Saturday night I picked Jock up in the Model "A", and drove to Fenton. The cold moon shone full and bright. The car had no heater, so we were glad to get to Dag's warm trailer.

When we arrived Dag had a beer, and offered Jock one. We sat around the gas heater telling dirty stories, and talking about girls. Dag showed us some girlie magazines. It didn't take long for Jock and me to get hot and excited.

Dag said, "You boys need your ashes hauled, then you won't have to play with yourselves. Let me know when you're ready, I know just the place to have it done."

Going back to Byron that night, Jock said, "Let's take Dag up on his offer soon." I agreed.

*   *   *

Each winter Dave bought a half ton of soft chunked coal. He mostly used wood in the big potbellied stove to heat the dining room and downstairs bedrooms. At night he tossed in a couple of pieces of coal to bank and hold the fire all night. Coal burned hotter and longer, but was hard to get and expensive. Every time we opened the stove door a black sooty cloud of smoke came out into the room.

It had been an unusually cold winter, and the coal was soon used up. Dave commented to me that we were fortunate to have plenty of wood to heat and cook with. John L. Lewis, president of the United Mine Workers of America, called a strike and shut down the coal mines.

*   *   *

Cassie and I dated frequently. She suggested that maybe we should date others.

"You know, Nick, my mother thinks that we are too young to be going steady. Maybe we should break up for a while. It might help us to know how much we really like each other."

"I think it's a dumb idea, Cassie. I don't need to date another girl to know how much I like you."

Cassie dated a couple of guys home on leave. It bothered me to think of her with other boys, but I went along with what she thought best.

Jock approached me while Cassie was experimenting with other dates and said, "Let's go to Fenton and see Dag. I'm ready to have my ashes hauled."

I felt ready for something, I didn't know what.

Dag offered us a beer when we got to Fenton. Jock accepted, I declined.

"Are you guys ready for some live action?"

He told us about a 'Cat House' on Water Street in Bay City, where we all would be well taken care of. I had second thoughts about going. I wrestled with my good conscience. Did I want to lose my cherry to some old ugly woman in a whorehouse? The devil won out, I agreed to go.

Dag and Jock drank beer on the way to Bay City. Dag had been there before. He talked a good story, telling what pleasures lay ahead.

Dag got a little high. "You boys are in for the time of your life. Just think you get the pick of the litter, and no commitments."

By the time we arrived, Jock and I were hot to trot. There were seven good reasons why the devil in me won. They were all young, nice looking girls, with friendly smiles, sitting around with just their panties on.

"What's your pleasure, boys?" Dag wasn't in a hurry, Jock and I were. I selected a small, light complexioned young girl with dark hair. She was in her early twenties and had big round breasts that pointed straight out.

Freda took me to a small bedroom, and collected my two dollars. "Drop your pants, I'm going to wash you good. My, you are ready," she said, grabbing and scrubbing me with hot soapy water.

"Not so rough."

"I'm almost done washing you."

Too late! The anticipation, excitement, and hot water done me in. I had an empty feeling in my stomach when I went out to the waiting room.

Nobody said much on the trip back to Fenton. Jock and I arrived in Byron late at night. I stayed at his house, then got up early in the morning. Dave didn't care how late I stayed out, but I had to be at the barn by milking time.

Marcus would have taken a turn with all the girls, and I was still a virgin.

NINETEEN

I received a letter from Sonya. She divorced her husband, and was working in a factory on war production. Hedy, pregnant, and with her husband overseas, moved to Racine to live with Sonya. Watt would be in Racine before shipping overseas. Sonya sent money for my train fare. I was excited! Two sisters and two brothers would be together for the first time in many years.

Hattie thought it great for part of the Sabitch family to be reunited. I would have to get excused from school.

The Superintendent said, "No problem, Nick, sometimes family matters are more important than school work."

I thought about Watt on the train ride to Racine. It had been over three years since he went to live with the Wiltons. The fun times we had together was in the past. We weren't kids anymore.

Watt had finished training from gunnery school, and assigned duty in the Pacific. He liked the Army Air Force, and looked forward to the overseas assignment. Watt hadn't seen Sonya since the family break up. With tears in his eyes, he gave her a hug.

Sonya couldn't get over how handsome he looked.

"My God, Watt, you're a dead ringer for Ziv."

The four of us talked long into the night, bringing each other up to date on what had happened in our lives. The reunion was short. As Watt left the next morning, I told him about my trip to Bay City with Dag. He laughed about my experience with Freda.

"Nick, you have lots of time for girls, and growing up."

*   *   *

After my trip to Racine, Cassie was ready to get back together. She didn't have fun dating other guys and really missed me. I wanted her all to myself. We were going steady again.

Dad showed up Easter weekend, almost four years since our last contact. He located me after talking to Clark Cooper. He drove a maroon 1941 Oldsmobile that looked almost new. Dad had a good job in Lansing, Michigan working at a Drop Forge Plant as a machine oiler on war production. He still lived in the small house, and missed his family.

"Nick, do you know where your brothers and sisters are?"

"Some of them. Haven't you heard from any of them?"

"No, and Mrs. Hardy won't give me any information."

I thought it strange that she wouldn't tell dad about his own children. I brought him up to date, telling him Joseph changed his name to Mason, and both he and Marcus joined the Army and were now prisoners of the Japanese in the Philippines.

"Watt has adopted the Wiltons as his family, and he's in the Army Air Force, stationed in the Pacific. Sonya's divorced, and Hedy is married, and living with Sonya in Racine. Hedy's husband is in the Army overseas. Jay and Alfred have been adopted."

Dad was quiet for a long time, and then said, "I sure miss all my children."

We went to Flint, and Dad let me drive his car; very smooth compared to the Model "A." Dad took me to lunch. We had soup, sandwiches and pie. After lunch he handed the check and a five dollar bill to the cashier. When she gave Dad the change, he said, "That's wrong."

The cashier counted back the money. "The bill is a dollar sixty five, and your change is three dollars and thirty five cents."

We later stopped at a clothing store, where Dad bought me a blue sport coat and a pair of light gray slacks. Again he told the clerk, "The change is wrong." She counted the change back to him, and he seemed satisfied.

During the drive back to Byron, it suddenly occurred to

me, Dad couldn't read or write, and didn't know how to count. That's why he questioned the cashier about the change; his way of knowing if he had been cheated. Late in the afternoon we arrived back at the Schmidts farm.

Easter morning I took Dad's car and picked up Cassie and went to Easter services at the Methodist Church. Dad visited with Dave while I was gone. He later told me he enjoyed the visit but was ready to go home. Dad wasn't comfortable around people.

As Dad left he said, "I haven't seen any of my family but you, since Marcus lived with me. I miss them." With tears in his eyes, he drove off.

*　　*　　*

Ely met a girl named Dinah. After a short courtship, they decided to get married. I was best man, Dinah's sister the maid of honor.

Dinah got a husband, but not her own home. Dave and I finished off a big bedroom upstairs at the south end of the house. We insulated the walls, and a stovepipe that went to the ceiling in the middle of the room, made it warm. I moved into Ely's room with the kerosene heater.

*　　*　　*

On my way home after school I ran out of gas and stopped at a farm to borrow a gallon of gas. From the barn I could hear the radio playing. A news flash came on, describing a race riot in Detroit. The National Guard had been called in. Thirty four people had been killed and hundreds injured. It was June, the start of summer.

*　　*　　*

It had been over eight years since I left the Whaley Orphanage. I decided to visit, and see if any of the kids I knew were still there.

On the drive to Flint, I thought back to the two years I spent at the orphanage. Other than mean Mrs. Gibson, living at the orphanage wasn't really too bad. I wondered about Pat Dugan. Did Janet and Annet Flowers still live there? As I drove through the gates, the Whaley Orphanage didn't look as large as I remembered it.

I had a short visit with Mrs. Hardy. She told me not to be foolish and try to join the service until after I graduated from high school. I told her about my visit to Racine with Sonya.

Mrs. Hardy commented, "I hope you poor souls can find some happiness in life."

She told me that she had lost contact with Pat Dugan. The only kids I still knew at the home were Janet and Annet. The twin girls, eighteen now, would soon leave the orphanage. I found them sunning out near the back orchard. They were glad to see me. I remembered them as the first girls I had a crush on. They had grown up, with short, curly black hair, flawless complexions and curvy, sensuous figures.

They talked for quite awhile about the residents at the orphanage and gave me information on their families. They asked me if I had a girlfriend. I told them about Cassie.

Annet said, "She's not here, so you'll have to pretend I'm Cassie."

The twins were very forward. They took turns kissing me.

Annet stood up, facing me. "Want to see my appendix operation scar, Nick?"

Before I could answer, she slowly raised her dress. Thin pink panties barely covered her smooth, white belly, where a slightly swollen, red scar showed through. The faint smell of sex excited me. I had never been all the way with one girl, let alone two. My good conscience didn't have a chance.

In the distance I could hear the gardener mowing the lawn and coming our way.

I stuttered, "I better go."

As I drove back to the farm, I thought of Marcus. I knew he was somewhere laughing at me and the situation I had left hanging in the air.

*　　*　　*

I received a letter from Sonya and Hedy. Both were doing well. Sonya worked long hours. Hedy was getting quite big with the baby. Could I spend some time with them? Train fare was enclosed with the letter. The hay crop was stored in the barn, wheat harvested, and the oats would not be ready until later in the month. Dave thought it would be a good time for me to take a vacation.

As I rode the train to Racine, I had time to think about my family. I wondered where my two younger brothers were. They would be teenagers by now. How could I find out about them? Mrs. Hardy told me the Probate Court would not give out any information as to their whereabouts. I thought about Mother in the asylum. Would I ever see her?

Sonya had a small apartment. Hedy needed to exercise so she and I walked daily. With her husband being in the service, I would represent the father when Hedy's time came. When it did come, we took a taxi to the hospital. Hedy was in labor a long time. The nurses commented that I seemed awfully young to be a father. I stayed with Hedy during her labor. She yelled a lot when the pains came. I held her hand and thought to myself I didn't want to put anyone through that agony. Hedy finally delivered a baby boy.

Sonya had met a man; a short, swarthy, good looking Italian. He liked to joke around and was a good-natured guy who laughed a lot, but also a Catholic, married, with a family.

He worked in the steel mills with Sonya. He told her he would soon be divorced, and then they would get married. He made two stainless steel heart shaped rings, "Cassie" engraved on one and "Nick" on the other. A present from him to Cassie and me.

Sonya and Hedy cried as 'Uncle Nick' left to go back to the Schmidt's farm. It was August 1, 1943.

TWENTY

I called Cassie when I returned from Racine, and told her I had a surprise for her. Sunday afternoon I drove over to see her. Cassie's mother and older sister looked alike. Both were big, tall, stern looking women. Cassie's mother, almost fifty, and her sister, thirty, didn't seem to be happy. Both thought Cassie and I should not be going steady.

They felt she could do better and were afraid Cassie and I might get married before she finished school and had a chance to experience life.

Through the doorway I saw Cassie in the back room talking with her mother. Mrs. Cole picked up Cassie's dress and said, "I'm just checking to see if you're wearing them. Remember, don't you ever take them off."

Cassie and I took a walk in the field behind their barn. I showed Cassie the heart shaped ring with my name on it, then put it on her finger. She gave me a kiss, and whispered, "I want to do it with you, Nick, but right now I can't."

Going back to the house, I wondered, when could she?

*   *   *

The senior class that fall consisted of five boys and seven girls, the smallest in many years.

Jock was glad he stayed in school. "With all the guys in the service, I can pick and choose most any girl I want to go out with, Nick. I'll go in the service next summer after I graduate."

Mr. Bath, the Superintendent, was also a teacher and coach. The song, "They're Either Too Young or Too Old," said it all.

Everyone who could be was in the service. There were young kids and old men left, with a few 4-F's. The war was not going well for the United States.

The school Superintendent announced that the high school would participate in a scrap metal drive. Everyone who could, bring a tractor and wagon to school Monday morning. We would cover the countryside for any old scrap metal or old implements. The scrap was to be unloaded at the football field. A scrap company would haul the metal away later. The school would buy war bonds with the scrap money. A bond drive was going on all the time. Ten cents and twenty five cents would buy bond stamps. Eighteen dollars and seventy five cents would buy a twenty five dollar bond.

Jock borrowed his dad's tractor and hay wagon for the day. Lois Bath, Cassie and I rode on the wagon, with Jock driving the tractor. At one farm, while we picked up scrap, a small dog came out to play with us.

I heard Lois saying, "Look, the dog likes me."

It was riding her leg.

Jock said, "Christ, Lois, don't you know the difference between playing and humping?"

By the end of the day the football field was piled with scrap.

The Superintendent commented, "You kids learned more collecting today than you would have in school."

Jock said, "At least Lois did."

*   *   *

I went out for football for the first time since I was in high school. Mr. Bath, the coach, made me captain. I played quarterback. The team consisted of six players as the smaller schools didn't have enough players for eleven man football, so they played six man conference. During one game, Jock, carrying the ball, was tackled and the other team jam piled on him. His leg was hurt, Jock couldn't get up.

Mr. Bath came out to the field, examined Jock and said, "It's just a sprain."

Jock was carried off the field on a stretcher, the bone sticking out the side of his leg. Most of the kids didn't know until Jock came back to school with his leg in a cast, that it had been broken. Byron's team finished at the bottom of the league that fall.

*   *   *

The early part of the winter came on cold, with no snow. The mill pond froze solid. Some men from the mill came down to cut ice blocks to store and use in the summer. A hand saw was used to cut ice blocks. Another man used tongs to pull the blocks out of the water. Sawdust was sprinkled on them and they were loaded on a truck and taken to a barn for storage. That winter there was plenty of ice stored for use in ice boxes during the summer.

*   *   *

The basketball team played a so-so season. Our minds weren't on the game. Most of the boys wanted to get through school so they could enlist in the service.

I came home late Friday night. Byron had lost the basketball game. Tired and cold, I put some pieces of coal and wood in the stove and banked it for the night. The noise woke Cindy up. A flickering light came from the isinglass in the stove door.

"Is that you, Nick?"

"Yes, I just filled the stove."

"Come in and tell me about the game."

"We didn't play very well, lost the game."

"You must be cold, why don't you get in here with me?"

Cindy reached out and took my hand, pulling me toward her, then slowly raised the blanket up. She was nude. The heat from her body, mixture of perfume and female scent, excited me. As Cindy raised up to kiss me, Dave woke up. He had been sleeping on the couch in the living room.

Sleepily he said, "Is that you, Nick? Who won the game?"

"We lost, I'm just banking the stove for the night. Goodnight, Dave. Goodnight, Cindy."

Frustrated, I went upstairs to bed. The cold, kerosene smelling bedroom soon dampened the excitement and pressure Cindy had stirred up in my testicles. I quickly undressed and climbed into bed, and soon fell sound asleep.

*   *   *

Ely and Dinah were moving to Byron. They would have their own apartment and privacy. I moved into their bedroom for the winter. It was a lot bigger and warmer. The heat from the stovepipe kept the room warm and cozy.

My high school days were coming to a close. I wanted to be a pilot, so before my eighteenth birthday I drove to Detroit to take a written test at the Army Air Force Recruiting Office, and have a physical examination. Jock went with me.

Before we returned home we wanted to see the sights of Detroit. I told Jock about Sonya taking me to the Burlesque Show in Chicago. We decided to see one in Detroit. We went to the Rialto to see Scurvy's act and the girl strippers. We had a good time laughing at Scurvy. Jock liked the strippers best.

A week later I received the test results from the Army Air Force. I passed the written test with flying colors, but not the physical. I had sugar in my urine.

*   *   *

Friday night I drove over to tell Cassie about the results of the physical test. Mr. and Mrs. Cole were going out. They asked me to feed the livestock. When I told Cassie that I had failed the physical test for the Army Air Force, she seemed quite happy.

She said, "Maybe now, Nick, you won't have to go in the service."

With three brothers in the service, I couldn't even think about not being in the war.

I finished the chores and went in the house to be with Cassie. She needed help to move a dresser in the upstairs bedroom. I helped, then started to go downstairs.

"Wait a minute, Nick, I can now."

She quickly undressed and stood nude in front of me. I gulped hard, trying to catch my breath.

Cassie jumped in her bed, "Aren't you coming?"

I was coming, but didn't think I could make it to the bed. Suddenly Cassie got up and put her clothes on.

She said, "I can't do it." Downstairs she went.

I stuttered and said, "I guess I better be going. See you tomorrow."

It happened so fast I didn't even have time to get excited. I wondered how Cassie could be so hot one minute and so cold the next. I went home shaking my head.

*   *   *

Mrs. Hardy came to Commencement to congratulate me. Not many of her boys from the orphanage graduated from high school. After the graduation exercises, the Superintendent announced a minute of silent prayer for the boys overseas. The Allied invasion of Normandy had begun. It was June 6, 1944, D-Day in Europe.

*   *   *

I found a job working at the Deere Implement Shop in Byron. I assembled new equipment and delivered them to the farm customers. It paid fifty cents an hour. I stayed at Schmidts, did chores morning and night for room and board.

Cassie had gone somewhere for a few days. Her mother wouldn't tell me where she was. "Just visiting some friends." I thought it strange that Cassie would go away without saying something to me.

Most of the boys in service came back after basic training to visit with their families and friends in Byron. The girls were wild about guys in uniforms. Finn Rider finished pilot's training and came home before leaving for overseas duty. He looked handsome in his Navy officers uniform.

Finn and I were good friends in school. After a few drinks his first night home, he smashed up his dad's car. Finn asked me if I still dated Cassie. I told him we were going steady.

"She sure is a pretty girl, Nick."

Cassie called after Finn left. She wanted to see me, said she had some news for me. I made a date to see her that night. She acted kind of funny, wasn't her old self. Cassie had been to Fenton, found a job in the office of a small factory, and rented a small apartment.

* * *

Jock Comstock phoned to tell me that if we enlisted before being drafted, we could pick the branch of service we wanted. Jock and I drove to the county seat the next day and signed up as selective volunteers. We had thirty days before we would be called to serve in the United States Navy.

* * *

Jock went with me to visit dad. He was still living in the small house, working at the Drop Forge Plant in Lansing,

Michigan. Dad was feeling good and doing all right for himself. He was going to night school, learning to read, write and speak better English. I told him I would be going in the Navy soon and this would be my last visit with him for quite awhile. Dad had visited Zora again. She was still quite violent and didn't know who he was and wouldn't begin to know me. Dad soon would have four sons in the service.

*   *   *

Cassie didn't talk much on our date, and didn't seem surprised or concerned that Jock and I had enlisted in the Navy. After our date that night, I took a stroll down the lane, with Tub, Schmidt's dog, walking by my side. The moon came up big and full, bright enough to see to walk by. Looking up at the moon shining through the trees, I gave a loud, shrill whistle. Tub, sitting close by, looked up with his head cocked to one side and his ears perked up as if to say, "I'm right here, who are you whistling for?"

I listened, hoping to hear a hound howl in the distance.

"Marcus, I know you're out there somewhere. I'll keep whistling until I find you."

I was eager to catch up with the war and fight the Japanese.

*   *   *

Jock and I received our induction orders. Dave drove Jock and me to the county seat. He told us we probably would never get to see any action. The tide of the war had turned in favor of the United States and its' Allies. Paris and Italy had been recaptured from the Nazis and Germany was being bombed regularly. General MacArthur had made a triumphant return to the Philippines.

Jock gave a yell, and I a loud whistle, as we boarded the bus for induction in the Navy. It was July 31, 1944.

TWENTY ONE

Jock and I were bused to the Navy Base at Green Bay, Wisconsin for twelve weeks of boot camp basic training. After being sworn in, all inductees were given a physical. I passed the urine analysis test. Albumin didn't show as it did when I had my examination for the Army Air Force.

A platoon of one hundred and thirty trainees lived in the same barracks. The rules and regulations were very strict. No visitors for six weeks, or leaves until the end of the basic training.

The barracks, a long one story wood building, had double bunks lined up in straight rows in the middle of the room, and along the sides.

My daily assignment was to clean and polish six thirty gallon galvanized trash cans. Stool samples stored in them were used in a medical experiment.

Jock's daily detail was to clean the urinals and stools in the head.

"Head, hell," Jock commented, "It's the ass end that I have to clean up after. I don't know who has the smelliest job, your shit cans or my shit house, Nick."

At the start of training all of us boots were given an endurance test, consisting of many different types of exercise. I finished first out of one hundred and thirty men.

*   *   *

The Captain's inspection, conducted each morning, meant extra guard duty for anyone whose bunk had not been properly made.

The training consisted of marching, drilling, work details, cleaning assignments and guard duty. Sunday afternoon I wrote letters to Hedy, Sonya and Cassie. Away from home and friends, I was lonely, as were most of the other boots.

I didn't get a reply to my first letter to Cassie. I wrote again. I received a letter from her, and kept it to read that night during guard duty. My excitement turned to shock as I read it. Cassie wrote that she and Finn Rider were engaged, and would be getting married soon. She had dated him for quite awhile, even before I left to go in the Navy. Now, as quick as the time she got in bed and jumped back out, it was over.

It didn't seem possible Cassie could leave me for someone else. I wrote her another letter. "Tell me it isn't true." I received a reply a week later, the heart shaped ring I gave her a year ago was enclosed with the letter.

I remembered the time Cassie wanted to date others, and later being gone for a few days when her mother wouldn't tell me where. I didn't want to believe it, but Cassie must have been with Finn both times.

Jock told me, "Forget Cassie. She's just a tramp and Finn is a real shit heel."

I wanted to, but I couldn't forget her just like that. The daily routine kept me busy, I didn't have time to feel sorry for myself, and wasn't the only one to receive a 'Dear John' during boot training.

*   *   *

The first six weeks went by fast. Sonya and Hedy showed up the Sunday visitors were allowed. Jock went along with me. Sonya brought chicken and cake. What a feast we had. Hedy asked about Cassie. I said she was okay, I didn't say anything about the letter and ring. Sonya and Hedy visited me several times during the last part of the training.

With basic training almost over, Jock was getting salty. He

could talk sailor language with the best of them.

I overheard him talking to his stepmother on the telephone, telling her he would be home on leave the following week. She asked him if he had been eating good. Jock's reply, "Your fucking aye."

I heard her gasp and say, "Jock, you shouldn't talk like that."

"But, Mother, that's how sailors talk."

When boot training ended, Jock and I went home on a ten day pass.

*　　*　　*

It seemed to me that I had been gone forever, not three months. The town of Byron looked smaller, the kids in school a little younger. My world changed quickly. The Schmidts missed me. Ely still worked in Byron. Cindy said I looked handsome in my Navy uniform. Dave found it difficult farming alone. Hattie told me she would fatten me up, that I looked poorly.

Jock's stepmother scolded him for using such language. She admitted men talked different than women, but he didn't need to swear all the time.

I didn't feel like seeing my friends. I helped Dave and Hattie on the farm, and spent a lot of time hunting squirrels and rabbits in the woods with Tub. I still hurt from Cassie's letter.

*　　*　　*

Jock found me moping around the Pool Hall on the last day of our leave.

"Nick, I've got a girl to cheer you up."

Dora sat in Jock's car with Ginger, waving out the window, "Let's go for a ride, Nick."

Jock and Ginger got in the front seat, Dora and I in the back. For once Jock wasn't in a hurry.

The moon came up full and bright as we rode the back roads in silence. Jock thinking about going overseas, Ginger and Dora wondering about the future, with all the young men in the service. I thought about Joseph, Marcus and Watt, and what lay ahead for me.

Dora knew about Cassie's 'Dear John' letter. "Cassie isn't your type, Nick. You need a girl like me, who will appreciate you."

It had been two years since I last saw Dora. Eighteen now, a pretty girl with a full figure, and light, clear skin. Her curly brown hair was cut short. Dora had never gotten over her crush on me.

Jock stopped the car in a hayfield. "Nick, why don't you and Dora go for a walk? I want to be alone with Ginger."

Dora and I got out of the car. As we started to walk away, we heard Jock tell Ginger, "Let's make the best of tonight. I'll be going overseas and probably be killed."

We walked down the lane in the bright moonlight.

"Nick, are you going to feed me the same line that Jock is giving Ginger?"

I laughed, "No, but who knows I might not come back."

Dora asked if I had seen the Perrys lately. I hadn't seen them since I left them to go live with the Schmidts.

Dora said, "Nellie had a baby boy after you left, and now she's pregnant again. She's bigger than ever, you should see her now."

I wasn't very talkative, so Dora quit trying to make conversation. We both sat on a tree stump looking up at the moon. I thought about Marcus, and suddenly let out a loud whistle.

Dora jumped up, startled, "Why did you do that?"

"I don't know. It just came out of me. Let's go back to the car."

As we walked back down the lane Dora said, "I'm going to work for the doctor in Byron. I'll be here, look me up after the war. You should be through hurting from your 'Dear John' by then."

After Jock dropped the girls off, he drove me home.

"Why in the hell did you have to whistle when you did? Nick, you scared the hell out of Ginger and beat me out of a good screwing."

*   *   *

Our leave over, Dave took Jock and me to the train station the next morning. We traveled by train to Virginia Beach, inland near Chesapeake Bay, for amphibious training. Jock and I were assigned to the same ship's crew.

The weather was damp and cold. We lived in tents, with a coal stove for heating. Training took a different form; small arms, landing boats, anti-aircraft guns, fire prevention and fire control.

The training ship, an LST (Landing Ship Tank), was as long as a football field. The inside cargo space, hollow from front to back, and the bottom as flat as a wash tub. The bow of the ship opened up with two huge doors. LST's are designed to carry troops and tanks up on the beach. A company of one hundred and thirty men trained, and lived together.

The city of Norfolk was a Navy town. Sailors from training ships in the port were everywhere. In the residential area some yards were posted, 'dogs and sailors keep off.'

Jock and I took leave at the same time, but didn't always stay together. I liked to go to the USO, sponsored by the townspeople, to dance, play Ping-Pong and pool. I wasn't into smoking, drinking, and whoring. Jock was. Enjoying his newfound freedom in the Navy, he liked to whoop it up and get drunk.

"Christ, Nick, you should live it up while you can, we're going overseas soon to get killed. I don't want to have any regrets about missed chances to get balled."

*   *   *

I liked to dance, and wanted to learn to jitterbug. Jock had burned himself out from drinking, and decided to tag along with me. He wasn't into dancing, but he might find a girl to take home after the dance. My instructor was Moon, a young Chinese girl with short, jet black hair, slanted, coal black eyes, chalk white skin, and a nice rounded figure.

Moon's husband, a sailor, had been killed when the Japanese bombed Pearl Harbor. Moon's grieving time over, she wanted a man. During a slow dance, she held tight to me and pressed her breasts against my chest.

"You are such a nice boy, Nick. I would like you to take me home, and stay overnight."

Somehow I couldn't get excited about a girl who had been married, and loved by another man.

"Moon, I have a buddy who would be glad to take you home." I pointed to Jock sitting in a chair looking bored to death.

"No, I don't want just any man. I want you."

Jock and I stayed in a downtown hotel that night. I mentioned Moon's offer.

Jock exploded, "Jesus Christ, you turned Moon down to stay in this flea bitten hotel with me. Goddamn, you can bet your sweet ass I wouldn't turn down an offer like that."

*   *   *

The final phase of training over, the crew boarded a train for Pittsburgh to pick up our ship. We were assigned quarters at the University of Pittsburgh for two and a half weeks, waiting for our ship to be finished.

I got a three day pass, and flew home. Ely, Dinah, Cindy and I had a steak supper in Byron, and then went to Flint to take in a show. Cindy sat next to me, and as the movie started, she slipped her hand into mine and held it tight all through the show.

She whispered, "Why don't you come down to stoke up the fire tonight. I'll have my bed all nice and warm for you."

I stuttered, "I'm afraid Dave would hear us."

As I left the next day, Cindy gave me a big kiss and said, "Happy nineteenth birthday." It was March 25, 1945.

*   *   *

Three days later I boarded our ship for a cruise down the Ohio and Mississippi. The trip from Pittsburgh to New Orleans took nine days. Spring rains flooded the river. The ship made good time. The first stop, an ammunition depot, to load the tank deck with five hundred pound bombs. By the middle of May the ship was loaded, and ready to sail. The crew called the ship 'Last Chance.'

A news broadcast came over the radio—The war in Europe is over! The crew celebrated the victory. We mourned the loss of President Roosevelt, who died April 12th, before he could witness the Allies triumph over Nazi Germany. I was anxious to get to the war in the Pacific and do my part.

*   *   *

Mail came aboard as we left port, heading out to sea. A letter from Sonya that said Marcus had been killed at the hands of the Japanese. There was no explanation as to how or where Marcus had been killed. My stomach churned with anger. What a waste. Marcus, my brother, was dead.

I thought about the postcard I received while living at the Perrys, telling me Marcus was a prisoner.

Marcus is dead! Gone! I would never see him again. The memories of the few short years, living together in Fenton were all that remained. I vowed I would never forget Marcus. Every month when the moon came up full and bright, I would think of him.

I could hear Marcus—a hound dog howl, baying at the moon, in defiance of his Japanese captors. It was May 8, 1945.

TWENTY TWO

Our ship, the Last Chance, cruised into Panama City harbor to pick up supplies, the first foreign port stop as we headed overseas. I had the security watch so I couldn't go into town with Jock. He could hardly wait to go ashore.

"Nick, I'm going to get roaring drunk and screw the tits off all the girls in the first whorehouse I come to."

Late that night Jock came staggering up the gang plank, pulling a Billy goat behind him. He was roaring drunk.

"No shit, Nick, this is the best liberty I've ever had."

Then he collapsed in a heap on the deck. I chased the goat down the gang plank, and managed to get Jock below decks into his sack without being discovered by the watch officer.

"Jock, you owe me one," I muttered as I hurried back to my post.

*   *   *

Life aboard the Last Chance became routine. An officer headed each unit of the crew. Jock was assigned to the deck gang, who were responsible for the general maintenance of the ship. The engine crew worked below decks in the engine room. The stores group and cooks were in charge of supplies and food. The gunnery group looked after the ammunition, weapons, the forty and twenty millimeter anti-aircraft guns. The last group, communications, radar and signal men kept in touch with the other ships at sea.

I was assigned to the signal gang with a Mexican in his middle twenties. He had a slight build with small bone structure, light brown skin, black hair and brown eyes. A First Class regular Navy Signal Man, he was born and raised in San Diego.

"Nick," he said, "When I attended high school, everyone treated me like shit. In the Navy I'm just as good as anyone."

I couldn't understand why anyone would treat such a smart, good looking young man like shit.

* * *

Everybody in the crew stood guard duty; eight on, sixteen off, on a rotation basis. All crew members had a post for battle stations. Mine, the only forty millimeter gun on the ship. We soon became an organized, well oiled crew that worked together.

The Pacific Ocean is an amazing body of water. One day the waves were so high the ship bobbed up and down like a cork. The next day the water so smooth, a penny dropped in the water caused ripples. Every time the Last Chance rocked and rolled, I became seasick.

The sleeping quarters below decks were small and confining. The beds, a canvas stretched over an iron frame, folded against the wall, two deep. The close quarters didn't bother me as much as the smoking. Almost everybody smoked. Between the cigarette smoke and the ship's motion, I was seasick a great deal of the time.

* * *

The next stop was the island of Oahu, Hawaii. With the ship's company divided into port and starboard sides, it allowed half of the crew to be off the ship, while the other half stayed aboard.

I took shore leave with Jock. We had to see Pearl Harbor and Waikiki Beach. It was a long, bumpy ride over a narrow mountain road. Pearl overflowed with service personnel, standing in line to drink, get tattooed, and then skivy-skivy in the whorehouses. Jock had to have a go at it. "It might be the last time I get liberty. This time I'm not going to get drunk. See you back at the ship, Nick."

The native girls didn't appeal to me so I went swimming at Waikiki Beach. The trip back over the mountains sobered up the sailors, but many had to go to sick bay for the real cure.

*   *   *

The Last Chance headed west into the South Pacific with a small convoy of LST's. The ships earned the nickname "large stationary targets." At top speed of twelve knots, about fourteen miles per hour, we charted a zigzag course in case of submarine attack. It was slow progress catching up with the war. Life boat drills were a joke. If bombed or torpedoed, with the tank deck full of 500 pound bombs, the crew would need parachutes instead of life jackets.

The convoy stopped in Eniwtok Atoll for food and fuel, then on to Ulithi for rest and relaxation at the beach of Mog Mog, a small flat island barely above sea level. Nothing to do but lay in the sun, swim, drink beer and pee into funnels stuck in the sand. The water was warm and crystal clear. Most of the crew got roaring drunk.

Then on toward Japan, with stops at Guam, Saipan, Iwo Jima, and finally Buckner Bay, Okinawa. Because of our explosive tank deck of bombs, we anchored the ship a long way out in the bay. The Japs were flying kamikaze missions. If the Last Chance was hit, anything near would go up. Cargo ships came in quick, took off some bombs and left.

Midway through unloading, the Last Chance and another LST were ordered out to sea. A typhoon came up, and the ships had to ride the storm out in the ocean. As the ship floundered in the storm, the whole crew was seasick.

The second LST, following the Last Chance a short distance away, took a seventy foot wave broadside. The ship shuddered, and slowly turned into the raging wind, rain and waves. The ship took on water. An emergency flare lit up the sky. A signal man furiously flashed an S.O.S. for help. The crew of the Last Chance watched helplessly as the floundering LST took another high wave broadside, breaking it apart. It quickly sank under the swirling waves. One hundred and thirty men aboard went down into a watery grave with the ship.

I couldn't believe what had just happened. One minute the ship could be seen, then it completely disappeared. Our Captain ordered all men below decks, and all hatches battened down. The Last Chance had to be sealed water-tight, the only way it could survive the raging typhoon. For three days we rode the storm. When it subsided, the Last Chance went back to Okinawa to unload more bombs.

*   *   *

A big convoy of ships were gathering in the bay, ours included, for the invasion of Japan. Information had it the Japanese were entrenched deeper in caves on their mainland than Okinawa. It would be a costly battle for the Americans to take Japan.

*   *   *

A news broadcast came over the radio; Japan would surrender any day. Suddenly over the ship's speaker; battle stations, battle stations, all hands to battle stations! The Last Chance put up a smoke screen, and the crew remained at battle stations, in the hot scorching sun.

Three Jap pilots, on the last suicide mission, dove down at our ship, screaming through the clouds. Strapped to the fore ward gun mount, I thought of Marcus as I fired at the torpedo

bombers. They veered away. One exploded on the battleship
Pennsylvania, and another on an APA transport ship, moored
nearby. The third Kamikaze missed us, and crashed into the
sea.

The crew gave a cheer, and I a loud whistle. The Last Chance
had fired its guns at the enemy for the first time, on the last day
of World War II. The Japanese surrendered. It was August 14,
1945.

TWENTY THREE

Another typhoon headed for the harbor, and again we were ordered out to the open sea. Typhoon Louise pounded Okinawa, destroying fifty to ninety percent of the buildings on the land bases. It sank eight ships, and grounded or damaged over two hundred ships in the harbor. Seven days the winds blew. All hands aboard ship were seasick. The Last Chance was blown backwards all the way to Subic Bay in the Philippine Islands.

The rest of the bombs were unloaded, and the tank deck reloaded with beer and canned tuna. The orders were to sail to Japan, by way of the Lingayen Gulf.

The ship pulled into port at Lingayen Gulf for the night, before heading to Japan. Three native girls slipped aboard. They had dark, dirty skin, long, unkempt black hair and were wearing short ragged dresses. They were skinny, underfed teenagers. The girls spent the night screwing most of the crew. The girls were a mess and in a sad way by morning when they left. Sick bay was busy all that day.

*   *   *

I had the midnight watch. As the ship headed for the Japanese mainland, a full moon came up, not so much as a small ripple in the calm sea. Off in the distance the islands looked dark and sinister.

My thoughts turned to Marcus. He spent the last years of his young life in a Japanese Prison camp, enduring only God knows what. Somewhere in this foreign land his body lay, but where? His soul surely must be up there on the moon. I wondered if I whistled loud enough, could I call him back? I gave a long, loud whistle.

The Watch Officer came out of the conn tower asking, "What was that?"

I said, "The ghost of all the men killed fighting for the freedom of the Philippines."

The Last Chance sailed into Nagasaki, Japan without incident.

A Japanese destroyer was the only other ship in the bay. The crew didn't know what to expect. We were told to stick together, not to stray far inland. The Japanese yen, ratio one hundred fifty to the American dollar, was useless. No stores, nothing to buy. Cigarettes and candy could be bartered for souvenirs. The people in the southern part of Japan were poor, hungry and homeless.

The atomic bomb, dropped there two months ago, blew up the city, killing thirty-five thousand men, women and children.

The only thing standing, in the center of the rubble, was a Shinto Shrine, the religious symbol of the Japanese people. I took some pictures, picked up a human skull, then sat down and cried, as the horror of it all overwhelmed me.

I thought of Marcus, and the many people tortured, maimed and killed by the Japanese at Pearl Harbor, Corregidor, Bataan, Guam, Iwo Jima, Okinawa, and all the other islands throughout the Pacific. Maybe it was God's way of punishing the Japanese.

*   *   *

Jock and I had the day off, and decided to go inland, to find out how the Japanese lived. We saw fields of rice and small gardens, not a foot of land wasted. Large earthen pots buried near the gardens were receptacles for human waste, used for fertilizer on the gardens. Soon we came to a small town.

We went into a theater and watched a short play. I was standing up peeing in the bathroom, when an old woman squatted next to me and peed into a slit trench in the ground. The Japanese in the country were a very primitive people.

We found a Geisha House and were entertained by two young girls singing, playing instruments and dancing. In Japan, some young girls are raised to be Geishas, for the sole purpose of entertaining men. Another group of young girls are raised as Gama Geisha girls, for the sexual pleasures of men. The Gama, or red light district where they lived, was out of bounds for the American service men.

Jock wasn't about to let the "restricted" notice keep him from the Gama district.

"Let's go, Nick. You missed your chance with Moon back in Norfolk. Now I'm gonna find out what these slant eyed girls are like."

The Gama area was in the run down part of town. Young boys were everywhere.

"Skivy-skivy my sister? Cheap, only a pack of cigarettes and a candy bar."

Jock signaled 'okay' to a small raggedy clad kid.

"Come on, Nick, you can stand guard, and watch for MP's."

We followed the boy into a flimsy one room shack where a small young girl, wearing a red kimono, lay on a pile of straw. The girl motioned for Jock to come to her. I stepped back outside.

I heard Jock telling the girl, "Take off that damn kimono, I want to get a look at you." He muttered, "Christ, you are no different than American girls, only skinnier."

*   *   *

Our ship proceeded to Fukuoka, located on the southern end of Japan, to unload the cargo of beer and tuna. A large portion of the precious cargo came up missing. It could not be accounted for.

The Last Chance was beached, and the cargo that could be found, unloaded. The crew, together a year now, would soon break up. The men in the service the longest were going to be discharged, back to their homes and families. Tonight was party night. The missing beer appeared from nowhere, out of the bilges, lockers and ditty bags. The crew got drunk.

Jock and I had the midnight watch. The tide came in and the Last Chance drifted out in the bay toward the mine fields. We managed to get the ship back on the beach without incident. It was December 31, 1945, New Years Eve.

*   *   *

The Last Chance had orders to take a group of Army personnel back to the States. With the extra men aboard sleeping quarters had to be rearranged. The signal gang, along with the deck gang, was assigned temporary bunks around the eating area of the stern of the ship. They had to be up and about before breakfast was served. Jock, a sound sleeper and hard to wake up, slept nude. One morning he must have been thinking of his girl back home, because his manhood stuck straight up.

I took a tube of toothpaste and squeezed it over the top of it. Jock looked foolish heading for the shower. He later told me, "You won't believe the wet dream I had this morning."

At the time I was issued Japanese yen, I was told that only seven hundred fifty yen (five dollars American money) could be exchanged when we left Japan. I had accumulated a large sum of yen playing cards, selling cigarettes and candy. That night I played poker, no limit. I played fast and loose and lost it all. The yen would not be any good tomorrow anyway. To my surprise and sorrow, the next morning the Captain announced that any and all yen could be exchanged for American money.

I lost seventy five thousand yen, five hundred dollars in American money. I was a sad, sick sailor.

*   *   *

We left Japan with one engine out, the other flank speed to travel non-stop to the United States. The crew and Soldiers partied the whole way on beer and tuna. I stayed outside on the bow deck shooting a rifle, exploding stray mines floating by.

The non-stop trip took thirty days and nights. The ship docked at San Diego, California. Most of the crew left, to be discharged and go home. A few short timers, and regular Navy men remained aboard.

For the first time in a month we had mail call. I received a letter from Sonya saying Joseph had been rescued, and released from a prison camp in Japan. He would have to recuperate in a Military Hospital for awhile, then planned to stay with Sonya in Wisconsin.

I thought back to the last time I had seen Joseph. It was five years ago, when he stopped by Perrys to tell me about changing his name to Mason. Joseph had been in a Japanese prison camp most of those years. Maybe Joseph could tell me about Marcus' death. I looked forward to seeing him in a few months, when I would be discharged from the Navy.

*   *   *

Jock asked me to go to Tijuana, Mexico with him. Tijuana is a short distance from San Diego, just over the Mexican border. A wide open foreign country full of service men partying on Mexican beer and tequila with Spanish senoritas. Jock had to have a couple of shots of tequila to face up to the job at hand. A taxi cab driver took us to the "cleanest whorehouse" in town. I declined, I didn't want to lose my cherry on a Mexican whore and take a chance of getting a disease. Jock selected a girl and went into a partitioned off area. I could hear but not see. The girl talked through the partition to another girl, telling her what a young man Jock was. She liked older men, they lasted longer.

Jock said, "My God, how can you eat candy at a time like this?"

He wanted her undivided attention.

*   *   *

The ship was ordered to Portland, Oregon, to be decommissioned. The Last Chance sailed into Portland Harbor on its last cruise. A civilian construction gang came aboard to moth ball the ship. The crew could come and go as they pleased.

I spent most of the evenings at the roller rink, where I met a pretty girl named Sue, two years older than me. She had short, curly hair, and a shapely figure. Her boyfriend, a sailor, had been killed overseas. About a week after I first met Sue, I told her, "This is a special night for me, let's celebrate."

She must have been lonesome. "Okay, let's go to my place, but you can't stay overnight."

We rode a bus to the edge of town to Sue's small, but nicely furnished apartment. We sat on the couch listening to music on the record player. Suddenly Sue got up, went into the bedroom.

Upon returning, she said, "My skating pants were too tight, I took them off."

Sue got hot. She gave me long passionate kisses, as she lay soft and warm in my arms. "Are you okay, Nick?"

I stammered, "I guess so."

I thought what's the matter with me? I couldn't become excited.

"I better go Sue."

I got up, and as I was leaving she said, "I'm sorry you weren't in the mood for a good loving, Nick. I wanted to give you something special to remember on your twentieth birthday." It was March 25, 1946.

*   *   *

I lay awake a long time. For months overseas my dreams were about a night like this. Why couldn't I get aroused? Was there something wrong with me? The next morning I told Jock about my night with Sue.

"You dumb Hunky, when are you going to grow up?"

*   *   *

The Last Chance was finally decommissioned and moth balled. I received my first stripe, I made Radar Man/Third Class. Jock and I received train tickets to the Navy base in Chicago, where we would be mustered out and discharged from the Navy.

I had lots of time to think about the past months, during the three day train ride to Chicago. The Last Chance had taken me half way around the world and back, with stops at most of the islands in the Pacific Ocean; the Hawaiian, Marshall, Caroline, Marianas, Bonin, Nansei, Philippines, and the Island of Japan.

What would I do? Where would I go? I thought about Cassie. I needed to meet a girl, and have a lasting relationship. I wanted a family of my own. It was June 9, 1946.

TWENTY FOUR

I called Sonya to see about visiting her before I went back to Byron. Joseph was staying with her, so I could see both of them. Sonya had bought a house on the south side of Racine, with lots of room.

My thoughts turned to Marcus as I rode the bus to Racine. The reunion would not be complete without him. What would Joseph be like? What a terrible ordeal he must have endured in the Japanese prison camp.

Joseph cried as we shook hands and hugged. He was very thin, not much more than skin and bones. He was almost bald, with wispy gray hair in a crew cut. Joseph, at twenty nine, had been through an incredible experience.

He hardly recognized me. The past five years had changed me more than him. At age twenty, I had jet black hair, piercing, bright blue eyes, and smooth tanned skin. When I smiled, a slight gap showed between my front teeth.

Sonya, a young lady of twenty seven, was as pretty as ever, full of life and fun. She still worked at the steel mills. Joseph and I had all day to visit, and catch up with our lives.

He talked about his life in the prison camp. "I survived because I ate better than most of the prisoners. I didn't smoke, and other prisoners would trade their rice for my ration of cigarettes. I also exercised any time I got the chance. The Japanese were barbaric in their treatment of us prisoners. I'll never be able to get out of my mind all the American prisoners brutally tortured, maimed, and executed by the Jap guards. Thousands of others died from malnutrition, dysentery, and lack of medical care."

Joseph paused a minute, as he continued to reflect upon his prison years.

I asked, "What about Marcus?"

"He contacted a tropical fever, and was a hospital patient when Bataan fell. We were separated after being captured. The Japanese divided the prisoners by alphabetical order. Marcus was sent to camp two to work on a pineapple plantation near Davao. I was taken to the Bilibid prison in Manila and later transferred by rail car, with five thousand other prisoners, to camp three.

"Marcus and I had a short reunion when I went with a detail of prisoners from our camp to his. We asked the Japanese prison commander to be allowed to stay together. Our request was denied. We parted, and I never saw Marcus again. I don't know how or where Marcus was killed."

Joseph's eyes moistened, "Six months later I was herded aboard a Japanese ship with other prisoners, and shipped to Osaka, Japan. I was transferred by rail to the prison camp Yodogawa Bunsho, to work in a steel mill until Japan surrendered, and the war ended. Changing my name to Mason before enlisting in the Army probably saved my life. I feel responsible for Marcus' death, because I talked him into enlisting in the Army."

He choked up, "I don't want to talk about it anymore."

"Joseph, I think we should be thankful that three of the four of us in the service returned. Even if our family is not living together, we are pretty lucky. We can be thankful that dad decided to leave Serbia, and come to America. Just think how people live in Europe and Asia."

Joseph's face flushed red, he turned and walked toward the house muttering, "Surely you know about Dad."

*　　*　　*

I didn't sleep well that night, thinking about Marcus, and

what Joseph told me about his prison years. When I finally fell asleep I had a weird dream; the Sabitches were one big happy, hunky family again. Then I heard Joseph saying, "Goddamn it, Nick, you must know."

Marcus was playing a jew's-harp and singing "Red River Valley" and baying at the moon. I woke up in a sweat, hearing a hound dog howl. It wasn't Marcus, just the neighbor's dog.

The next day I told Sonya and Joseph goodbye, and took a train to Byron. I had a lot of things on my mind to sort out.

* * *

Dave and Hattie Schmidt were glad to see me. They had aged considerably the past two years. Cindy and her husband, now home from the service, had moved to Flint to work at the Buick Motor plant.

Dave said, "Stay with us, Nick, until you decide what you're going to do."

The government paid unemployment to ex-service men, twenty dollars a week for fifty two weeks. I could help on the farm, and draw unemployment.

I went out to the shed to see what condition the Model "A" was in. The tires were flat, and sunk deep in the dirt. Chicken shit covered the ground, and hens nested in the shredded upholstered seats. The Model "A" was a mess.

Dave let me use his Ford until I could buy a car of my own. I had to see Watt, Hedy and Dad.

Watt and Bert were back from the service. Mr. Wilton had hired Bert at the Buick plant in Flint. Watt managed a gas station in Fenton.

I visited Hedy. Her husband worked at the McDonald Dairy. They were buying a small home in Flint, a short distance from where our family used to live.

Dad, the last one I went to see, was in his early fifties, and starting to show his age. He lived in a small house, and worked at the Forge plant in Lansing. He seemed to be in good health, and doing well.

He was sad, and remorseful. "You're the only one who keeps in touch, and treats me like a father. I miss all of my children. Have you been to see your brothers and sisters lately? What are they doing?"

"I've only been home from the Navy a short time, but I've managed to visit Joseph, Sonya, Hedy and Watt. Marcus was killed during the war."

Dad said sadly, "I only had him a little while."

I went on, "Sonya is divorced and living in Racine. Joseph is there with her now. Watt is out of the Navy and living with the Wiltons. He's kind of forgotten his family. Hedy is living in Flint. Her husband has a milk route. I don't have any idea where Jay and Alfred are."

I felt sorry for Dad, living alone, isolated from his family. When I told him goodbye, he said, "Come visit me again."

*   *   *

I couldn't get enthused about helping Dave on the farm. I didn't have a future there, and needed a more challenging job that paid better.

Dave was going to Byron on business, and asked me to go with him. We could look at some used cars.

I had saved five hundred dollars in War Bonds while in the service, to be used to buy a car.

Most of the cars were old and worn out. I finally found what I was looking for; a 1939 two door V/8 Ford. The price, nine hundred dollars.

Dave said, "That's a lot of money for a car eight years old, that cost six hundred dollars brand new, Nick."

There were not many used cars to be found. Automobile factories had quit building news ones over four years ago. Any car available, sold at a premium. If I wanted transportation, I had to pay the asking price. Dave didn't have the money to lend me, but agreed to cosign a note at the bank for four hundred dollars.

I had a year to pay the note, plus interest, back to the bank. I paid forty dollars for full insurance coverage on the Ford for a year through the Citizens Insurance Company.

Basic transportation, the '39 Ford had a stick shift, no heater, defroster or radio, but a big step up from the Model "A."

*　　*　　*

At the time Marcus enlisted in the Army, he had designated Sonya as beneficiary on his insurance policy. His other brothers and sisters were listed as next of kin. The government had sent checks to Sonya for Marcus' Army back pay. From his $10,000 insurance policy, she would receive a hundred dollars a month, for the next eight years. The back pay was divided among the five brothers and two sisters, each to receive a hundred and sixty three dollars. Sonya telephoned me to tell me about the government checks.

"I'm having trouble with my boyfriend, and can't get away from Racine for awhile. I'm mailing the checks to Hedy. See if you and she can locate our brothers, so they get the money. Don't worry about my problems. We'll get together later."

*　　*　　*

How could we locate Alfred and Jay?

I called Joseph. He was leaving for Washington to testify before the War Crimes Court against the Japanese.

"I'll pick my check up later. Let me know if you locate our adopted brothers."

Watt, curious, but indifferent, said, "Wiltons are my family. Let me know if you locate Jay and Alfred."

Hedy said, "Let's start with the Probate Court. The Judge will know what to do."

We drove to the County Court House in Flint to see the Judge of Probate. Judge Mackey had a thick shock of unruly, curly hair.

He said, "I can't tell you the whereabouts of your adopted brothers. That's confidential information. Why are you bothering me?"

Hedy showed Judge Mackey the checks. "I think it's important that Alfred and Jay know they had a brother who died fighting for their freedom, don't you, Judge?"

Mackey softened a little. Smiling he said, "I was starting practice on this bench when I separated you Sabitches. Maybe it's time I helped you get together."

The Judge gave us the address of Alfred and Jay. Jay lived on a farm between Fenton and Flint, with the Lewises. Alfred resided in Bay City with the Dobsons.

Judge Mackey said, "I better call the Dobsons and Lewises, and let them know you are coming." He laughed as we left, "You may be sorry you're opening this Pandora's Box."

* * *

We decided to visit Alfred first. Excited, Hedy and I drove to Bay City. Laughing to myself, I thought back to four years ago, and my visit in Bay City with Freda.

I wondered what Alfred looked like. I had no memory of him. When the family broke up, he was a baby and sent to live at the State Home.

Mr. And Mrs. Dobson weren't happy when they received Judge Mackey's phone call, telling them about the government check for Alfred, and Hedy and I coming to see them. They knew Alfred would find out someday about his birth family, but hoped he would be much older.

The Dobsons shocked Alfred when they told him about

his brothers and sisters. He was just a baby when Dobsons adopted him. Hedy cried when we were introduced. Alfred looked a lot like me; the same height, features and build. He had a larger nose, and his eyes not quite as blue and piercing as mine.

Alfred couldn't believe he had a family other than the Dobsons. He wanted to see the rest of his family right away. I calmed Alfred down long enough to explain to him the whereabouts of our family. No way could we ever live together. Hedy told Alfred maybe he could live with her later when he was older. We said goodbye to an unhappy Alfred, confused that the Dobsons had kept his birth family a secret from him.

*   *   *

The Lewis' were quite disturbed when they received Judge Mackey's phone call. They told him they didn't want any interference from Jay's birth family. The Judge insisted. Jay, at eighteen, was old enough to know about his family.

We finally located the Lewis'. Something was vaguely familiar about Mr. And Mrs. Lewis. I couldn't quite put my finger on it. Jay had been told in advance about us coming to see him.

When we met him, he said, "I don't believe it, it's some kind of a joke."

Jay, the biggest of the Sabitch family, had big ears, like Marcus, a large nose like Alfred, and big, bright blue eyes like mine. He needed some time to think about what he just learned. Hedy thought it might be best that Jay see, and talk to Alfred before meeting the rest of our family. Hedy cried when we left. She gave Jay the names and addresses of all the family members.

Marcus, by his death, had managed to have the adopted brothers located. Maybe he didn't die for nothing after all, but where and how did he die? Somehow I had to find out.

*   *   *

Hedy telephoned Sonya after our visit with Jay and Alfred. Sonya had some news; she was planning to sell her home in Racine and move to Flint to be closer to the family. She hoped Alfred and Jay would come and live with her. She left Hedy with the happy thought that with her move to Flint, the family was getting closer together.

Sonya's Italian boyfriend continued to string her along. He kept telling her that someday his divorce would come through, and then they could get married.

I spent some time visiting with Alfred and Jay. They were getting over the shock of finding out about their family. Alfred looked, and acted a lot like me. Jay was moody and withdrawn. Alfred had another year in high school, Jay would graduate in the spring. Both boys were anxious to get out of school, and spend more time with their brothers and sisters.

* * *

Sonya moved to Flint, and bought a small house on the outskirts of town. Joseph, after visiting her for a few days, called me up, and asked me to visit him. He introduced me to Pearl Maddon, a girl he had been dating. She had long, brown hair, wide open blue eyes, and a small, turned up nose. Pearl talked tough, and flaunted her well stacked figure at me.

Joseph cornered me in the garage, and asked me for a favor. "I'm thinking of marrying Pearl, but I'm not sure how faithful she'll be to me."

I said, "Yeah, she's impressed me already."

"Here's what I want you to do. Sonya and I are going downtown shopping. You stay here with Pearl, and make a play for her. If she won't have anything to do with you, then I'll know she'll be faithful to me."

"Christ, Joseph, I'm your brother. It wouldn't be right."

"Please, Nick, I've got to know about Pearl. Do it for me."

Sonya and Joseph hardly got out the door when Pearl took

my hand and said, "If I'm going to join your family we better get acquainted." She pressed her breasts against me, and kissed me hard on the lips. I tried to pull away, but Pearl held tight.

"Don't you want me, Nick?"

"You're a sexy girl, Pearl, but Joseph's girl, not mine. I think I better go."

Pearl pouted, "Maybe next time we'll get better acquainted."

Joseph called me the next day. "Pearl's sure a neat girl isn't she? I knew she'd handle herself okay. She told me about you making advances on her, but she resisted. Pearl will make me a good wife. Thanks, Nick."

I thought to myself, Joseph really didn't want to know the truth about Pearl, or he would have asked me what happened when Pearl and I were alone.

Joseph took time to look up and visit Alfred and Jay. His curiosity satisfied, he left to re-enlist in the Army. His POW status allowed him to choose his base location each re-enlistment period. Joseph married Pearl in Texas. None of us brothers or sisters knew about the wedding. I wondered why they didn't have the wedding in Flint, where Pearl's family lived.

*   *   *

Jock threw a party while his folks were gone for the night. Most of our high school friends came, ready for a good time. It didn't take much booze to get the group high. Jock and I got to talking about the future.

"Let's go to Mt. Pleasant College, Nick. The GI Bill will pay our tuition, books, and give us sixty-five dollars a month for room and board."

"Okay, we'll check it out soon."

The party got wild. Jock took all of us for a ride on the back of his dad's truck. He drove along the edge of the road, clipping the tops off mail boxes with the corner of the flat bed. Nobody wanted to be involved in Jock's escapade.

It was a short lived party that New Years Eve, 1946.

TWENTY FIVE

Ely and Dinah Schmidt were still living in Byron. They asked me to spend the weekend with them.

I, like most of the service men recently discharged, still wore my Navy clothes. My tailor made dress blues fit me like a glove.

Ely and Dinah had a small apartment, comfortably furnished. They were happy, doing well, and wanted a child, and a house of their own.

Sunday night we went to the movie theater. I noticed Lois Bath getting a ticket to see the show. I asked her to sit with me. We couldn't talk during the movie, so I invited Lois back to the apartment. She had grown up, and blossomed since I last saw her at Byron High School. Built like a dream, Lois had all the curves in the right places. She wanted to get away from Byron, and live in a big city.

Working in a small town, she didn't meet many boys, or have much fun. Ely and Dinah went to bed. They both had to get up early to go to work. Lois and I sat on the day bed, and talked for quite awhile.

"I'm sorry about your breakup with Cassie, I've heard that Finn Rider is staying in the Navy, making a career of it. He and Cassie are living at a base in Florida. Just think, if they hadn't got married, we wouldn't be together tonight, would we, Nick?"

Lois had her hand around my neck, under the flap of my Navy blouse. "Nick, you don't smoke, so that isn't a box of matches I feel." She reached in the little pocket, and pulled out a box of rubbers, Navy issue; just in case. Lois asked if I had ever used one. I never had.

She said, "Let's try one out."

Lois, hot to be loved, reached down and unbuttoned the flap of my trousers. "Let me help you put that thing on. Wait, Nick!"

I couldn't. When I took her home, Lois said, "Let's try it sometime without one of those things. When you're ready, look me up."

*   *   *

Summer faded into fall, and the work at Schmidt's farm slowed down. I needed a job making more money, in order to pay off the bank loan on my '39 Ford.

Jock stopped by, driving a '41 Plymouth he bought during the summer. He had a cute little blonde in the car with him. He introduced me to Annie Boyd. She was quite a bit younger than him, a senior in high school. Jock told me he still dated Ginger, but was playing the field.

He had borrowed money from the bank to buy his car, and needed a steady job, too. We applied for work at the Buick factory in Flint, and were hired to work on the final assembly line, for ninety-seven cents an hour. We could take turns driving back and forth to work. Jock asked me to stay at his farm.

We could do chores for room and board. Jock and I slept on the third floor of the farmhouse. There was no heat upstairs. Jock was a fresh air nut and slept with the window open all winter. Sometimes the wind blew snow in the window and the top blanket would be covered with snow in the morning. It didn't take me long to get up and out to the warm barn to milk the cows and do chores before going to work.

*   *   *

Jock's job on the assembly line was to put tires and wheels on the car chassis. I inspected car bodies and did final repair on the line. For small town farm boys the work was boring and tiresome. I knew it was not the type of work I wanted to do the rest of my life.

The Buick plant worked overtime daily and weekends to meet customer demands. Any daily work over eight hours paid time and a half. The pay was good, but the long, confining hours hard to get used to. I paid my bills off and was saving a little. I didn't have time to spend it, with getting up before sunrise to help Jock's father with the farm chores, working at Buick all day, then chores again before going to bed. Sunday was a day to rest up before starting another long, tiresome week.

Buick, up to now, had been an open shop, and not mandatory to be a union member. An organization as large as Buick, without formal rules and regulations, fostered favoritism. Without a structured plan to deal fairly with all employees, the bosses' relatives and friends received preferential treatment.

It also wasn't right that some workers paid union dues and other didn't. We all profited by the benefits, and higher wages won by the negotiations during contract time. I had three months before I had to join the union.

*   *   *

I ran into Dora Simpson at the Drug Store in Byron. Dora was wearing a nurse's uniform, and looked quite slim and trim. I hadn't seen her since the last night of my leave before going overseas.

She commented, "I see you didn't get killed in the war, Nick."

I laughed, "No, neither did Jock."

Dora lived with her parents, and worked at the hospital in Byron. She worked most weekends. I asked her if she wanted to go skating some night, when we both had the same time off.

"Yes, I guess you are over that 'Dear John' letter you received from Cassie."

"Yeah, Cassie is an old married woman now."

*   *   *

Jock and Ginger were planning a picnic, and asked me to go along. Lois Bath wanted another date with me. She had called me a couple of times, and teasingly asked me if I still kept the box of matches in my Navy blouse. Jock told me I would be a fool not to date her. "She's a sexy girl."

We drove to the top of a big hill, overlooking Fenton. The girls had packed fried chicken, potato salad and beer. After a few drinks, Lois got amorous. We laid on a blanket, looking up into the blue sky, and necked a little. Lois wanted to go all the way. She was quite forward, and demanding. I couldn't get excited or in the mood. Lois was disappointed.

"This is the second time you left me all up in the air, Nick. We should go out alone sometime, and I'll make sure you do the job right."

That night I lay in bed wondering, what is wrong with me sexually? The first time I was with Lois at Ely's apartment, she had me so excited I did something before she was even ready for me. Then today I couldn't get aroused.

As I fell asleep I heard Marcus saying, "You're not a kid anymore, Nick. Who are you saving yourself for?" Then he gave a hound dog howl and disappeared.

I laid in bed and thought about all the lost opportunities I had in the past to prove my manhood. I consoled myself, that maybe I hadn't found the right girl yet.

*   *   *

Friday night I drove to Byron to watch the high school basketball game. Annie Boyd, the girl that Jock dated a few times, was a cheerleader. During half time, I talked to her.

"Have you dated Jock lately?"

"No, Jock's a pretty wild guy, not really my type."

I took Annie home after the game. She lived on a farm not far from the Schmidts. A pretty little gal, only five feet tall. She had long, blonde hair, a tiny waist, blue eyes, and smooth complexion. Annie was very shy.

I told Jock the next day about my date with Annie.

"Annie is too young for you, Nick. She's only sixteen."

*   *   *

Jock and I drove to Mt. Pleasant to look over the college campus. Mt. Pleasant, a small town in the center of the state, was located at the base of a long range of high hills extending north. Flat farm country extended south. To the east and west were oil and gas fields.

The small town and friendly college campus appealed to us. I enrolled for classes in business administration, and Jock the teaching curriculum.

I gave Buick Motors two weeks notice. With Marcus' government back pay, and the money I saved while working at Buick, I bought a used '41 Pontiac.

*   *   *

College life was a lot like the service; ex GI's going to classes in barracks, and living in barracks. Due to the age, and service experience, the Dean of Students decided not to have freshman initiation. Most of the freshmen were older than the upper class men.

Student enrollment starting in February was 3,500, with almost 1,000 freshmen and most of them were ex-servicemen. The GI Bill paid tuition, books, supplies and sixty-five dollars a month living expenses. We would have to stay in the new barracks being built for veterans. The rooms were small, with two double bunks per room. There were bathroom stools, sinks and showers at each end. A hall ran the whole length, with oil stoves, tables and benches outside each room. The room cost each student thirty dollars per month. Jock and I bunked in the same room.

Mt. Pleasant turned out to be a suitcase college. Everyone went home Friday afternoon, and returned Sunday night. We were no exception. I always had a load of kids to take to Byron and Fenton. I continued to stay at Jock's place.

Jock partied all weekend. His stepmother didn't approve, but Jock had been in the Navy, was twenty one and going to college. There wasn't much she could say. Jock's dad thought it was a good time for him to 'sow his wild oats.'

*   *   *

Hedy had another baby boy. Dora and I baby-sat sometimes, so she and her husband could go out. One evening we laid on the couch, our bodies pressed close together. Dora got hot. She whispered to me, "I know you want to, so do I, let's do it."

I mumbled, "No, I don't think we better, you might get pregnant."

Later that night I lay awake a long time. I had the empty feeling in my stomach. Dora had let her guard down for the first time, and wanted to go all the way, giving me a present on my birthday that I would never forget.

I fell asleep dreaming that Marcus and I were in Cooper's old outhouse talking.

"I don't know what's the matter with you, Nick. You're twenty-one years old. If you're saving yourself for a special person, you better find her soon."

"I know, if I don't find someone soon, I'm going to explode inside."

Marcus opened the outhouse door, and gave a loud howl at

the moon. I tried to whistle back, but I woke up hissing through my teeth.

*   *   *

The first semester of college went pretty fast. Most of the veterans stayed close to the barracks, partying. The younger students lived in dorms, belonged to fraternities and sororities. The ex GI's weren't into college clubs yet. The vets were having enough trouble adjusting to civilian and college life.

When classes were out for the summer, Jock and I had to get jobs and earn some money. We made application at Buick Motors, and were hired for the summer as vacation replacements.

*   *   *

Jock and I went to a dance hall on the outskirts of Flint Saturday night. Lois Bath was there. She had started training to be a nurse, at a hospital in Flint. I took her home. Lois reminded me of our two previous dates, when I had left her emotions all up in the air.

"You are not going to do that to me tonight," she pouted, "it's my time of the month, and I've got the 'curse.'"

She laughed when I reminded her about the dog riding her leg during the high school scrap drive.

"I was pretty dumb then, I'm a lot smarter now, Nick. I think you are the dumb one."

We dated a few times. Lois wasn't ready for a serious relationship, she wanted to finish nursing school.

*   *   *

Jay, my adopted brother, confused about his two families, went to live with Hedy. Mr. and Mrs. Lewis had been good parents to him; he had been happy until he found out about his birth family. Now he didn't know what to think or do.

I visited Alfred often, and let him drive my car. He was a different guy than Jay, liked to joke, and have a good time. He didn't have the hang up that Jay did about having two families.

Alfred said, "Nick, next year after finishing school, I'm going to live with my sisters."

* * *

Watt met a young girl from a small town in Wisconsin. She was taking classes in Flint, to earn a teaching degree. She convinced him he ought to further his education, and do something with his life. Watt told me that next year he wanted to attend college at Mt. Pleasant with me.

I had money troubles starting college that fall, never enough to pay my bills. The big Pontiac I had bought during the summer cost a lot to run and repair. I talked to the Dean of Veterans Affairs at the college. He gave me the job of barracks master. My duties included keeping the oil stoves filled, cleaning the rest rooms and barracks area. I earned thirty dollars a month, just enough to pay my room expenses.

* * *

The first weekend home, on Saturday night, I went to Byron Lake. A group of kids I knew were having a party. Annie Boyd was there with a boy I knew from high school. He drank too much, and got sick early in the evening. I helped get him in the car. Annie told me she worked in Detroit, and lived with her sister.

"Maybe we could go out together sometime, Annie."

"I'd like to."

Dora took me aside after Annie left. "Annie is too young for you. I'm your type. When are you going to realize it, Nick?"

I took Dora home. On the way, I parked the car in a lane, down a back road. We watched the moon play hide and seek with the clouds. Dora wanted a serious relationship. She became amorous.

"Remember when we were baby-sitting for Hedy, and I wanted you to go all the way?" Dora pressed her warm body tight against mine. She whispered, "Try to control yourself." Dora ground her hips against me. "Do you want to do something, Nick?"

I said in a raspy, husky voice, "Yes."

Suddenly Dora pushed herself away from me and said, "Not until we're engaged."

The heat and passion left me. I stammered, "Give me some time to think about it."

She kissed me goodnight. "Keep thinking about what we could have done tonight. I don't want a very expensive ring. A small diamond will be fine."

The devil was egging me on. Why didn't I tell Dora we will get engaged later. That's all it would take for her to let me release my pent up emotions inside her. That wouldn't be honest and Dora didn't deserve to be lied to. My good conscience prevailed.

The ache in my groin kept me awake most of the night, thinking about Dora. I had known her, and we had gone together on and off, for the past eight years. I liked her a lot, but I wasn't ready for marriage. I needed to finish college, and get a good job.

*   *   *

I took a trip to see how dad was doing. He had good news for me. He had been taking night classes to become a Citizen of the United States, and had received his naturalization papers. He also changed his name to Burke.

"Nick, I no more hoky, I Amarrkan."

I congratulated him. "I have good news, too. I found Jay and Alfred. Jay is living with Hedy, he's the biggest of the family, a combination of Marcus, Watt and me. Alfred is still living with his adopted parents. He looks a lot like me. Next year he will finish high school, then he wants to live with his birth family."

Dad was silent for a long time. "They were just babies when I lost them. Did you tell them about me, their father? Will they come and see me? Nick?"

"Yes, Dad, I told them, but let's wait and see what they want to do."

Driving back to Byron I thought about dad. He had left his native land to live in a country foreign to him. He had been through a lot. It never occurred to me that he had a problem with the name Sabitch, or being a hunky. Now we had another new name in the family. Watt and I were the last ones with the Sabitch name.

*   *   *

I hadn't seen Watt for some time, so I drove to Fenton. He had finished classes in Flint, and wanted to take the entry exam for college. A bunch of veterans were having a big celebration.

"Stay and party with us, Nick."

I declined, it was getting late. On the way home I stopped to see Bessie Cooper. I hadn't seen her for eight years. When she came back from Arizona, she lived with Clark and Ella. They were out for the evening.

Bessie cried a little when I talked about Marcus getting killed in the war. "I'm happy to know you're going to college, Nick."

I told her about finding my two adopted brothers, Jay and Alfred.

She had tears in her eyes, "Yes, I knew about your younger

185

brothers being adopted. I'm glad you are finally getting to see them. What a tragedy your family has gone through."

Bessie, in her late sixties now, told me she and Mr. Otis were getting married. I congratulated her. She gave me a hug and a kiss.

"Happy New Year, Bessie." It was January 1, 1948.

TWENTY SIX

I received a letter from Sonya, asking if I could come to Flint to see her. She needed some help. Her Italian boyfriend had gone back to Wisconsin. He wasn't going to divorce his wife after all. Hedy and her husband weren't getting along and were talking divorce. Sonya had been laid off from her job. A note I had cosigned with her at the bank was due. When I saw Sonya I told her I was barely getting by myself.

Sonya suggested, "Let's ask Joseph, maybe he will help."

I said, "I haven't been able to figure Joseph out. He always says if you need any help let him know. His only help has been verbal advice, or a lecture on how well he is doing. Joseph has never given financial assistance to any of us and he's never around when there is a family crisis. No, he's too far away and wouldn't approve of you borrowing the money in the first place."

I sold my war souvenirs, a M-I carbine, two Japanese rifles and five hundred rounds of ammunition for twenty dollars. I had recently received a three hundred dollar Veterans bonus from the State. I paid up my car bill of a hundred and twenty dollars at the Byron garage and gave some money to Sonya. It would keep her going until she found another job.

*   *   *

Watt drove up to Mt. Pleasant in the spring to visit me, and to take the college entry exam. He was accepted, and enrolled for the fall term.

I was glad classes were soon to be out for the summer. Dave Schmidt had asked me to help him work the farm again during the summer. Buick wasn't hiring summer students for vacation replacements. I could still draw the twenty dollars a week from the GI Bill. I told Dave this would be the last summer I could help him farm.

On a trip to Byron to get supplies, I met Annie Boyd in the grocery store. She was home for the weekend. I asked her to go to a show with me that night.

"I would like to, Nick."

After the show, when I walked Annie to the back door, I bent down to kiss her goodnight. She was a little runt. I had the next day off, so I drove Annie to Detroit, and met her sister. They both worked for the New England Life Insurance Company and rented a small apartment. Her sister, a tall girl with short, dark hair and brown eyes, had recently been widowed. Annie's oldest brother died in a car accident during his senior year in high school. Her mother died two years later, from cancer, when Annie was seven years old. Annie's dad married his second wife several years later.

Leon, Annie's dad, wasn't happy about her going with me. He wanted her to marry a farmer. I had all the farming I wanted at Perrys and Schmidts.

*   *   *

Jock was spending more time with Ginger and less time playing the field. Jock, Annie and I drove to Flint where Ginger was working, to take in a show and then have something to eat. It was late when we went back to Byron. Annie and I were sleeping in the back seat and Jock was driving my car. Suddenly I woke up, the car was heading for the ditch. Jock was slumped over the steering wheel. He had fallen asleep.

I yelled at Jock, "Wake up!"

It was too late, the car went into the ditch. The soft dirt slowed the car down, then it dropped over a culvert and stopped.

The right side, back fender and wheel were smashed up. Luckily no one was hurt, only shaken up.

A car stopped and took us to Byron. For insurance reasons, I decided not to tell anybody Jock was driving. Jock's stepmother was not happy when he told her about the accident.

She was angry with me. "Jock could have been seriously hurt, Nick. You should be more careful when you are driving."

I never did tell her Jock was driving the car. The Insurance Company paid the bill to repair the car.

*   *   *

Late in the summer Watt stopped by, driving a new slant back Buick. "Let's go, Nick, I'm ready to start college." Watt had a problem adjusting to the daily class schedule, but was determined to stick it out and get a degree. I told him each semester became easier.

I was starting my fourth term, Watt his first. I was the pro, Watt was the rookie. Watt moved into the barracks with Jock and me. I was barracks master again this year. Watt helped with the cleaning and filling the oil stoves.

A lot of veterans had dropped out of college. Too much partying, not enough studying. Watt followed my example, he did his homework at the Library.

I was dating a couple of girls at college, but was spending more and more weekends with Annie. Her likes, dislikes and ambitions were very compatible with mine.

The annual Mt. Pleasant College Homecoming was a week away. Annie had never been to Mt. Pleasant and wanted to visit the college. I made arrangements for her to stay in the girls dorm. I was growing very fond of Annie and she of me. Annie arrived by bus on Friday night. She wished she could attend college, but no way, she had to work. Her father thought college was a waste of time.

*   *   *

The Presidential Campaign was in full swing. I registered to vote. Thomas E. Dewey, Governor of New York, a Republican, was the heavy favorite in the polls. The Chicago Tribune prematurely announced Dewey as the winner. Harry S. Truman, Vice President, had taken over the reins when Franklin Roosevelt died, and was not expected to be reelected. A surprised nation awoke the next morning to find that Truman had defeated Dewey.

I, like thousands of ex-service men, voted for our commander in chief, Harry S. Truman. It was the fall of 1948.

*   *   *

The fall term went fast, and classes were soon out for Christmas vacation. I was driving some kids home for the holidays. We were almost to Byron when another car ran a stop sign, and smashed into the back quarter of my car. It was totaled. An ambulance took us to the hospital. We just had minor cuts and bruises.

Jock called his dad to come to the hospital and pick us up. It was late when he dropped me off at Sonya's. The next morning I took her car, and drove to Byron to see Annie, and tell her about the accident.

"Let's take Sonya's car back to her, Nick, and you can stay here at the farm with me for the holidays."

Annie's stepmother seemed pleased that I planned to stay at the farm. It would give her a chance to get to know me. Her dad acted indifferent.

Her stepmother, a tall, thin woman, with braided gray hair, always had a cigarette in her mouth. She kept the house spotless, and liked to cook.

Leon, a short man, had a bald head, with wispy blonde hair around the sides, and blue eyes. He chewed tobacco, and loved to joke around.

Annie's brother lived upstairs with his wife. Three years

older than Annie, he was a big guy, who resembled their older sister. His wife, an attractive blonde, with thick, long hair, kept busy cooking, cleaning and raising their little girl.

Leon was a small time farmer. The barns were old, and in need of repair. The out buildings were faded, and falling down. Two horses, five cows, a couple of pigs, and a few chickens were Leon's livestock. An old John Deere tractor, and a few pieces of broken down farm implements were the only means to make a living.

Annie's stepmother kept house more efficiently than Leon managed the farm. The old house had been remodeled, with an inside bathroom, and a coal furnace in the basement. Leon preferred going outside to the two hole outhouse, rather than use the new water closet inside.

*   *   *

The Insurance Company replaced my car with a white four door Ford. The night Annie left to go back to Detroit, and I to Mt. Pleasant, she said she had something for me to think about until we got together again.

"I like you a lot, Nick, and want to keep going with you, but no more dates with other girls, or we are through. Think about it." She gave me a kiss and left.

I did think about it a lot the next couple of weeks. Annie wanted me all to herself, no nonsense about going with other girls. I liked that. I thought back to my crush on Addie in Fenton, the infatuation for Dora when I first knew her, the thing I had about Cassie in high school. What was it about Annie that was different?

Annie, nineteen years old, was more mature than me, at twenty three. Did I love her? I wasn't sure. Passion and desire I knew, and understood, but love was a word I never heard spoken, or discussed much. I thought more of Annie than any other girl I had dated.

The next time we dated she said, "Well, Nick?"

"Yes, I'm ready for a commitment."

*   *   *

College took on a new meaning. I studied harder, and looked forward to being with Annie. She bused to Byron from Detroit on Friday nights. I picked her up, and we spent the weekends on the farm, talking about the future, marriage and family. Her stepmother teased me a lot about getting married.

"I'm not ready yet, I still have two years before I finish college."

Leon seemed glad. Annie had time to change her mind, maybe get another boyfriend, possibly a farmer.

By taking classes the next two summers, I could finish my degree work in a year and a half, and graduate a year from August. I borrowed some money from Watt, and bought Annie an engagement ring. I could hardly wait to give it to her.

I picked Annie up Friday night in Byron. I decided to wait until the right time to give her the ring. The next morning I showed the ring to Annie's stepmother. She was happy, but didn't think Leon would be.

I took Annie for a drive down a back road. An early spring moon came up, full and bright. Lost in thought, I gazed out the window.

"Nick, I'll bet you're thinking about your brother Marcus."

"Yes, I am." I got out of the car, and told Annie I would be back in a few minutes. I looked up at the moon, and said, "I know you are out there somewhere, Marcus." Then I let out a loud, piercing whistle. In the distance a hound dog howled back. No, it can't be Marcus. He was dead, somewhere in the Philippine Islands.

When I got back in the car, Annie said, "I know how you feel. I've been thinking about my brother, too, younger than Marcus when he died."

"I've got something for you, Annie. I've been thinking a lot lately. I love you very much." I put the ring on her finger. "We don't have to wait until I graduate to get married, let's plan on getting married this August, before my last year in college."

We talked long into the night. The moon, ring, and dreams of the future overpowered reason, and good judgment. Our emotions flamed, her passion more than a match for mine. A warm and tranquil feeling flowed throughout my body. Yes, Annie was the girl I wanted to spend the rest of my life with. In the distance a hound dog bayed at the moon. I looked up at the clear, star studded sky. "Marcus, I have finally found that very special person." I was at peace with the world and myself.

*   *   *

Annie had been busy all summer making wedding plans. She had saved a little money; enough to pay for the minister, church and wedding expenses. The wedding ceremony took place in the Methodist Church, across from the Byron High School. Ginger was maid of honor, and Watt the best man. Leon bought the food and beer for a reception at the farm. Mr. Wilton, or Ringo as he preferred to be called, had a great time partying with the other guests. Maggie, Mrs. Wilton, had to be the center of attention or she didn't have a good time. She was impatient to go home. Maggie sat in the car blowing the horn for Ringo. Finally Leon went to the car and told Maggie to go back in the house with the guests, he would stay in the car and blow the horn for her. She didn't think that was very funny. It was a hot, humid day, August 27, 1949.

TWENTY SEVEN

Our wedding night wasn't awkward for either one of us. Annie was shy, but not backward. We undressed facing each other.

"Are you happy with me, Nick?"

She was small, but well built. Her round breasts pointed straight at me. Her slim waist flared out to smooth, round hips. God, she was beautiful. "Yes, Annie, I couldn't be happier."

Together in the shower, we made love standing up. Later in bed we talked of the future. We were two young people very much in love. The flame in her body was still burning hot. I released the frustrations of my youth into a willing lover and wife. We fell asleep in each others arms. During the night, Annie awakened me with passionate kisses. "Show me again how much you love me."

Annie had waited for the right man to give all her love to. I would find out that love would last a lifetime. Fulfillment, at last. I had no stomach ache or empty feeling. Our honeymoon was a week in a cottage on the shore of Lake Michigan. We swam in the surf, and sunned on the beach, but mostly we made love.

*　　*　　*

Annie and I decided the practical thing to do would be for Annie to keep her job in Detroit and stay with her sister. I would continue living in the barracks and finish college.

We were practical for two weeks. No way could we be married and live apart. Annie quit her job. I found a furnished apartment about ten miles from the college.

As a married student, I received ninety five dollars a month from the GI Bill. Annie hired in at the Chemical Plant as a stenographer. I found a job working part-time at a farm implement and car dealership. We could barely make ends meet.

Annie and I had just nicely got settled in our apartment, when Jock and Ginger stopped by. On the spur of the moment they had gotten married, and were looking for a place to live. A small upstairs apartment, over ours was vacant. Jock and Ginger Comstock moved in the following weekend. Jock would finish college, and Ginger planned on finding a job.

*　　*　　*

One night, Annie and I lay in bed, talking about the future, our hopes and dreams.

"What about your past, Nick? I know so little about you, and nothing about your family. I've never met your father or mother, tell me about them."

I was silent for a long time. "It's only right that you know about my family background." I went on to tell Annie what little I knew about my dad, mother and my brothers and sisters.

"I'd like to meet your father, and some day, your mother. Maybe we can make life a little easier for them."

"Yes, Annie, let's start with dad."

*　　*　　*

We drove to Lansing to visit him. I introduced dad to Annie. He apologized for not speaking good English, then told her that he attended night school, learning to read and write. Dad was proud of me being in college. He didn't get to go to school in the old country. Dad asked me to tell him about the rest of the family. I brought him up to date on what I knew about his children.

"Sonya has a new boyfriend. He looks and acts like a big,

overgrown kid, but Sonya likes him, that's what counts. Hedy divorced her first husband, and has remarried. He is a postman for the City of Flint. Joseph and Pearl are living in Texas. He writes to all of us, telling how great things are with him, and how well he is doing in the Army. His advice is endless.

"Watt's living with Wiltons, and going to college with me. Alfred and Jay have enlisted in the Navy. They want to get away from their adopted parents, and see the world."

Dad thanked me for telling him about the family. "I miss them."

He told Annie, "Maybe you will give me some little hunkies that I can visit and play with. As we left to go home, Dad said, "Thanks for visiting me."

Deep in thought on the drive home, I wondered how Marcus would have fit in the family. He would be twenty eight years old now, probably living out west and working on some big cattle ranch.

I could visualize Marcus as a cowboy, on a big horse with a six gun strapped to his waist, late at night on the open range riding herd on a cattle drive. When the moon came up he would be singing "Blueberry Hill" and "Red River Valley," and howling like a hound dawg. Why did he have to get killed in the war? What a waste of such a fun loving young man.

*   *   *

Annie soon became pregnant. Expecting our first child, I talked to her about changing our name. She didn't care, whatever I wanted to do. What name should we select? All of the rest of the family had different names, except Watt and I; Ziv and Zora Burke, Joseph Mason, Sonya Carson, Hedy Gordon, Jay Lewis and Alfred Dobson. I tossed some names around; Annie's maiden name of Boyd? I had lived with the Coopers, Perrys, Schmidts, and stayed with the Comstocks. I really didn't care, just a good, easy American name, that couldn't be made fun of.

I approached Watt, he wanted to change his name to Wilton for years, but never did. To my surprise he said, "I'll change my name to any name you do. At least two of our family will have the same last name."

When I told Annie, she said, "You decide. Any name will be all right with me."

We petitioned the Court for a name change. I didn't mind being a hunky, or called one. It bothered me being called Skab-bitch, Son-of-a-bitch, Cab-bitch, Little bitch or Big bitch. Our children wouldn't have to go through the name calling I did. Watt was quite happy when I told him the name I had selected. Annie and I legally changed our name to Wilton. It was July, 1950.

*　　*　　*

Annie kept getting bigger every day. We were excited, a baby of our own. We didn't care if it was a boy or girl. We could hardly wait, the baby would be born in late October or early November.

Ginger was also pregnant. She was expecting about the same time as Annie. Jock bragged to me that he was a sleep-walker and had taken care of both girls. I told Jock if he had ever been downstairs with Annie he never would have had the strength to make it back upstairs.

Jock invited Annie and I to see their new TV set. I had heard about them, but never seen one. It had a six inch screen in a two foot by two foot box chassis. You could barely make out Sid Caesar on the black and white screen.

Jock said, "Someday I'll bet they will have a TV with a twelve inch screen and in color, Nick."

*　　*　　*

I had made application for work at the Chemical Plant in Mt. Pleasant, and the Fisher Body Plant in Flint. I received a letter offering me employment at the Fisher Plant. I took the job, working in the payroll office, starting salary of two hundred dollars a month.

We located a small, furnished apartment in Byron, for thirty five dollars a month. We packed up our belongings and moved to Byron.

*   *   *

General Motors was the main employer in Flint, Michigan. The city had grown and prospered with the corporation's expansion. Flint had the largest employment and concentration of GM automobile factories of any city in the United States. Over seventy-five thousand people were employed in the fabricating, body, press, parts, engineering, sub-assembly and assembly plants located throughout the city.

My job at Fisher Body wasn't very exciting or challenging. Part of the day I audited hourly time cards, the rest I spent checking to see if the employees were actually on the job. Fisher Body built and shipped car bodies to the Oldsmobile and Buick assembly plants. The Fisher plant worked according to the assembly plants schedules. The Fisher Body Division had few decisions to make. The automobile final assembly plants had the say in running the body plant. Some day I hoped to work in one of the division assembly plants. I would have more chance for exposure and advancement.

As I wandered about the plant, I thought about Dad. Twenty years ago he worked at Fisher Body, hanging doors on car bodies as they went down the assembly line. We could have been working together here now.

*   *   *

My Degree from Mt. Pleasant College finally arrived. My change of name had delayed issuing the certificate. A letter was enclosed. The outbreak of the Korean War in June had prompted the Navy to recruit recently graduated Navy veterans. The letter inquired if I would be interested in re-enlisting in the Navy as a candidate for Officers Training. It was urgent, please reply promptly.

Annie and I talked it over. A career in the U.S. Navy as a Commissioned Officer was a tempting offer. We were married just over a year, with the responsibility of a baby on the way. I had a new job with a giant, prospering corporation. No, we were not about to be separated. I returned the letter, saying no thanks.

*   *   *

A large house in Byron had been converted into a hospital. A doctor owned and operated it. The baby would be delivered there. Annie, five feet tall, weighed 98 pounds when we were married, now she was almost as wide as high. She looked forward to having the baby, and being a mother.

On a cold, snowy morning in November, her water broke, and the labor pains started. I took her to the hospital, and she delivered a baby boy. I went off to work, leaving Annie's sister with her. Later I received a call at work. Come to the hospital right away.

When I arrived, Annie was in a coma. She had gone into convulsions after I left. The doctor had no idea what caused them. I paced the hospital floor the rest of the night, while Annie lay in bed, still and quiet. She looked beautiful, even in a deep sleep. I hadn't realized until now how much Annie meant to me. I couldn't lose her; she was my whole life.

In a few days Annie pulled through, but couldn't remember anything after entering the hospital. She remained in the hospital several days. When she regained the feeling in her legs, and could walk, she came home, carrying a blue eyed baby boy, we named Adam, who was born November 4, 1950.

TWENTY EIGHT

Our apartment was cramped before the addition of the baby's chest of drawers and bassinet. We slept on a Murphy bed pulled down from a wall closet in the living room. The chairs and end table had to be moved to the edge of the room when we pulled the bed down for the night. We placed the bassinet at the foot of the bed.

Adam had colic and didn't sleep well at night. I was still on second shift and arrived home about two o'clock in the morning. Annie would be up with the baby. I stayed up so she could sleep awhile, then Annie would take over and I went to sleep.

We needed more room, and I wanted to be closer to work. I transferred to days, working eight to five. Annie found an upstairs, unfurnished apartment, about five miles from the Fisher plant.

Jock graduated from Mt. Pleasant College, and took a teaching position in Byron. The Comstocks were looking for a place to live. They stopped by to visit with us. They had a baby the same age as Adam. I told Jock we were moving to a larger apartment, closer to work.

"Great, I'll help you move out, if you help me move in."

"Jock, this apartment is too small for a family of three."

"It will be okay for us for awhile. We are living with Ginger's folks, and anything will be better than that."

*   *   *

Maggie and Ringo Wilton, Watt's adopted parents, stopped by to see baby Adam, and our new apartment.

Maggie said, "This apartment is awfully small, Nick, but I suppose it's all you can afford."

I had the feeling that Maggie wasn't happy when we changed our name to Wilton. Watt changing his was proper, but why did we? I asked Ringo about their son, Bert. I hadn't seen much of him since I left Fenton.

"Bert's married, and going to General Motors Tech studying to become an engineer."

Ringo had made the mistake of seeing a young lady years ago in his travels. Maggie found out, and caught them together in a motel room. She never divorced him, but their marriage died that day. Maggie never let Ringo forget about it, and she verbally abused him all the time. She told Annie all men were alike, they can't be trusted. Her favorite expression was, "A stiff prick has no conscience, and knows no relation."

*   *   *

Annie, Adam and I were getting along great except for one thing, the money always ran out before the month did. Annie went back to work to supplement our income. She wanted a good reliable baby sitter to take care of Adam. A sixty-five year old farm woman lived around the corner from us. She was short and stout, and looked much younger than her age. She would take care of Adam.

Annie was hired at the Red Feather Agency in downtown Flint. She drove our car and left Adam with the baby sitter on the way to work and picked him up on the way home. I rode in a car pool with a group of people who worked at the Fisher Plant.

*   *   *

After Adam took his first steps, he was into everything. He was an active little boy, with big blue eyes and a devilish grin. Soon after he started walking, first one eye then the other turned in. The doctor said it was a stigmatism, nothing could be done about it now. Adam would soon have to wear glasses. If that didn't correct it, eye surgery would.

Adam was examined by several eye specialists. They all said the same thing, glasses now and corrective eye surgery later. Adam started wearing glasses at the age of eighteen months.

*   *   *

My job at Fisher was going well. A superintendent wanted me to work as a foreman in the plant. It would be a promotion, and a big discount on a new automobile every year. Personnel had a new policy, a testing procedure, before any advancements. I took the aptitude test.

"Can you believe it, Annie, I've been picked to be a plant foreman."

"I'm so happy for you, getting a promotion so soon."

That night she questioned me about the test, "Did you do well, Nick?"

"There weren't any right or wrong answers. The test determines what kind of personality you have, your likes and dislikes, and how well you get along with your peers. Whether you pass or fail is a judgment call that the person giving the test makes."

The next day the Personnel Supervisor interviewed me, and talked about everything but the test.

I finally said, "I've got to get back to work, how did I do on the test?"

The Personnel Supervisor said, "I guess you did okay, but I don't think you would make a good foreman."

I asked why.

"It's a decision that I have to make. I'm sorry, maybe you'll get another chance."

I was hurt, disappointed, and disenchanted. How could I tell Annie that I had failed to get the promotion?

She sensed when I arrived home that I didn't have good news. I told her about my interview. "My chances of being somebody in General Motors upper management are gone, Annie. I've got to leave GM and try a new field of work."

"But, why quit your job just because of one persons opinion of your ability?"

"His opinion of that test has been put in my personnel file. No superintendent will ever consider me for a foreman position now. I can stay on my present job, but it's a dead end."

It wasn't an easy decision to make. If I didn't get another job right away, we would be in trouble financially. We didn't have anyone to turn to for help.

A friend of mine who worked in the Personnel Department, later told me that a relative of the Personnel Supervisor got the promotion.

I quit Fisher Body, and took a pay cut to work for a Public Accountant. The office was a block away from Annie's office. We rode back and forth to work together. Working only a block apart, we usually had lunch together. Annie was bookkeeper and secretary to the Executive Director, and supervisor over the other secretaries in the office.

I worked in the office and traveled throughout Flint doing the bookkeeping for one hundred accounts. It entailed doing single and double entry ledgers, payroll, sales, unemployment, social security, income taxes and audits.

My new boss was a large heavyset man, with a bald head and coarse, fat facial features. He was a crude, dirty old man in his sixties. He chain smoked big brown, stinking cigars. I went home every day smelling like I had been barbecued in the city dump.

*   *   *

We were outgrowing the apartment. The outside steps were tiring for Annie and a hazard for Adam. Jock told me about a Minister he knew who had built a small house to retire in. The Minister said we could rent it until he retired. It was a one story house, with two small bedrooms, a living room, kitchen, bathroom and utility room. The rent was fifty dollars a month. A Free Methodist Church park was directly behind the lot. Jock helped us move.

The small house was a big improvement over the upstairs apartment. Adam could go out and indoors easily and had a large yard to play in. The backyard was so big I decided to put in a garden. A neighbor worked the land up with a horse, plow and spring tooth drag. I planted corn, tomatoes, potatoes, cabbage, carrots, onions, radishes and melons. Keeping the garden up was good exercise. I found I hadn't forgotten my farming background.

*   *   *

Dad stopped by for a visit. I hadn't seen him since I took Annie to Lansing, shortly after we were married. The first look at Adam, his grandson, he was a proud grandfather. Dad wanted to know about his children.

"Do you spend much time with your brothers and sisters?"

"Not really, Dad, they are spread all over the country, and are busy raising their own families."

"Tell me what you know about them."

"Okay, Sonya's husband was caught by the police for breaking and entering a jewelry store. Sonya had to sell her house, and used the money to pay lawyers to defend her husband in court. He was convicted, and sent to jail. Sonya is living in a small apartment in Flint.

"Watt's married, and has an apartment in Flint. His wife teaches school. Watt has a year of college left. He stays in Mt. Pleasant during the week and visits his wife on weekends.

"Jay is out of the Navy. He lived with Sonya for a short time, then lived with Hedy for awhile. He got restless, and went to Oregon. He's working as a lumberjack. Alfred's out of the Navy, too. He's working in a coal mine in West Virginia. Joseph is back in the Army, and living in Texas."

I told Dad about changing our name to Wilton, and that Watt was going to soon. He commented that Sabitch was 'old country'. We all have American names now.

He said, "Drop me a line, just a few words, write real plain. I can read and write a little now." His visit was short, but enjoyable.

TWENTY NINE

I had never kept anything from Annie, she knew all the family background, and accepted the facts as they were. She felt it unfortunate the way things happened, but no use to be bitter or grieve about the past.

Annie had been thinking about my family, too. "Nick, it's time we went to see your mother."

I had procrastinated for years about seeing Mother. Why hadn't I gone to see her years ago? The few times that Dad and Joseph had visited Zora, they told me how violent she was, and how she didn't know them. I always felt relieved, but guilty that I hadn't gone to see for myself.

Annie and I took a drive to the State Hospital. On the way I tried to think back to the time when the family lived together. Being only four years old, I had no memories of my mother. She was committed to the Insane Asylum twenty years ago. The closer we got to the hospital, the better I felt about going to see my mother. Annie certainly knew how to do the right thing, even if I didn't.

She had been silent most of the trip. "Nick, just think, seeing your mother for the first time; she must be at least fifty years old."

"Yes, I'm excited. I hope there is something we can do to make life easier for her."

The State Hospital was located outside the city of Detroit. I pulled into the driveway, and stopped the car in front of a high iron gate. A guard, in a gray uniform, came out of the gate house and asked me my name, and who I wanted to see. The guard told me where to go to get a visitor permit. Then he unlocked the gate, and waved us through.

The hospital, a large gray-stone building, with iron bars on all the windows, sat in the center of a big open field, surrounded by a high chain link fence. I slowly drove the car up the driveway. My excitement had subsided, and I felt queasy in my stomach. The hospital looked like a prison.

Annie sensed my uneasiness and said, "I'm sure it's bright and pleasant inside."

I parked the car in front of the hospital. We got out and walked toward the entrance. Suddenly a man, looking out a window on the second floor, let out a loud scream, and started swearing, and made obscene gestures at us. An attendant, in a white uniform, pulled him back from the window.

"Nick, it's okay, let's go inside."

Annie rang the bell. A guard let us in, after asking who we were, and who we wanted to see. We sat on a couch in the hallway. A sign on the wall stated, "Visitors must be accompanied by an attendant at all times. Ring bell for attendant."

Some people, down the hall, could be heard laughing and talking. Suddenly a female patient ran out of the room, yelling, crying and screaming. Two male attendants ran after her, and quickly bundled her in a straight jacket. They dragged her to a small room at the end of the hall.

I was feeling ill. "I can't do it. I don't want to see my mother violent, or tied up like an animal. Let's get out of here. I'm sorry, Annie, but I just can't bear to see her that way."

On the ride back home, Annie cried, and I had tears in my eyes. We were both thinking of poor Zora living like a caged animal.

I had a weird dream that night. The family was all back together again, except Dad. Mother staggered around in a straight jacket, yelling obscenities.

Then Marcus said, "Annie made a man out of you, Nick. I won't need to take your turn anymore."

Marcus' head stuck out of the water, howling at the moon. I tried to whistle back. I woke up in a sweat.

"Are you all right, Nick? You were making some awful funny noises."

"I had a bad dream. Go back to sleep, Annie."

*   *   *

Adam had a difficult time keeping his glasses on even though they were strapped to a band around his head. He sometimes took them off and forgot where he put them. Annie and I spent a lot of time looking for Adam's glasses.

Doctors in Flint and Detroit recommended eye surgery. Operate on one eye now and the other in a couple of years. Annie and I settled on an eye surgeon specialist in Flint. The doctor explained the operation. A small incision would be made on the side of the eye. The eye muscle would be tightened, straightening the eye. The doctor made arrangements for the surgery and hospital room.

Adam was too young to explain to him what the operation was about. He was a brave little guy. When he left for the surgery, Annie told him when he woke up she would be with him. I was not a very religious person, but I said a prayer for Adam during the operation, something from my Masonic Bible. "In the beginning God created the heavens and earth, there was darkness upon the land. God said, let there be light and there was light." It seemed appropriate for Adam's situation.

Adam came through the operation fine, but what a bruised bloody eye he had. He would have to wear a patch over it until it healed. I had no medical benefits, but Annie did. It was an expensive operation. Annie's insurance paid most of the cost. The eye operated on did straighten up, but Adam still had to wear glasses. He was just three years old.

Adam was growing fast and a handful for the baby sitter. Annie enrolled him in a nursery school to prepare him for kindergarten.

*   *   *

Annie and I wanted another child, a playmate for Adam. We thought two should be just as easy to raise as one. It wasn't that simple. Annie didn't get pregnant. She thought perhaps the complications after Adam's birth had something to do with it, and visited a doctor. He put her on the pill, a new type of birth control, but also a method to regulate her periods.

The doctor said, "Annie, you're young, you have lots of time to have another baby."

That night she told me about her visit to the doctor, and about the new birth control pill.

"But, don't you want to get pregnant?"

"Yes, Nick, the pill will regulate my periods, and maybe help me to conceive. Just think, your parents had eight children in twelve years. Your mother had to be pregnant most of the time the family was together. They must have had an active sex life. Living in the one room basement house, the kids never out of sight, how and when?"

* * *

On the weekend we drove out to Byron to visit with Annie's family. Her dad, Leon, was always glad to see Annie and play with Adam. He treated me well, but I still had the feeling that I wasn't the son-in-law he wanted.

* * *

Maggie Wilton asked us to visit them, and help celebrate Bert graduating from General Motors Tech. He had a job at the Proving Grounds, working as an engineer. Bert, a heavy drinker, talker, and party person, took after his mother. His favorite word was "fuck." He used it frequently.

After Maggie had a few drinks, she reminded Annie of Ringo's fling with the "chippie," using a few choice words.

"The old bastard should have known better, I'll never let the son-of-a-bitch forget it."

Bert's wife was a quiet, shy person. It always took a few drinks to loosen her up. Ringo confided in me, "Someday Watt is going to share equally in my estate with Bert."

Soon the gathering turned hostile. Maggie berated Ringo, and Bert got vulgar. Annie drank a couple of gin martinis. She told me we had better go home, and check on Adam. At home, the baby-sitter gone, and Adam tucked safely in bed, her passion flamed long and bright. After, we lay together in bed, savoring the loving.

*   *   *

Working as an accountant was challenging, but not rewarding. In order to become a CPA, I would have to work as an apprentice for three years at low pay, and then pass the state exam.

Bill Brown, the owner and Manager of Brown Finance and Loan Company, had an office nearby. His son left to open his own office. Bill offered me a job, with a pay increase, and year end bonus. I moved across the hall to work for the Brown Finance Company.

Bill, a staunch Republican, told me the only good Democrat was a dead one. I decided that I couldn't be a Democrat or a Republican. I had to vote for who I thought best for the job. In the last Presidential Election, I voted for Harry Truman, a Democrat. In this election I voted for Dwight Eisenhower, a Republican. I never told Bill who I voted for. Politics was a personal preference, and not worth getting into an argument over. It was the fall of 1953.

*   *   *

Bill Brown lived east of Flint, near a new subdivision. He

told me I should move there, then I could ride to work with him in the company car. The end of the year I received a bonus of seven hundred dollars. Bill advanced me seven hundred dollars on next year's bonus. The fourteen hundred dollars made the down payment on a house. The local contractor built us a three bedroom house for thirteen thousand dollars. The payments were eighty-five dollars a month, including escrow, insurance and taxes.

Jock and Ginger helped us move in. Jock still taught school in Byron. They were renting a small house in the country, and hoped to build one soon.

The new subdivision consisted of mostly young adults, just starting careers, and families. Bill picked me up in the morning, and brought me home after work.

Annie managed to work part-time in the summer at the Agency in Flint. She kept the payroll and books up, by sometimes going to the office, or doing the work at home, in order to be with Adam most of the summer. When school started she worked full-time. Annie felt strongly that her obligation was to me and Adam, supplementing our income should not interfere with being a wife and mother.

Things were going real well at work. Between Annie's and my checks we made expenses and sometimes had a little left over at the end of the month. I fixed up the basement into a recreation room. I put tile on the floor, a false ceiling overhead and a bar in the corner. We bought a pool table and an old player piano. After the recreation room was completed, we invited the whole neighborhood over for a party. Loud singing and the noisy piano music continued into the wee hours of the morning.

*   *   *

Adam would be starting kindergarten after Labor Day. The doctor made arrangements for Adam's second eye surgery. He

wanted it done before Adam was five years old and in school.
Adam, Annie and I knew what to expect and were more prepared. Adam was a real trooper and came through the operation without any complications. His eye had healed by the time
school started. He still had to wear glasses.

*   *   *

Bill Brown was a deacon in the Baptist Church. A member passed away and left half a million dollars to the Church.
She was impressed with the Minister and wanted the money
invested and used to serve the Church, under his direction.
The Minister was a well liked man in the community. He practiced what he preached and was a good Christian. His radiant
personality was contagious.

I was asked to set up the books and administer the funds. I
agreed. It would be a new experience for me and I could work
evenings. Most of the money was in the form of unsecured 3%
notes, loaned to local residents and business people. I suggested to the deacons that as the notes came due, the money be
reinvested in Land Contracts and secured notes at the market
rate. They wanted the notes called immediately and reissued at
6%. The Minister agreed with me, but was overruled by the
deacons. The townspeople were put out by the deacons decision to call and reissue the notes. They had no choice, as they
were all on demand.

I continued to do the bookkeeping for the Trust. The Minister suffered a severe stroke and was completely incapaci-
tated. He was a man in his middle forties, with a wife and two
children to support. I suggested to the deacons that a portion of
the earnings from the Trust be used as a pension for the Minister. The deacons said no, the Trust must be run as a business,
not as a charitable organization. The Minister's wife would have
to find work and support the family.

I was disenchanted with the deacons and the Church. The

check I received for setting up the Trust and books was for five hundred dollars. It was a lot of money, but Annie agreed with me that the Minister needed the money a lot more than we did. I signed the check over to the Minister's family and quit the Trust and the Church.

*   *   *

One night, after a sound loving, I fell asleep warm and tranquil. Suddenly Marcus rode by on Webb's stud horse, Hugo, his head held high, baying at the moon. I tried to yell at Marcus to stop. I wanted to talk to him, but the words wouldn't come out of my mouth. I awoke with a start. Annie was poking me in the ribs. "What were you dreaming about, Nick?"

"I had a weird dream. Marcus was in it, but it didn't make any sense. Go back to sleep. I love you."

THIRTY

Annie wrote dad a short letter, asking him to come for a visit. A week later his answer arrived. "I am fine, see you soon."

It was his first letter to us. The following week dad stopped by. He liked to visit with us, but mostly he enjoyed seeing, and playing with his grandson, Adam. Dad had good news, he had bought a small house with an unfinished upstairs. His job at the Drop Forge was going well.

"Tell me about my children."

"Dad, most of your children are married and have children of their own. We rarely see each other. Annie keeps in touch with them with letters and telephone conversations. Watt graduated from Mt. Pleasant College, and is working in a bookkeeping office in Flint. He and his wife are house hunting. Alfred is married to a girl from the deep south. They have a baby boy, and are buying a house near Fenton. He is still working for the railroad.

"Sonya divorced her husband who was in jail, and she married another man. They now live on her father-in-law's farm in northern Michigan. Joseph and his wife have two sons and a daughter. He has been stationed all over the country; California, Arkansas, Alaska, and is now back in Texas. He is always on the move, but never near his family.

"Jay is back from lumber-jacking in the northwest. He drifts about, doesn't go to see his adopted parents, and very seldom visits his brothers and sisters. Hedy has another husband, with a drinking problem. She quit her job, and has her hands full with three boys and a baby girl."

Dad thanked me for keeping him informed about his children.

He said, "All those grandchildren, Nick, and I only get to see Adam. I've given up any hope of my children ever having anything to do with me. You are my only son. Let's keep in touch."

*   *   *

Bill Brown's grandson graduated from college, and was taken into the business. My working relations with Bill took a turn for the worse.

"Nick, I want you to teach my grandson all you know about this business."

"Sure, but there is hardly enough work for the two of us, let alone three people."

"Yeah, well we'll talk about that later."

I knew right then my future with Brown Finance was uncertain at best. When I told Annie about me helping Bill's grandson learn the business, and his comments to me about the future, she said, "If you are not going to be happy at work, you might just as well quit, and look for work somewhere else. We can make out until you find another job."

I gave Bill two weeks notice.

December in Michigan is no time to be looking for work. Too cold and snowy for construction work and General Motors automobile factories generally laid workers off. I made application to the State of Michigan for a job as a geologist. Geology was my first choice for work when I graduated from college. Michigan was having a financial crisis at that time and was now. I was told my application was on file.

*   *   *

Everyone in our subdivision knew I had left Browns, who were old time wealthy residents, not well liked by the newcomers. The guys at the monthly poker party felt bad that I was out of work, but glad that I no longer worked for Brown Finance Company.

A local residential builder and developer was looking for a superintendent to help run his business. He asked me to work for him. I could be his accountant, manage the office and in the spring be superintendent to the building trades. Annie thought it would be good experience for me and the job would keep us going until something better opened up. I accepted and started work the following month.

Construction and residential home building had been booming since the war, but recently the Michigan economy was in a downswing. The General Motors plants were laying off employees and homes were not selling. I found out quickly that the developer's business was shaky at best. Income came from land contracts, various accounts receivable and construction draws from three banks in Flint. Every week I had to do a juggling act to collect enough money to pay bills and meet the weekly payroll.

The construction job kept Annie and me going, but wasn't anything I could make a career of. As most small companies are family concerns, this one was no different. The developer hired his relatives to keep peace in the family.

* * *

Annie became pregnant soon after she had taken a job working for an Insurance Company in Flint. We were happy, as was Adam. He would no longer be an only child.

* * *

Hedy called and told me that her husband had quit his job. He drew out his retirement money and was on a drunken binge. She asked me to take thirty five hundred dollars of his retirement money and hold it for her until he sobered up and dried out.

"Nick, don't give him money under any circumstances."

Two weeks later Hedy called me and said, "Give me back fifteen hundred dollars, Nick."

Her husband took the money and pissed it down the drain in another three day drunk. A month later Hedy called me and said she needed the rest of the money. She gave it to her husband and he got drunk and blew that money too.

Hedy and her husband separated. He went into bankruptcy. Things were tough for her. She had no income and four children to take care of.

We were having a rough time financially, but we still helped Hedy. We gave her some money. I told her it might be best after the first of the year that she keep the two youngest children living with her, one of the boys to stay with Sonya and one boy to live with us. Hedy agreed to try it for a little while.

Hedy's second child, had dark brown hair, a baby face, small features and large droopy blue eyes. He adjusted quickly to living with us. We made the den into a bedroom for him. An all "A" student, he got along fine in school and was a big brother to his cousin Adam.

I received a letter from the bankruptcy court. I had to appear and testify because I had banked Hedy's husband's pension money. All moneys earned and spent prior to bankruptcy proceedings had to be accounted for to the court. The bank had record of the pension money via my savings account passbook. When I drew the money out, I gave cash to Hedy. The court hinted that I had tried to conceal the money from creditors and should pay the sum of the pension fund to the court. I was shocked and hurt. I had quite a time convincing the judge that all the pension money was given back to Hedy and I had in fact helped Hedy's family out with my own money and was currently supporting one of the children.

Hedy got a divorce, and desperately needed help. She called me and said, "I've talked to Dad, and he agreed to let me and my children live with him until I can get back on my feet."

She didn't want her children to go through a family separation like she had.

*   *   *

The Flint General Motors factories were expanded into many manufacturing and assembly plants. A large Corporation, getting bigger, with many factories throughout the United States.

Our neighbor behind us was manager of one of the Flint manufacturing plants, a GM Components Division. He asked me if I was interested in working at the AC plant.

I said, "Let me think about it."

Annie and I talked it over. "Do what you think is best, Nick. We'll make out whatever you decide to do."

AC was hiring and I obtained an application for salary employment. I told the developer I would be leaving the first of the year. His construction business was barely surviving. I was thirty-three years old. It was time to settle down to a job I could make a career of.

The salary personnel manager at AC interviewed me and arranged to have three department heads talk to me about job opportunities. The first interview was with the department head of purchasing. I sat outside his office for half an hour while he picked his nose and made personal phone calls.

The interview was short. "I don't think I can use you, Nick."

I was hot. I told the personnel manager that if the other men to interview me were like the purchasing director to forget it, I didn't want any part of AC. The personnel manager told me not to be hasty, to check the other two interviews out.

The second interview was with the superintendent of government contract manufacturing. He needed a budget supervisor. I wasn't interested, I wanted manufacturing supervision.

The third interview was with the manufacturing manager. He took me out to dinner and said, "You are just the guy I'm looking for, Nick. Would you be willing to start as a management trainee?"

I thought back to my earlier employment at Fisher Body Division, the time a supervisor in personnel department turned me down for a management position. Now the manufacturing manager of AC, a GM components plant saying, "You are just the man I am looking for."

I was told my starting salary would be five hundred dollars a month. After a year of training I would be assigned to supervise manufacturing activities. Exactly the job I was looking for. I accepted.

The future looked pretty bright. Annie knew I would be a good foreman. The salary and benefits at General Motors had greatly improved since I left Fisher Body.

I knew a woman in the neighborhood who worked in the office at AC. I could ride to work with her while I was in the training program. Annie could drive our car to work.

*   *   *

My job experiences at the CPA's, Brown Finance and the construction company helped a lot. I had good relations with all the people associated with the training program. I was interested and eager to learn and do a good job.

One of my bosses, an assistant superintendent, liked my work so well he took me out of the training program after six months and promoted me to a manufacturing foreman. Things at work were really going my way.

Then I had my first exposure to shop, and national politics. The superintendent called a meeting of all supervisors. The Presidential Campaign was under way, and the party needed campaign funds.

Laughingly the superintendent said, "I don't care who you guys vote for, as long as it's a Republican. You all know they side with business, and GM is as big as it gets."

I told Annie about the meeting. "If I'm going to be a loyal company man, I guess I better vote like one."

"You do what you think is right, but when you're in that voting booth no one ever knows which lever you pull." Annie was a free thinker.

There must have been a lot of free thinkers in the country, because a Democrat, John F. Kennedy, in spite of the prejudice against his Catholic religion, was elected President, over Republican, Richard Nixon.

*   *   *

Watt was looking for a different job. Ringo wouldn't help him get a job at General Motors. He told Watt, "If I help you get in the business, you will never get any credit for anything you do yourself."

I had become good friends with the guys in personnel. They played poker at my house. I arranged for Watt to be interviewed by the AC salary personnel manager.

Watt called to thank me, and tell me he had been hired, and assigned to work in the Accounting Department. Before he hung up he said, "Did you know Bessie Cooper Otis passed away?"

I hadn't seen Bessie since her marriage to Mr. Otis. I attended the funeral to pay my last respects. As I gazed at Bessie lying in the casket, my eyes grew moist, when I thought back to the good times Marcus, Watt and I had living with her during the Depression years.

I visited with Clark and Ella. They were still living in Bessie's house on East Street. They had two children, a daughter in high school, and a son in college. Clark worked in the Fisher Body Factory in Flint. During our conversation, he told me that the hired man, suspected of murdering the Davis' over twenty five years ago, had never been found.

That night I lay awake thinking about the time Watt and I ran into Juno in the barn, across from Davis' farm.

Finally I fell into a deep sleep. I couldn't breath, and was sinking into a pile of oats. Juno stood over me laughing, his face turned sideways, his right eye staring at me. I tried to yell for help, but my mouth was stuffed full of oats. I awoke as Annie gently shook me. "Are you all right? It sounded like you were calling for help."

"I had a bad dream."

* * *

One day after work I came home and Adam and Annie were crying. Pal, the family dog, had died suddenly. It was a real loss. Pal was a member of the family.

I took Pal to be buried in a field next to the subdivision. Adam dug a shallow grave and I gently laid Pal to rest. Adam cried as he covered Pal with dirt.

"Say a prayer for him, Dad, maybe it will get him into dog heaven."

Tears clouded my eyes as I slowly recited the Lords Prayer. "Let's go home Adam, there's nothing more we can do for Pal. He'll rest in peace here."

* * *

Annie's doctor had an office outside of Flint, on Fenton Road. Dr. Maltor, a young man just out of the Army, was smart and confident. His boyish grin, and easy smile, masked his professional medical ability. Annie felt comfortable with Dr. Maltor, and his office was close by.

Finally Annie had labor pains. At the hospital, the doctor examined her, and said she was having false labor pains, but should stay in the hospital. I went home to stay by the phone until Annie went into labor. Later I received the call, but our daughter, Sarah, was born before I arrived at the hospital.

It was Thanksgiving day, November 24, 1960.

THIRTY ONE

Annie enjoyed being home with Sarah and Adam. She had kept house, juggled working hours when Adam was a baby and for ten years to supplement our income. Now she just wanted to be a mother and stay home with the kids. She had the time to nurse Sarah and fuss over her. Annie was mother and father to the children.

What little free time I had I spent with Annie and the kids. I wasn't into shop politics. I preferred a private family life.

*   *   *

Being a new foreman, I had to work the graveyard shift, twelve midnight until eight in the morning. I didn't see much of my family. I could drive the car, but Annie would be without transportation. The past ten years we had managed to work different hours with only one car. Sharing the ride wasn't practical anymore. I bought a used Jeep station wagon to drive to work and use for hunting.

I replaced a young foreman who was the only college graduate out of the work force of three hundred and fifty manufacturing foremen. He didn't make it, the other foremen wouldn't cooperate or help him in any way. He was an easygoing, likable person. Too easy according to his bosses. Now I was the only foreman in manufacturing with a college degree.

Most of the other foremen I worked with had been promoted from the hourly work force. They said within thirty days I would be glad to get out of manufacturing, and work in the front office somewhere.

The United Automobile Workers Union had come a long way since the thirties. It was a powerful force throughout the General Motors plants. The union contract controlled all aspects of the hourly work force; shift preference, job changes and promotions. Full-time union representatives roamed throughout the plant to see that the contract was followed to the letter. I had a lot to learn, in a short time, in order to survive as a foreman.

The General Manager and Vice President of AC Components worked up from the manufacturing floor. He knew the ropes. He was the most progressive plant manager in the General Motors Corporation. He knew that in a division as large as the AC plant, with 15,000 employees, competitiveness was important and it was necessary to recognize and promote employees who excelled in their working environment.

*   *   *

Manufacturing was the backbone of the AC organization. The General Manager instituted a Management Improvement Proposal Program. Any ideas that improved productivity, and saved AC money, initiated by a foreman, and completed, were awarded points. The foreman with the most MIP points would be given recognition by the General Manager at the annual salary party.

I was foreman of the new die cast department, supervising men casting zinc, aluminum and magnesium into automobile parts. I implemented a lot of new ideas and improvements, often staying at the end of the shift to write up and report to personnel the progress of my MIP's.

At the end of the first year, I had earned the most points of all the foremen in the plant. After I was given recognition at the AC annual party, my superintendent called me into his office. He talked to me about the production, and union problems in the department.

"I've got good news for you, Nick. You are being promoted to a general foreman. You have done a good job, but I want you to know, I had other foremen who have worked for me a lot longer that you have, that I wanted to promote. My boss made your promotion, not me. You have a lot of obstacles to overcome in your new position."

I couldn't have been happier; a promotion after only three years at AC. I told my superintendent in due time I would be his number one top rated general foreman. I was anxious to get home, and tell Annie the good news. She wasn't too surprised.

"You worked awfully hard on the Management Program. I knew, in a matter of time, you would receive recognition for it. I'm so happy for you."

*   *   *

Alfred called shortly after my promotion. He had read about it in the Flint Journal. He congratulated me, then asked for a favor.

"Nick, can you get me a job at AC? The railroad business has slowed down, and I'm getting laid off."

"I'll see what I can do, Alfred, but you have to understand the automobile business goes up and down with the economy, and if I do get you a job at AC, when business slows down you could get laid off."

"Sure, I understand, but I'll take that chance."

We talked a little about our family, then I told Alfred to go to the personnel office Monday, and I would have an interview arranged for him. I hadn't seen much of Alfred and his family, but we kept in touch. He was hired the next week for a job on Plant Protection.

Watt came to my office after he heard that Alfred had been hired to work at AC. He wasn't very happy.

"Nick, what's going on around here. My boss told me I

was being transferred to the new plant AC is starting up in Milwaukee. If I don't go, I'll get laid off."

"Yeah, I heard about it. You don't have much choice, do you?"

"I'm glad to hear Alfred is getting a job here, but it doesn't make sense to me that AC is laying people off, and hiring at the same time."

Watt sold his house, and moved his family to Milwaukee. His wife obtained a teaching position there.

*   *   *

Dad's sixty-fifth birthday was in February. We drove over to congratulate him, and give him a present. He had retired from the Drop Forge plant, and bought a motorcycle. "I always wanted one, but couldn't afford it until now. I'm calling it my 'white pony.'"

Dad's solitary existence, and his age were showing. He had gained a lot of weight, and his once bright blue eyes were dull. Still a heavy smoker, he had trouble breathing. His grandchildren delighted him. Sarah reminded him of Hedy as a little girl. He said Adam would carry on the Serbian bloodline.

Dad didn't have much to say about the short time Hedy and her children lived with him. His only comment, "My house is too small for six people, and I couldn't afford to keep them."

He wasn't sure about retirement. "I have too much time on my hands and nothing to do, Nick."

*   *   *

Annie's father Leon's second wife became ill and died. She had been a good stepmother to Annie. Leon missed her a lot. A warm, loving person, he didn't like to be alone. His son, and his family occupied the big farmhouse. Leon lived alone, down the road, in a small house. But not for long; he started courting a woman he had known for many years, and was seventy years old when they were married. Her husband had died years ago, and left her to raise a family of three. They were grown up now, and on their own.

*   *   *

Roy Henry stopped by my office to see me. A tall Negro, in his middle thirties, Roy was the night janitor in charge of cleaning the rest rooms and offices. He had a soft smile, and a pleasant personality.

He was uneasy as he said, "Mr. Wilton, I'd like you to help me. You have a reputation on the floor for being tough and firm, but fair. A job setter position is opening up in your department. According to the union contract, I should get that job. I have the most seniority, and I can do the work. If you're as fair as I hear you are, you will promote me to that position."

"I'll see what I can do, Roy." I checked the promotion list, and Roy was next in line. I looked over the union contract. It stated, promotions would be made on the basis of merit, ability and seniority, in that order. I decided to give the promotion to Roy. I wasn't going to ask my boss, but I informed him of my intention. He wasn't too happy.

"Nick, you're promoting a Negro to a job setters classification."

"Yes, he has the most seniority, and is best qualified for the job."

My boss thought a minute, then said, "You can disqualify him by saying he doesn't have the ability to do the job. Then you won't be violating the union contract."

I knew I was sticking my neck out. There were no Negroes at the plant with the job setter classification. They had jobs as janitors, or stock handlers.

An unhappy union representative came to see me the next day. "Nick, you can't promote that Negro."

"Why not?" I looked him straight in the eye. "He's next in line for the job, and the most qualified."

The union rep left in a huff, muttering to himself.

THIRTY TWO

Watt received a letter from the Probate Court. He called me in a panic.

"Nick, Zora has been transferred from the State Asylum to Winchester Hospital on the outskirts of Flint. The letter states she has organic brain changes, high blood pressure, arteriosclerosis, hypertension heart disease and diabetes. Under institutional care she is doing extremely well, but must have a court appointed guardian."

Watt didn't want any part of being mother's guardian. His loyalties belonged to Wiltons.

Annie and I talked it over. No question about it, if we could help in any way, we certainly would. I called Winchester to make arrangements to see mother. On the way to the hospital, many thoughts went through my mind. The guilt feelings I had over the years resurfaced. I remembered the time I backed out when I arrived at the hospital to see her. The letter stated she was doing extremely well. What did she look like? Would she know me? Could she leave the hospital? Mother had been institutionalized for thirty three years.

*   *   *

Winchester Hospital, a large red brick building, with flower gardens, fruit trees, and a huge green lawn surrounding it, was located in the country. A pretty sight compared to the dismal gray stone State Asylum.

In the visiting area, a nurse pointed to a little lady sitting in a rocking chair. "That's Zora over there."

She had snow white hair, and bright blue eyes. She gestured, and talked to the people walking by.

I said, "Mother?"

She stared back at me, smiled, and said, "Brother."

Mother couldn't comprehend that I was her son. She talked in English, then lapsed into several foreign languages. Annie and I stayed for a long time, then we left with tears in our eyes. Mother wasn't violent, she seemed happy, but did not remember me as her son.

I felt remorse that I hadn't visited her in the past. She certainly wasn't the violent person that Dad always told me about. Could I have helped? She was sixty six years old now. Annie suggested that maybe her aging process, and new medication helped to calm her down.

"Nick, your Dad had no reason to mislead you about your mother's condition."

Annie and I continued to visit mother on weekends. We soon realized that she would never know me as her son. Most of the time she was bright, cheerful, laughing and joking a lot. We started calling her Zora; it seemed more appropriate. Mother called me 'boyfriend', Annie 'girlfriend', Adam 'boy', and Sarah 'baby'.

Our conversations with Zora were limited to a few words in English, then she would ramble on in different languages. She swore fluently; "Got damn goot, heem son-of-beech, shet, you goot louking bastard," were some of her favorite expressions. It seemed strange to hear such language coming from a petite, elderly lady with white hair. We were amazed, that in spite of all her illnesses and diseases, she was quite spry, and active.

We decided to take Zora for a ride in the country, and then a short stop at our home.

The head nurse at Winchester said, "Okay, but I'm going to give her some medicine to make sure she stays quiet. Zora hasn't been away from the confines of a hospital for so long, I'm not sure how she will act."

Zora sat in the back seat of the car, looked out the window mumbling, gesturing and smiling. She was enjoying the ride. I looked back at her, and asked if she wanted to see our house. Zora just smiled, and nodded her head.

As we drove in the driveway, Zora said, "Me live in hoose with you?"

I looked at Annie with a sad expression, and replied, "No, Zora stay for a little while."

"Hokay."

I commented to Annie as we drove Zora back to Winchester, "Most of the English she knows is swear words."

"Nick, I suppose Zora's heard them used many times over the years in the Asylum."

*   *   *

I told my brothers and sisters about seeing, and visiting with our mother, that she was non violent, and doing well. When I told Dad about seeing Zora, he seemed pleased that I wanted to help her.

"Zora is your mother, and always will be, Nick. She stopped being my wife when she was admitted to the hospital."

Dad had no intention of seeing her again. Annie and I asked him about their early married life.

He told us Zora was a happy person, liked to dance a lot, and buy things. She couldn't hold onto money, and spent all he made. They were married in Ambler, Pennsylvania, and had a three day wedding. Later I called the Montgomery County Courthouse, and requested a copy of Zora and Ziv's marriage certificate. The clerk said it would take awhile to locate, based on the sketchy information I gave him.

Sometime later, I received a copy of the marriage certificate. Zora and Ziv were married October 30, 1916. I had a difficult time making out the names on the certificate. The signatures were scribbled so badly, they were meaningless marks. Evidently when Ziv spoke his last name, it sounded like "Sabitch." Ziv and Zora couldn't read, so they didn't realize their name was incorrect.

*   *   *

I contacted the Probate Court concerning Letters of Guardianship for Zora. I finally got a date to appear.

Judge Mackey looked us over, and said, "I have known about the Sabitch family for over thirty years. Nick, you are the only goat in the family to come forward to be a guardian for your mother."

I was taken back by his abrupt manner. "She's my mother, Judge, what else can I say? How come Watt received a letter from the Probate Court, and the rest of the family didn't?"

"He was the easiest member of your family to locate."

I asked if I could see mother's medical papers. The Judge said, "No, but I've read them over, and I'll tell you what's in them, Nick. It won't change anything now, but you've got a right to know what's in her records.

"Zora, your mother, suffered a nervous breakdown after having her eight children. She was sent to St. Mary's Hospital. Zora couldn't speak English well enough to communicate with the doctors. They obtained an interpreter for her, but it didn't help. Your mother can speak many different foreign languages, and she would lapse from one language to another. Nobody could understand her. Ziv, your father, wasn't any help. He couldn't speak English, or understand the foreign languages your mother knew.

"Zora became very violent in the hospital. She wanted to be home with her family. Because of her radical behavior, ranting and raving in many languages, the doctors assumed she

TED WILSON

was insane, and committed her to the State Institution. They kept her restrained, and heavily medicated.

"Nick, it's easy for me to second guess what happened years ago. I'm sure the doctors did the best they could under the circumstances. It's sad, being institutionalized for thirty three years. Your mother is not violent anymore, but must be medicated and supervised at all times."

I cried out, "But Judge, Annie and I have been able to communicate with her."

"Yes, over the years she learned enough English, mostly swear words, to communicate with the doctors and nurses when she wanted to."

*   *   *

The Judge went on, "Before you decide to take this guardianship, there is something you should know. The State can, and might try to get you to make restitution for your mother's care the past thirty-three years. In the eyes of the court you are the only member of your family who is liable. The rest of your family are exempt; your sisters by marriage, Joseph by his service status, your brothers, by adoption, and your father is retired, and living on a small pension.

"You are the goat of the family. I'll tell you this, as long as I chair this court, the State will not collect from you. I can't promise anything when I'm gone. Do you still want to be appointed guardian of your mother, Nick?"

I asked Annie what she thought. "Nick, we are morally obligated. If the state tries to collect, we'll cross that bridge when we get to it." The Judge appointed me Zora's guardian.

*   *   *

On the drive home, I was all choked up, and Annie cried

softly. Finally she said, "What a terrible injustice, for Zora, that could have been prevented."

Annie turned the radio on to listen to her favorite country music station, to soothe her troubled mind. Suddenly a special news bulletin interrupted the program. President Kennedy had been shot and killed, while on a trip to Texas. What a tragedy!

It was November 22, 1963.

THIRTY THREE

Dr. Maltor had an office outside of Flint on Fenton Road. After finding out all of the health problems Zora had, Annie and I were concerned that I might have inherited some of them. Dr. Maltor gave me a complete medical checkup. I tested positive for diabetes. The doctor put me on a low sugar diet and daily use of Orinase.

He said, "Nick, it's nothing serious yet, but someday it could be."

*   *   *

Dad came to visit his grandchildren. He asked about Zora. I told him that I purchased a cemetery lot, and someday both he and Zora would be together there.

"I know you will take care of us. Adam, Sarah, Annie and you have been the only happiness I've known for a long time. The rest of my family won't have anything to do with me."

We had a picnic in the backyard. Dad gave me an envelope before he left, and told me to put it away.

"Nick, if something should happen to me, open it." Then he left, saying, "Visit me soon."

Annie was curious about the contents of the large, plain white envelope, sealed, with just 'Nick' roughly printed on the front. "What do you suppose is in the envelope, Nick?"

"I don't have any idea, Annie. Maybe it's something from his past that he doesn't want me to know until he is dead. I'll put it in the lock box and someday we'll know what's in it."

I got to thinking about dad's retirement. He had a small

pension from the Drop Forge plant and was receiving Social Security. Zora was legally his wife, and should be entitled to a spouse's portion. I contacted the Social Security office. They said she was entitled, but I had to bring in proof that she was his wife. Dad had nothing, but I had a copy of their marriage certificate. It was proof enough that Zora was his wife. I used the monthly check to help pay Zora's care at Winchester.

*   *   *

School was out for the summer. I had promised Adam to go camping with his Boy Scout Troop, at a camp near Lake Michigan. We packed our sleeping bags and tent in the car, and headed north for a week of vacation. We slept in tents, and cooked our meals outdoors. Adam competed in Scout activities during the day.

A thunderstorm came up during the night. I lay awake, snug in the tent and warm sleeping bag, thinking of Annie. This was the first time since our marriage that we were separated longer than overnight.

Suddenly above the thunder and lightning, I heard Zora saying, "I no krazy wollmen, me kan saay Nick seben diffren wayys! Whyy no un lissen to me?" Then I saw Marcus looking up to the sky, the rain pouring down on him, giving his hound dog howl.

Adam was shaking me, "Wake up Dad. Listen, I hear coyotes howling in the woods."

Annie did miss me. The first night back, she tucked Sarah and Adam in bed early. She was ready for make up time. Her kisses were passionate. Later as I was falling asleep, Annie kissed me goodnight, and whispered, "We're still behind."

*   *   *

Annie received a card from Dad. He couldn't make it for

her birthday. He had fallen off his 'white pony', and bruised his shoulder. A month later, on a Saturday, two days before dad's seventieth birthday, we drove over to see him. He didn't answer the door when I knocked. I opened the door to go in, Adam following behind me. It was deathly quiet, and a rank, pungent odor filled the air, choking me. "Adam, go back to the car."

I put a handkerchief to my nose, and walked through the house to the bedroom. Dad lay in bed, his face black, and his body all bloated. I barely made it back outdoors, where I gagged and threw up. Annie ran from the car to my side.

"Dad's dead, Annie! The odor is awful. You don't want to see him. Let's go to the neighbors, and call the funeral home."

The county coroner told me that dad had been dead three or four weeks. The body was decomposed so badly, that burial should take place very soon. Before we left, we made arrangements with the funeral home, and the Orthodox Church to have services on Monday at 1:30 P.M.

We arrived home late Saturday night. I lay quietly in bed. Annie cried softly.

"What a shame, Dad must have died right after he sent your birthday card."

Annie called my family and hers to tell them about Ziv's death, and the funeral arrangements. "I know it is short notice, but under the circumstances, we have no choice." She told them it would be a closed casket service.

A few members of my family and Annie's attended the funeral. Dad was buried in the plot I had for him and Zora, in the cemetery outside of Flint.

The death certificate stated date and cause of death, 'unknown'. The coroner's remarks were, bronchial pneumonia, pulmonary emphysema, right side failure. We suspected the fall from his motorcycle, and subsequent injured shoulder, put him in bed, and he developed pneumonia and died.

It had been a traumatic, hectic three days. I thought of the lonely, empty life he lived. I broke down and cried. A cold, bleak day, February 23, 1965.

*   *   *

I received a nasty letter from Joseph two weeks after dad's funeral. Why wasn't he consulted in making the arrangements? Joseph, stationed overseas at his request, had never been around to help in any family crisis. He never visited or even liked dad, now this letter.

"Joseph, is suffering a guilt complex, Nick. He wasn't around to help the family when he should have been, now he wants to play big brother only if it doesn't cost him anything. He is always conveniently away, and insulated from the family's problems. We have been married sixteen years, and I've never met Joseph and Pearl. Yet, through their letters, I've got to know them quite well. Joseph has been in the Army too long. He's out of touch with the real world."

*   *   *

I remembered the envelope Dad had given me last year. It wasn't about his past. He had made a will, and named me the only heir, and executor of his estate. Dad mentioned the rest of his sons and daughters, but stated that he had no intent for them to receive any part of his estate. I had mixed emotions about the will. It would only cause trouble, and bad feelings with my brothers and sisters.

I went to see the attorney who had drawn up the will. He was sorry to hear of Ziv's death. The attorney thought it strange that he didn't want to leave anything to his children, other than me.

Dad hadn't told the attorney that his wife, Zora, was still alive. The attorney told me she couldn't be disinherited and that the State would be notified of the contents of the will.

As Zora's guardian, and the executor of dad's estate, I had

a conflict of interest. I needed to hire an attorney to represent Zora, and be her guardian, until the estate was settled.

I went back to dad's house to check it over. The smell of death was still overpowering. I found a bunch of papers in a desk drawer, stuffed them in a big manila folder, and quickly left the house. I drove back to Flint, and hired an attorney and guardian for Zora.

I hadn't told my brothers and sisters about the will. After I heard from the State regarding reimbursement for Zora's care, I would contact them.

The letter arrived from the Attorney General of the State of Michigan. A claim for payment for Zora's care all those years.

Annie said, "Nick, it's time to cross that bridge we talked about earlier."

* * *

I called my brothers and sisters for a get-together at our house, telling them I had information about dad's estate that they should know about. Annie wasn't looking forward to the occasion. She knew, under the circumstances, it would not be a pleasant meeting.

Joseph, still overseas, could not be at the reading of the will. His letter clearly stated that his share of the estate should be banked for him until he was back in the States. Jay could not be located. None of the family had seen him for quite awhile, or knew of his whereabouts.

Sonya, Watt, Hedy and Alfred arrived at our house in a good mood, anticipating their share of dad's estate. When I passed out copies of the will, there was a long silence in the room.

Finally Watt spoke up, "Maybe I'm not entitled to a share, but my daughters are!"

Hedy spoke next, "It's not fair, I need money badly, and my children should get something."

Sonya chimed in, "Everyone should receive equal shares. It's not right that Nick should get it all!"

Alfred was the last to speak, "I can't believe what's going on here. Now that Ziv is dead, suddenly he's our father, and we are all family. That's a bunch of bullshit, and you all know it. Nick's the only one in the family who ever visited, or treated Ziv as a father. We all had a chance to be Zora's guardian, but no, Nick was the only one to take on the responsibility. None of us have even taken the time to see her, or help financially for her care."

Watt, Sonya and Hedy sat silently staring at Alfred, as he continued to talk.

"If anybody has anything coming to them, it's Nick. Sonya, you seem to have forgotten the times Nick helped you financially, and with your marital problems. Hedy, he helped you through bankruptcy, and divorce. Watt, you and I wouldn't have the good jobs we have at AC if Nick hadn't gotten them for us. Sure I'd like a piece of the pie, but Nick's the only one in the family entitled to Ziv's estate."

I was silent all this time, then I spoke up, "I'll tell you what, I'm willing to share dad's estate with all of you, but only if you are willing to help with the expense of Zora's care for the thirty five years she was in the State Asylum."

I explained to them about the letter from the State's Attorney General's office. I didn't say anything about the worth of dad's estate, or the amount of the bill for Zora's care. My brothers and sisters quickly decided that I indeed was the sole heir. They knew the State's bill would be greater than Ziv's estate. They made no offer to share in the expenses.

*   *   *

A week later, when I returned home from a visit with the attorney, Annie said, "I received a telephone call from Hedy, Nick. She told me that you must have made out Ziv's will, and disinherited everyone in the family but yourself. She said Ziv couldn't read or write, you had to make the will out for him. She and her children should have received a portion of the estate.

"Hedy went on to say, you and I tried to break up her family when she was having trouble with her husband. She is thoroughly disgusted with you, and never wants to see or hear from you again."

Then Annie handed me a letter from Joseph. The telephone call from Hedy was bad enough, she knew Joseph's letter would be worse.

Joseph's letter read, *"Nick, as the eldest of the family, Ziv's estate belongs to me. I've checked with the Adjutant General's office, and being in the Army, I'm not responsible for any part of Zora's bill from the State of Michigan. I've got the Army checking on my behalf to see if the will can be broken."*

"Annie, can you believe my family?"

Dad's estate consisted of an automobile, motorcycle, lawn tractor, a small bank account and his house. After appraisers, real estate, funeral expenses and back utility bills, the estate came to $7,400, Zora to receive $3,000, attorneys $2,000 and me $2,400.

*   *   *

The bill I received from the State of Michigan for Zora's care was itemized by the year, starting in 1930, costing ninety six cents a day, to a low of sixty one cents a day in 1933, up to twenty five dollars a day through June of 1965. The total cost of Zora's care was $50,000. I sent a check to the State of Michigan for $3000, Zora's share of dad's estate. I received a letter back, saying the balance of Zora's bill would be temporarily forgotten, but not forgiven.

THIRTY FOUR

Annie had enjoyed staying home for the past six years. When Sarah started the first grade, and was in school all day, Annie had time and wanted to keep in touch with the working world. She started working at the school as secretary for the Junior High Principal. She could be home with the kids after school, weekends and summer vacation.

Adam was growing up, maybe too fast. He had an average build, long blonde hair and fair complexion. He was old enough to have a drivers license. He started dating girls and working at a restaurant after school to earn extra spending money. Adam lost interest in his school work and his grades took a beating. He liked music and started up a small band. Adam played the drums and the band practiced at our house in the basement. The music was always loud.

*   *   *

I was too involved with my career at AC, putting in long hours, to really know what was going on with Adam's generation. Annie joined the PTA, and attended school activities.

We couldn't understand the long hair, mini skirts and try anything attitude the school age kids were going through. Adam started smoking. He ran around and stayed out late at night with a group of boys I didn't think were a good influence on him. It was difficult for me to understand what Adam was going through. There was no comparison between the era when I was a teenager and Adam's. He was an exceptionally intelligent boy, but didn't always use common sense. I had good common sense, but not the intelligence that Adam possessed.

I remembered back when I was a teenager and the old Model "A" I fixed up to drive around. Adam was allowed to drive, but he had to buy gas for the car. I had always wanted a fast, fancy car. I bought an SS Super Sport. It was blue, with wide oval tires, bucket seats, automatic console shift, 450 cubic engine. A real honey of a hot rod. Adam would be the envy of his friends. He only drove it a few times. The super sport used too much gas, so he preferred to drive the Corvair.

* * *

Alfred moved into a house near Fenton. He invited Annie and me to attend a party, along with a group of his friends. The party was going strong, when Alfred received a phone call. He seemed shook up, but didn't say who called.

As we were going home, Alfred said, "Nick, Hedy's oldest son, Tracy, has been in an accident. He was killed when a car he was in, hit a cement pillar late tonight."

I asked why he waited to tell me about the phone call from Hedy. Alfred said he didn't want to spoil the party for anyone. It was New Years Eve 1965.

* * *

I called Hedy New Years day. She was emotionally distressed. I offered my condolences, and told her Annie and I would be there for the funeral. Annie suggested I call Sonya, she could explain the details of Tracy's death. Sonya was cordial. She explained that Tracy was coming home for a weekend leave from the Navy. His buddy, who was driving the car, fell asleep, and the car crashed into a cement pillar. Tracy was killed instantly. The driver survived with minor injuries.

We drove up to the funeral. It had been nine months since

the reading of dad's will. I hoped the hard feelings over the will, had been forgotten. Hedy was distraught, but seemed glad I was there. Sonya and Alfred were also at the funeral home.

I looked at Tracy, lying in the coffin, with tears in my eyes. I remembered the first time I saw him, twenty-two years ago. I was seventeen years old, posing as Hedy's husband, when Tracy was born, during the war.

Just recently married, Tracy's wife was beneficiary of his Navy insurance policy. She was given the flag that was draped over his coffin. Hedy was left only with memories.

*   *   *

When I returned to work after the funeral, my boss recommended me for a job in another division, working for a different superintendent. He didn't want to lose me, but I needed more exposure and experience before I could handle a superintendent's job. I was in the new division a short time, when my boss called me to his office, and told me that the Manufacturing Manager wanted to see me. As a result of doing so well on my job, I was given a bonus, in stock and cash. Only a select few general foremen received a bonus.

Annie and I had a real celebration that night. We toasted our good fortune in having each other, and almost twenty years of a happy, compatible marriage. I was on the fast track at work, with unlimited potential for promotions. The future couldn't have looked brighter.

*   *   *

General Motors was growing and expanding departments, divisions and plant facilities to meet the growing demands of its customers. As with any large organization, as a whole it dealt fairly with the community, customers and its employees. The tier after tier of upper management is often insulated from the salary and hourly work force. Top management only hears what lower management tells them, not what they should know. Unfortunately, individuals in top management often get quite ruthless in the treatment of the employees, while climbing the ladder to success.

The AC Components Division management, in its quest to make bigger profits, so fatter bonuses could be handed out yearly, became a back stabbing group of individuals. One in particular, Ben Hooper, had been assigned to the Production Division, that I recently transferred to.

The Cable Division I supervised was in the process of being moved from an old plant to a new one. It was a real challenge to keep production going and moving equipment and people at the same time. My division boss retired and Ben Hooper assumed his responsibilities.

Ben called me to his office for a get-acquainted meeting. He was tall, slim, with faded brown eyes, and a blank stare that seemed to be looking nowhere. He had thick gray hair, and a thin mustache. Ben fancied himself a ladies man, but his pock marked face, and oversized nose, didn't qualify him for that distinction.

"I do the thinking around here. All you have to do is follow my orders. Do I make myself clear? Don't let that bonus you were awarded go to your head. If you'd been working for me, you wouldn't have received it. Well, Nick?"

"You're my boss, I'll do the best job I can for you."

I told Annie that night about Ben Hooper.

She said, "I'm sure that he is the exception, and not the rule of what AC's management bosses are like."

"I sure hope so, Annie."

*   *   *

The Speedometer Cable Division, my assigned area of responsibility, had not been a money maker for AC. I told Ben

Hooper that the division should work overtime to bank up cables for their GM customers, before they went into the model changeover. The engineers said the change could be done on a three day weekend. I told Ben it couldn't. We would run out of parts, and the Cable Division would be in trouble with GM headquarters.

Ben's dislike for me showed, as he said, "Nick, you're just trying to make overtime work for yourself, and the division."

The model change went on. What a disaster! The equipment change hadn't even started, when we ran out of cables, and bumped the GM assembly plants. AC management was in trouble with GM headquarters.

Ben called me to his office. "I'm in trouble, because you didn't plan ahead. I am going to put you on the night shift, and if your performance doesn't improve, you will be demoted. You know, Nick, the only reason I can't fire you now, is that damn bonus your last boss gave you. I'd have a hard time explaining and justifying to Corporate Headquarters firing you just after receiving a bonus, but I'll get you yet."

My career was ruined. I was stunned, angry and devastated, and could lose my job. Three months ago, as top general foreman, I received a bonus, and now my job was in jeopardy.

Annie cried out, "How could this be happening. You've received raises, promotions, a bonus, and all your appraisals have been rated number one. One man can't do this to you, can he?"

"Yes, he can, and he did. It's the end of any future for me with the GM Corporation."

*   *   *

The Superintendent of the Plastic Division asked to have me as a General Foreman on second shift. I replaced a man that I had recommended for promotion to General Foreman.

My new boss called me into his office and told me it was too bad Ben Hooper put me under the gun.

"Do a good job for me, Nick, I'll take care of you."

He said he knew what I was going through. He showed me a letter that his boss had given him a few years ago. The same deal I had just been through. It read, "Improve your performance or I'll fire you." The Superintendent said as soon as he got a new boss he was promoted. I couldn't accept what I had been told. Loss of pay, bonus, promotion and put on night shift all because my boss didn't like me.

I wrote a rebuttal to Ben's appraisal of my performance. I told Ben I wanted to talk to his boss, the Manufacturing Manager. All the Manager said was that he had to believe what Ben said about me. They were both concerned about their own jobs. It was the classic shop saying, 'CYA,' cover your ass. Somebody had to be blamed, I was the fall guy.

*   *   *

Three years earlier the Plant General Manager announced a program available to all salary personnel at AC. It was called the Management Career Degree, equivalent to a Masters Degree. Classes consisted of in plant training, college courses and out plant training. I was the first to complete the program at AC. Later Ben gave me an envelope containing a plague and told me he thought it was mine. Ben didn't open it or look at it.

*   *   *

The work and responsibility on the night shift wasn't as much pressure as first shift. I had twenty foremen and four hundred hourly workers, on second and third shifts, but it bothered me how and why I ended up there. Not being with my family, loss of pay, prestige, and no promotion, kept eating at me. I continued to have headaches and stomach pains. A visit to Dr. Maltor confirmed that I did have ulcer disease.

As I was leaving his office he commented, "You are the only case I know of where a person with a diabetic condition improved to the point where medication is no longer necessary."

*   *   *

Annie was eager to build a house, and move to the country. We bought a lot on the Spring Meadows golf course, about twenty miles south of Flint. We looked at many model homes, and found one we both really liked. I hired a contractor to start building.

Leon, Annie's dad, was pleased when she told him about building a new house. When he saw the plans, he told me it looked like more house than we needed. Over the years, Leon had finally accepted me as a son-in-law. He knew Annie was happy, and being well cared for. I enjoyed his good humor, and down home personality.

Our old house sold for a nice profit, which we used for the down payment on the new house.

Annie was excited about the new house. It looked awfully large. Did we really need a house that size? Adam would be graduating soon. We had managed for thirteen years with only one bathroom. The new house would have three.

Leon didn't live to see our house built. His son found him out behind the barn, dead from a heart attack. His son and wife, with their six children, took over the responsibility of managing and working the farm. It was October 6, 1967.

THIRTY FIVE

Winchester Hospital closed down due to a shortage of funds. I transferred Zora to a private nursing home in Flint. It turned out to be poorly run, and in a bad neighborhood. I put Zora's name on a waiting list, to live at a nursing home near us.

I took a copy of dad's will, and Zora's bill from the State to Judge Mackey. He laughed when I told him about my brothers and sisters reaction when I offered to share my inheritance with them, if they would help pay Zora's State bill.

The Judge was curious about my brothers and sisters. "Tell me about them. I use to keep track of them when they were younger."

"Well, Judge, I always hoped we could be a family, and live together. The older we get, the farther apart we are. When dad named me sole beneficiary of his estate, that really broke us up.

"Joseph tried to contest the will. Evidently the Army advised him to forget about it. He has been assigned to Alaska for the next two years. His wife and family will go with him.

"Sonya and her husband are living on a farm in northern Michigan. Hedy is having a rough time over the loss of her son. She's been through two divorces, and is struggling to keep her family together. She lived a short time with dad, but it didn't work out. Now she is working, and living near Sonya. Hedy has little contact with the family.

"Watt is working at AC Milwaukee, but soon will be transferred back to AC Flint. He's married, and has two daughters. His wife is a teacher. He still visits the Wiltons often. Mr. Wilton has retired, and is ill with cancer.

"Alfred is married, and has a son. He's working at AC. Jay has dropped out of sight. He has lost all contact with his brothers and sisters, and adopted parents."

The Judge gave me an envelope. It was a personal inventory of the things I had when I first went to the Whaley Orphanage. Just the clothes on my back. Judge Mackey commented, "You have come a long way from nothing, Nick."

Judge Mackey said as we left, "Your father put his family through a lot, but he paid the price when he lost them."

On the way home, I wondered what the Judge meant about dad.

*   *   *

Adam was going through a difficult time. He had been an honor student through the tenth grade, now Annie and I were wondering if he would graduate. I use to have hopes of Adam going to college. Maybe a job and being on his own would give him some direction in life. Adam wasn't as thrilled about the new house as Annie and I were.

Sarah hadn't put roots down yet. She was still very young, only in the second grade. The new house would be great, a bathroom of her own and lots of fields and woods around to play in.

*   *   *

We had the television on and were watching Robert F. Kennedy, the Senator from New York, at a Presidential campaign rally. Suddenly shots were fired and he was fatally wounded. God, how could it be happening? Right in front of a television audience of millions.

Annie and I were shocked. Two months ago, on April 3rd, James Earl Ray shot and killed Dr. Martin Luther King, Jr., the civil rights leader. It was June 5, 1968.

*   *   *

I received a good appraisal from my superintendent. Ben Hooper went over the appraisal with me.

"According to this piece of paper, you've got your act together, Nick. That doesn't change anything between you and me. I'm keeping you on nights, and I'm not giving you a cost of living, or merit raise."

Ben had ruined any chance of me ever getting an executive position at General Motors. He had a reputation for demoting, or firing foremen. Ben's position in management allowed him to cover his ass, by laying the blame on someone in a lower level in his organization. Fortunately there weren't many like Ben on the AC management team, but one was too much in my life.

The only way I could bring my plight to the attention of AC Corporate Executives, and make Ben accountable to the organization, was to file a lawsuit.

Annie disliked Ben with a passion, for what he had done to me, but wasn't sure I should pursue a lawsuit against him.

"It's the only way, Annie, to keep Ben from ruining anyone else's life and career."

I contacted a lawyer, to start action in the form of a lawsuit against Ben Hooper, and the GM Corporation.

I was unhappy working nights. I had little communication with my family, due to overtime, and weekend work. It was a sad Thanksgiving, 1968.

*   *   *

My right knee had been bothering me for sometime. Dr. Maltor diagnosed a torn cartilage, that required an operation. After the surgery, I had to walk with a cane, but enjoyed being home. Annie was also home for the summer.

I told her we were going away for a quiet weekend, but I didn't tell her where. As we left, she questioned me about our destination.

"It wouldn't be a surprise if you knew. You'll just have to wait until we get there."

The Mature Adult Motel was in a nice quiet suburb. When Annie spied the "Adults Only" sign, she said, "If I had known where we were going, I probably wouldn't have come. We're here, so let's party. I'll show you such a good time, I'll probably have to drive home tomorrow."

The motel room had mirrors everywhere, a console on the headboard, befitting the cockpit of a commercial jet. A movie screen, music, a well stocked bar, a basket swing hanging from the ceiling, over the bed, and a bidet in the bathroom.

I fixed us drinks. This would be an evening like none before. Soon Annie was ready to show me how the basket swing worked. I got up to go to the bathroom, and suddenly the room started spinning around. My stomach churned, and my head hurt. I threw up all over the bathroom floor, then passed out on the bed.

Annie did drive home the next day. I was still weak and dizzy.

She smiled, "You missed some good movies last night. You better see Dr. Maltor right away. One drink shouldn't make you sick."

After Dr. Maltor examined me, he said, "With the stress of your job, your ulcers are getting worse."

He gave me a sheet of paper, with a diet to follow, and a prescription for some medicine that would ease the pain of stomach cramps when my ulcer acted up.

I told Annie what the doctor said about my ulcers and stress on the job.

"Maybe you should quit AC. We'll manage somehow."

*   *   *

Maggie called to tell us Ringo was losing his fight with cancer. He had been in and out of the hospital for sometime.

We went to visit him. Ringo lay in bed, a skinny skeleton of a man, with his hair gone. The only feature recognizable, was his prominent square jaw. When we left, Ringo could hardly breath.

"Annie, that rasping sound is the death rattle."

Ringo died right after we left his room. He was finally at peace from the pain and suffering of cancer, and Maggie's many years of berating him. It was August 18, 1969.

THIRTY SIX

After Adam graduated from high school I helped him get a job at AC. He rented an apartment so he could be independent and not live at home. He was eighteen, still a teenager. Adam didn't know what he wanted to do in life, but after working in the factory, performing a repetitive boring job that any child could do, he decided he wanted something else.

Adam registered with the Draft Board. I encouraged him to go in the military to serve his country. He volunteered to go in the Army. Later he could go to college on the GI Bill. Annie and Sarah cried as he boarded the bus.

"Annie, I hope I did the right thing encouraging Adam to enlist."

I remembered back to the day when I was eighteen and boarding a bus to enlist in the Navy. Things were different then. I was going off to a war that the whole world was engaged in. Adam was going to fight in a political war that nobody wanted.

Annie said, "Nick, Adam enlisting in the Army might settle him down and help him decide what he wants to do with his life."

*   *   *

Annie read in the newspaper that my brother Jay's adopted father, Mr. Lewis, had died. "Let's go to the funeral home and pay our respects after work tomorrow."

I didn't know the Lewis family very well, but maybe Jay would be there, and we could visit with him. He didn't show up for Mr. Lewis' funeral. Mrs. Lewis hadn't heard from, or seen Jay, for almost fifteen years.

When the funeral was over, I told Annie, "It's a shame, Mrs. Lewis is heartbroken. With Mr. Lewis gone, she's all alone. I wonder what she'll do now."

"Oh, I forgot to tell you, Mrs. Lewis is coming to see us this weekend."

She was a short, plump woman, with large, round, piano type legs, and white hair. She tearfully talked about Jay's early boyhood.

Mrs. Lewis shocked me when she said, "You probably don't remember when you were living at the Whaley Orphanage, Mr. Lewis and I took you to stay with us for a weekend. We wanted to adopt you. Mrs. Hardy decided at the last minute not to let you be adopted. She suggested we adopt your brother Jay instead."

Mrs. Lewis went on, saying she had kept track of me, and followed my progress through the years. "You have done very well; this nice home, a fine family, a good wife, and a management position at General Motors." She started to cry, and blurted out, "I wish we could have adopted you, Nick, instead of Jay."

I didn't know what to say. Annie comforted Mrs. Lewis. As a mother she could feel for her. She hadn't lost a husband and a son, but could understand what Mrs. Lewis must be going through. Annie asked if we could help in any way.

She answered slowly, "Yes, you can help me. I'm moving to California, away from all the memories I have here. I haven't got too many more years to live. It would give me peace of mind, if you would find Jay, and see that he is taken care of. I know he's mixed up about his families, but he always was a good boy. I'll always love him as my son. I have some pictures of Jay, as a boy and young man, I want you to keep." Mrs. Lewis kissed me as she left. "I would have been proud to have you for my son."

Annie commented, "My heart goes out to that woman. All

Mrs. Lewis wanted was to be a mother to Jay, and he won't have anything to do with her."

*   *   *

That night we were glued to the television set, as astronauts Edwin Aldrin and Neil Armstrong, landed on the moon. It was July 20, 1969.

*   *   *

The work and responsibilities on the night shift wasn't as much pressure as first shift. I had twenty foremen and four hundred hourly workers on second and third shifts. It continued to bother me how and why I was put there. Not being with my family, loss of pay, prestige and no promotion, kept eating at me. I continued to have headaches and stomach pains. Dr. Maltor stated that my ulcer disease was getting worse.

Right after I left the cable division, the management was completely changed. The superintendent was demoted to a general foreman and put on the night shift. A general foreman was promoted to superintendent. Another superintendent was put on a special assignment to help on days. Three general foremen took my place. Ben Hooper was reassigned and a new division manager took over the responsibility of the cable area. It didn't make me feel any better to know three general foremen took my place. I was still on nights and Ben Hooper was still a manager over my boss.

*   *   *

For summer vacation, we rented a pop-up trailer, and camped a week in a State Park in northern Michigan. I visited a saw mill, the only activity in town. The mill supplied wood packing skids for AC. The mill owner had 640 wooded acres, surrounded by a National Forest. He wanted to retire, and the property was for sale; $10,000 per forty acre parcel. I had always wanted some northern property. This area seemed ideal to me; isolated, secluded woods, next to a National Forest, not too far from Flint. I asked if it would be all right to drive out and look the property over.

"Sure, it's okay."

I drove five miles out of town, and turned down a weed grown dirt road. A sign nailed to a tree read, "Private Property—640 acres for sale." I parked my car, and spent a couple of hours walking through the forest. Throughout the woods, there were huge stumps. The pine trees had been logged off years ago, in the 20's. The CCC boys planted seedlings in the 30's, and the pine trees were again mature enough to be harvested. I decided to buy the outside forty acres from the mill owner.

*   *   *

Alpine Nursing Home called, and said they had a room for Zora. We drove to Flint to pick up Zora and her belongings.

During the drive to Alpine, a thunderstorm came up. Zora got nervous, and in real plain English said, "Don't leave me, I want to stay and live at your house."

"It's too bad Zora can't live with us, Annie, but she needs constant supervision. Alpine is the best managed nursing facility around. We can visit her daily until she feels comfortable in her new home."

"I wonder if Zora really was as violent as you have been told all these years, Nick? She's such a sweet, lovable person, with a great sense of humor. What a terrible waste."

I lay in bed, thinking about Zora. She didn't know me as her son now, but maybe earlier she might have. As I fell asleep, I heard her saying over and over, "Me live in hoose with jew?

I want to stay and live at your house. I no krazy wollmen, whyy no one lissen to me?"

*   *   *

Dr. Maltor had written a letter to Adam's Commanding Officer, stating he shouldn't be placed in a situation where his eyesight was critical for his survival. Adam could see okay, wearing glasses, but without them, he couldn't see beyond the length of his outstretched arms. The Army sent him to Vietnam anyway.

Annie wrote to him regularly. We didn't receive a letter from Adam for months, and we were worried. Finally a letter arrived, he was in an Army hospital with malaria. When he recovered, and his tour of duty over, he flew home.

Adam was one happy guy to be back in the States, and out of the jungles of Vietnam. The Vietnam soldiers didn't get the welcome that the World War II service men did. Adam wouldn't talk about his experiences at all. He just said that he had done things he shouldn't have had to, didn't want to, and didn't feel good about doing. The Vietnam Veterans were casualties of a political war. I was sorry I encouraged Adam to serve.

He gave me his service record, and papers to keep. I found out he earned the Air Medal, Combat Infantryman Badge, Meritorious Service Award, and Letters of Commendation from his superior officers.

Adam didn't want to follow in my footsteps as a GM man. He wanted to be a writer, artist, and musician. He bought a used Chevrolet, with the Bonds he had sent home while he was in the service. Adam moved to Florida, and went to the State College on the GI Bill. The Vietnam Conflict had changed Adam from a boy who wanted to fight for his country, to a disillusioned young man who needed to find out what life was all about.

On a trip to visit him, Adam introduced us to Syna Steel, a

girl he met at college. She was a slender girl, with long, dark hair, brown eyes, and lightly tanned skin. A shy, bashful, talented artist and pianist, Syna was studying music.

*   *   *

Sarah was almost eleven now. She had let her hair grow and it hung down to the middle of her back. She had an impish smile and liked to joke around. She was pretty, outgoing and had a pleasing personality. Sarah was out of dolls and into ponies and wanted one for herself.

We bought her a pony named Kate. Kate was a sleek, shiny brown mare, with a mind of her own. We kept her across the road in a barn with another pony that a minister kept there for his daughter.

Kate came in season and Sarah wanted her to have a colt. A man down the road from us raised and trained ponies. He had a stud pony. When Kate was ready to be bred, Sarah wanted to go along. I thought back to the time when I watched Hugo breed the mare at the Herman farm. It wasn't anything a young girl should watch. I would be uncomfortable with her there. Sarah insisted it was her mare and she had a right to see Kate get bred.

We walked Kate down the lane and to the barnyard where the stud pony waited. When the stud pranced up to Kate and sniffed her behind, she kicked and nipped at him. Kate wasn't ready to be bred. I was relieved. We left her in the barnyard with the stud. We would go back and pick her up in a couple of days. Sarah wanted to watch and was disappointed.

*   *   *

I received a short letter from Mrs. Lewis, who was living in California with her younger sister. She wrote that she had terminal cancer, but would go to glory with peace of mind, knowing I would see that Jay was taken care of.

I had tried, unsuccessfully, to locate Jay. Annie told me we were morally obligated to find, and look after him. We just had to try harder. Jay was nowhere to be found. The best clue to his whereabouts came from the town drunk, where Jay used to live. According to him, Jay bummed around the country, preaching religion to whoever would listen.

*   *   *

I received a frantic call at work from Annie. Sarah had been hit by a car while riding on a bicycle. I drove home as quickly as I could. The Chief of Police was there. Annie had gone to the hospital with Sarah. The Chief told me Sarah was okay and asked me to stay a few minutes to answer some questions so he could make out an accident report.

I then drove to the hospital. Sarah was in the Emergency Room and Annie was with her. A specialist had been called to look her injured leg over and perform any surgery necessary. He hadn't arrived at the hospital yet. I noticed blood was dripping through the bandages and Sarah was very white. I was getting impatient waiting for the specialist and asked the Emergency Room Doctor to give Sarah a blood transfusion. When the specialist arrived he was furious. Sarah should have been prepped for surgery. The doctor had her taken to the operating room immediately.

Sarah had a broken leg, torn muscle in her leg and a head concussion. She had a rough time for a few days. Annie stayed with her most of the time. The doctor wasn't sure if she would be able to walk normally on her leg. When Sarah went home she had to wear a special leg and foot brace and use crutches to walk.

She had a lot of spunk and told me, "Don't worry, Dad, I'll be walking without the brace and crutches soon."

Sarah told us how the accident happened. She was riding a bike on the shoulder of the road and a friend was riding a bike behind her. A car, driven by a woman with some children with her, struck Sarah and threw her off the bike onto the pavement. The car had been in an accident before and the front bumper was bent and the metal all jagged. The driver of the car claimed Sarah fell off the bike into the car. Sarah's friend's father wouldn't let her give testimony as to how Sarah was hit. Sarah was riding his daughter's bike and he didn't want to get involved.

True to her word, in time Sarah was able to walk normally without the brace or crutches.

*   *   *

Annie and I took a few days vacation to drive to Florida, and visit Adam and Syna Steel. They were still in college, but I was concerned that Adam hadn't structured his courses, leading to a degree. He had enough credits to graduate, but not the required ones.

We were from the conventional establishment, while Adam was drifting about, not making any sense with his life.

On the drive home, I thought about my college days, and the fun I had with Jock Comstock. I had not seen Jock since we moved to Spring Meadows. The last letter Annie received from Ginger, told us that they had bought an old farmhouse in the country, near Lansing.

Annie must have been thinking of the Comstocks, too. "Let's stop and see Jock and Ginger, it's not very far out of our way."

"You must have been reading my mind. That is just what I've been thinking."

Jock looked good for a man in his late forties, stocky, but not fat. His blonde hair showed no signs of graying. Ginger was as sexy as ever.

Jock hadn't changed a bit, "Nick, you old son-of-a-bitch,

it's good to see you. I'm still trying for a boy, but I guess I'll have to admit, that with six girls, Ginger is more woman than I am man."

He was an administrator in the school system, not far from where they lived. When we left to go home, he said, "Let's get together more often."

*   *   *

I took a trip north to our forty acres. Sarah went along, to get some driving experience on the highway.

The north woods was peaceful and quiet. An Acme Oil Company survey truck blocked the entrance to our forty acres. The Oil Company was scouting for land to use for oil and gas exploration. They asked if I would be interested in leasing my land. I agreed.

Sarah, a budding environmentalist, wasn't happy. The drive back home was not as pleasant as the trip up. Sarah grumbled all the way, about my decision to lease the property.

*   *   *

I bought a headstone for Dad's grave and signed an agreement for a pre-arranged funeral for Zora at the Brown Funeral Home in Flint. I put five hundred dollars in a joint savings account with the Funeral Home and myself. The agreement stated that when Zora died the five hundred dollars, plus interest earned, would pay for all expenses and arrangement necessary for her funeral. Zora was 73 years old.

THIRTY SEVEN

A new superintendent was assigned to the Plastic Division, the area I supervised on nights. He was a go-getter, on the fast track, and his mentor was Ben Hooper's boss. He recommended me for a first shift job. Ben Hooper again refused to give me a merit raise, or let me go on first shift.

My headaches, and stomach pains persisted. In my mid forties, I had too much to lose to quit AC. I had to stay, and tough it out until I was old enough to retire.

I consistently received high appraisals, and was again recommended for a first shift lead off job. Ben Hooper wasn't satisfied with the performance of the Plastic Division. He demoted the first shift general foreman to a line foreman, but the man couldn't stand the humiliation, and quit AC. Ben could no longer ignore the recommendations of his superintendents. After three years on the night shift, he reluctantly transferred me on days, to replace the first shift general foreman.

Annie was happy when I told her the good news. "Now we can live like normal people again."

"I'm going ahead with the lawsuit against Ben Hooper, Annie. He's ruined my career, and wrecked my health. Ben just forced another general foreman to quit AC. The guy's inhuman, he's got to be stopped."

My first shift responsibility was manufacturing air filters. Some of the old time foremen, working in other divisions, requested to be transferred to my department. I soon had the best producing, and money making department in the division. I received a raise, my first pay increase, since getting a bonus four years ago. Ben Hooper had to sign the paperwork. It was September, 1971.

*   *   *

Roy Henry, the Negro I promoted to a job setter, stopped by to see me. "I'm glad to see you back on first shift, Mr. Wilton. You were too good a general foreman to be lost on the night shift. I'm asking for your help again. You have an opening for a foreman on the assembly line, and I want that job."

I looked at Roy, "What do you have to offer, besides wanting the job?"

"I've been going to classes at night, and recently received a Business Degree from the Flint City College. Besides I'm the best, and most experienced worker in your division."

"I'll see what I can do, Roy."

I talked to my superintendent, and told him about Roy wanting to be promoted to a supervisor, and work for me. "I know he's a Negro, and a damn good one. It's time we gave the minorities a chance at management level jobs."

The superintendent thought a minute. "Yes, let's do it, Nick. It couldn't happen at a better time. Make up the paper work, and walk it through to Personnel, and have the general manager sign it."

Once the paper work had been signed, I called Roy into my office, and congratulated him on his promotion.

He thanked me, saying, "I know some people will give me a hard time, but I'm going to make you proud of me. Just one more thing, Mr. Wilton, we don't like to be referred to as Negroes, we're Black, refer to us as Blacks."

My job at AC couldn't have been better. I had a great production team and my department ranked as the top money maker in the division.

My boss called me into his office, and handed me a piece

of paper. It was a promotion to assistant superintendent, for continued outstanding performance.

Annie couldn't believe it when I told her I had been promoted. "What about the lawsuit? Does Ben and AC know?"

"No, not yet. It'll take a long time for the Court to serve paper, and set up a hearing date. I'm still going ahead with the suit against Ben."

I put in lots of daily, and weekend work at the plant. The Air Cleaner Department was rated at the top at AC. Ben Hooper received a promotion, and transferred to a factory out of state.

When I told Annie, she said, "Let's drink a toast to Ben, to good riddance."

"Let's hope not, but Ben could come back to AC with a higher position in management. I'm still going to pursue the lawsuit. The higher up Ben goes, the more dangerous he is."

* * *

The frustration and aggravation of being on nights the past years, because of Ben Hooper, finally got to me. I suffered severe stomach cramps. Doctor Maltor put me in the hospital. I took a sick leave, stating that the ulcers were caused by stress and strain at work. The plant doctor called me at home, and told me that as a member of management, I couldn't say the ulcers were work related. He changed my sick leave papers to say the reason for ulcers was 'unknown'.

* * *

The last five years, when I could, I attended classes. Now on sick leave I used the time to write my final thesis for my Masters Degree from Central Michigan University. My paper was about the AC Management Team and manufacturing procedures. I used Ben Hooper as an example of how power of leadership can be abused, with the resulting affect on the work force. Annie helped type the paper and commented that she hoped AC Management wouldn't get to read the thesis.

*   *   *

When I returned to work, I built up a management team that consistently performed as one of the best at AC. My boss called me into his office to review the plant's performance. Costs were down, production up, and surplus money in the budget. He congratulated me on receiving my Masters Degree, and said it was a real achievement, considering the night shift hours I had endured over the years, and the many hours of time I spent studying, and attending classes.

"It finally paid off for you, Nick. I'm promoting you to Plant Superintendent. The promotion is a little late, you should have received it a few years back, when you completed, and received the AC Management Career Degree. Ben Hooper cheated you out of a promotion then, but he's not here to stop it this time. Congratulations again, Nick. We make a fine team."

*   *   *

Celebration time. Annie and I talked long into the night. How long could we continue to enjoy each other? Married over 25 years, we were two happy people.

Annie questioned me, "Aren't you going to drop your lawsuit now, Nick?"

"No, I'm not. I'm fifty years old, and finally have a management position at AC. Ben Hooper prevented me from becoming an executive manager, where I could have been involved in policy making for the corporation. I've suffered mentally, physically, and monetarily. I won't be satisfied until Ben Hooper is out of the GM plants."

After being thoroughly and soundly loved, I lay in bed thinking about my past. Life had been good, having a wife like

Annie; a great lover, companion, and my best friend, it couldn't get any better than this.

Suddenly Marcus appeared, saying, "You're one lucky hunky, Nick, having Annie for a wife. You have made up for the loving I should have received." Marcus gave his hound dog howl, and slowly slipped under water. I shouted, "No, Marcus, no," then I tried to whistle back, but only a garbled sound came from my mouth.

"Nick, Nick, wake up, are you all right?" It was August, 1975.

*   *   *

I called Roy Henry to my office after my promotion to Plant Superintendent. He was an outstanding supervisor.

"Roy, I have a general supervisor position open. You're my pick for the job. How about it? Do you want to be a general supervisor, working for me?"

"You bet, Mr. Wilton, I know you'll give me all the cooperation and help I need."

*   *   *

My boss, and many of the other superintendents were chain smokers, addicted to cigarettes, pipes or cigars. Closed up in meetings, lasting two to three hours, became more than I could stand. The lack of oxygen, and the stinking smoke, caused headaches, and aggravated my ulcers.

An opportunity came up for me to move to second shift, as a plant superintendent. Again nights, but by choice not by mandate, with more flexible hours, and away from the daily smoke filled meeting rooms. If my health continued to deteriorate, I would never make it to retirement. I took the night shift assignment.

The move improved my mental and physical condition.

Reporting to the General Manufacturing Manager, and on his staff, with all the Plant Managers, I had management responsibility to both the second and third shifts, with over 5000 employees. Ironically, the move put me into Ben Hooper's former office. I vowed never to abuse my position in management, as Ben did.

*   *   *

Sarah, a good student, especially in math and science, was accepted at AC as a high school co-op student, for the AC Engineering Program. Out of 27 co-ops, only Sarah and two other students passed the GM Institute entrance exam. When she graduated from high school, she could go to GM Institute, and become an engineer. As a co-op student, Sarah attended school in the morning, and worked at AC in the afternoon.

Sarah did not do well in the program. Her goal wasn't to be an engineer and work for AC. Sarah wanted to be an environmentalist. I was disappointed. She had an opportunity to get a paid education and receive a degree that guaranteed a management position at AC.

The last year in school Sarah's grades suffered. She was dating, running around with not much interest in anything. One day without letting Annie or me know, she took one of our cars and drove to Florida to see Adam and Syna. Annie and I were frantic, not knowing where Sarah had gone. Adam called and told us Sarah was with him. She had no money and was afraid to let us know what she had done. Annie and I managed to take a few vacation days and fly down to Florida.

On the flight down we had time to talk and think things out. Sarah had always been a very good child and student. We decided to ignore her sudden departure and trip to Florida. She was ready to come home. We made a vacation trip of driving back in the car. Sarah was glad to be home and soon was her old self again.

Sarah graduated from High School, and I managed to get her into AC on a production line in the plant. She moved into an apartment near Flint with a high school girlfriend. A short, but good experience. Sarah was working nights and taking classes at the University. Her girlfriend was into noisy music and partying. Sarah soon moved back home to peace and quiet.

*   *   *

Annie was promoted to payroll clerk and transferred to the school administration office. She had been the top secretary in the school system and always worked in the buildings with the students. The payroll job was the most demanding one she had. She would be involved in setting up the payroll to a computer system.

The Office Manager told Annie her salary would stay the same as she had been receiving as high school secretary. Annie didn't need the added responsibilities and grief without a pay incentive. The Superintendent agreed to give Annie a raise. He knew she was the best person for the job.

*   *   *

GM Corporate Headquarters issued a mandatory training film for all AC salaried personnel to view. I called a meeting of all the supervising personnel in my plant. The film indicated that a new policy of hiring and promoting had been instituted. Any future bonuses would be tied directly to the number of female, and minorities hired, trained, and promoted in a manger's area of responsibility.

Roy stopped by my office after the showing of the film. "I can't believe the contents of that film, Mr. Wilton. Any raise, or promotion, that a female or minority receives, will not be by merit or ability, but tied to a bonus the boss gets. No way will I, or any Black person, ever get credit for doing a good job. It's just a Corporate numbers game. I've never been so disgusted in my life. I'm glad I received a promotion before GM had that training film made, and required it to be shown to all salaried employees."

*   *   *

Big businesses were going through trying times. Foreign competition had reduced automobile sales. The politicians in the government were telling General Motors what to build and how to build it, who to hire, promote and what numbers they had to work with. The shop union was getting stronger and management was becoming younger, inexperienced and weaker.

Corporate Headquarters sent word to all its divisions to actively recruit colleges, to look for graduating talent willing to work in the plants as Management Trainees. It was almost a corporate mandate that all future supervisors have a college degree.

I and the older managers disagreed with this policy. We knew when the supervision work force had all degree employees, there was no way they all could get promoted. Soon the entry level positions would become overeducated, with disgruntled employees working at a dead end job. The word from GM Headquarters was, don't question this policy, just do it.

Civil Rights was changing the way GM structured its management team and the way it did business. Females were in managing positions and situations that never existed a few years ago. Annie firmly believed a female was limited in her ability to function unrestricted in a working role and still have a happy, healthy family relationship. Not because of mental abilities, but rather physical restrictions and family obligations.

All Plant Managers and Superintendents were given recruiting assignments at different colleges. I was assigned to my old college in Mt. Pleasant, Michigan.

The Department Deans invited me to a happy hour and prime rib dinner, prior to interviewing the students.

Only the top ten percent of the senior class was interviewed. A few from each graduating class from colleges all over the country were offered employment at AC.

The manufacturing organization soon had a highly educated, disgruntled work force, with limited advancement opportunities. After a period of time many left to seek employment elsewhere.

*   *   *

Annie and I gave a surprise anniversary party for Jock and Ginger at their cabin up north. We invited their family and friends for an outdoor barbecue. During the day, I suffered severe stomach pains. Annie took me to the hospital emergency room. The doctor gave me some strong pain pills, and told me it was probably stomach flu. "See your family doctor when you get back home."

Doctor Maltor put me in the hospital with bleeding ulcers.

I returned to work a week later. Buck Roe, my boss, said, "What's the matter, Nick? Did I give you ulcers?"

"No, if you had been my boss, instead of Ben Hooper, I wouldn't have ulcers."

Buck, in his middle fifties, had a big nose, ruddy complexion, and thinning, sandy colored hair. He was in a position of power, and liked it. Buck had a sharp tongue, and talked rough. He wasn't well liked, but everyone respected him. He treated all his managers fairly, and showed no favoritism. My former boss expected me to communicate, and work for all the plant managers and superintendents. Buck Roe had a different approach.

"Bullshit, Nick. You report to me, and you're a member of my staff, with the plant managers. You'll be rated on how you perform for me, not the plant managers, or superintendents."

I told Buck of a previous conversation with my former boss, requesting that a company car be assigned to me.

"A man in your position, should not have to scrounge around for a car, or required to use your own car for company business, Nick. I'll see that you are assigned a car at once. You're a good manager, I like the way you run the night shift."

Having a company car, with gas and insurance paid, was a bonus I never expected to receive.

Annie was happy, "You deserve it, after all Ben Hooper put you through."

My performance appraisal was on a one to one basis with Buck Roe. Buck's main concern was how he could help me be more effective with my plant responsibilities. I voiced my concerns about the plant managers resentment to my position on Buck's staff with my lower title and classification. I also stated that I did not feel that my function on the staff fit within the comfort zone of the plant managers.

He replied, "Nick, you have an obligation to tell me how things really are and what actually is happening on the factory floor. I don't give a damn what the plant managers want to hear or listen to."

When Buck Roe called me into his office to review my yearly performance appraisal, he suggested that a title change to Manager of Night Operations would be more appropriate with my position on his staff and my job responsibilities. At the close of the interview, Buck stated he would approve and put the change through right away. The paperwork for my title change went to the Personnel Department and the General Manager.

Before I received the title change, Buck Roe was promoted to a General Plant Manager and transferred out of the state. Temporarily, Buck's position at AC remained vacant. The plant managers and I reported to the general plant manager. I asked about the paperwork changing my title. The general manager said, "It's all signed and in my desk waiting for Buck Roe's replacement."

* * *

Sarah decided she had enough of working on the assembly line at AC, and was ready to enroll at Michigan State College. We were glad that she was going to use her mind instead of her back. We agreed to help out with college expenses. Annie and I took a few days off work, to help her get settled at the college.

Sarah was excited, and nervous when she enrolled for fall classes. Going to a college of over 50,000 students, would be a whole different experience than attending a small high school. Freshman students were not allowed to keep cars on campus so she had to park off campus. She could use her car to drive back and forth home on weekends.

I spent a day with Sarah, and a group of new students being briefed on safe conduct around the campus. As I left to go back home, she said, "Don't look so worried, Dad, I'll get along just fine."

* * *

Sarah's old car was wearing out and she wanted a new one. She had saved some money and we agreed to help. The car she picked out was a new red Chevrolet with white interior and a stick shift. I hadn't driven a stick shift car in years. I managed to drive the Chevrolet home without any trouble. Sarah had to go back to college the next day. I took her on some back roads for a lesson. What a time Sarah had trying to coordinate the clutching and shifting. She was frustrated as she ground the gears and jumped the car, stalling several times. Sarah was in tears when we arrived home. She left the next day, grinding, jumping and jolting down the road.

Sarah managed to work summers at AC, keeping her seniority and saving a little money. She heard about an Environmental Science degree at a college in California. She wanted to transfer there to finish her degree work.

Annie and I talked it over. California was a long way off and Sarah, as an out of state student, would have to pay higher tuition. We lived comfortably and were not wasteful or extravagant and managed to live within our means. My salary after stock, pension and taxes didn't allow for a lot of extra savings. We decided to help Sarah go to California, as long as she continued to get good grades.

I took a week of vacation time to drive with Sarah to California. The red car was loaded down, plus a cargo container on top. There was just room for Sarah and me in the front seat. It was a father and daughter fun trip, until the second day. We couldn't stand each others music. I like country, Sarah liked loud rock. We stopped for lunch, Sarah on one side of the restaurant, me on the other, not talking to each other. We reached a compromise. Whoever was driving could play the music they wanted. It ended up being an enjoyable trip, with sightseeing stops along the way.

I helped Sarah get settled into an apartment off campus. She cried when I left for my flight back home, realizing how far away she was from her family.

*   *   *

I had a surprise when I went back to work. Ben Hooper had returned to AC to replace Buck Roe. He was my boss again! Annie couldn't believe it when I told her.

She tried to console me, "You have twenty years with AC, and you are fifty five years old, what can Ben Hooper do to you now?"

Ben called me to his office, and I congratulated him on his recent promotion. He grinned, "Yeah, I'm your boss again,

Nick. The promotions, and top ratings you have received prevent me from canning you, but I can restructure your job responsibilities. I want you out of my old office at once, turn in your company car. You will stay on nights, out of my hair."

I asked Ben about the signed paperwork changing my title to Manager of Night Operations. He laughed, and told me he hadn't seen it, must have been misplaced.

When I told Annie about having to turn in the company car, she said, "Can he do that to you?"

"Yes, he is the big boss. Ben can do anything he wants to."

*   *   *

I moved into an office in the plant. The work force was considerably less than the 5000 employees I used to be responsible for on second and third shifts. My night shift organization now consisted of one general supervisor, six supervisors and a total of fifty hourly employees all on second shift. The third shift had been eliminated.

I hoped my lawsuit would be on the docket soon.

THIRTY EIGHT

Joseph came to visit an old friend near Flint. He stopped by, unannounced, as casual as if he had seen us yesterday.

"Hi, Nick, how are you doing? I was in the vicinity, and decided to stop by for a visit. I'm retired now, all done with the Army."

I shook Joseph's hand, and stammered, "It's been a long time since we saw each other."

Joseph thought a minute, "Let's see, I guess it must have been before I got married, and enlisted in the Army the second time. Where's your wife? I never met her."

"She's downtown shopping."

"Oh, it's just as well she's not here. We can have a better visit. Pearl always interrupts when I'm talking, and keeps correcting me. She's with her folks."

The soft life in the Army showed. He was bald, except for a few short white hairs around the back of his head. He wore glasses with thick lenses, and his right eye turned in slightly. Joseph, the oldest of the brothers, was also the shortest.

"I know you're Zora's guardian, Nick, and taking good care of her, so I don't worry about her. I'm going to visit our brothers and sisters, and then spend my retirement traveling throughout the country in my new trailer."

Joseph continued to talk endlessly about his life in the Army. He said little about his wife and children, and didn't ask about mine.

I finally interrupted him and said, "Yes, you can be proud of your accomplishments in the Army. The rest of us have also done quite well. We can thank dad for that. Just think of the sacrifice, and trauma he went through coming to this country, not even able to read or write. What a time he must have had keeping the family together when mother was hospitalized. I can't begin to think how I would handle a situation like that."

*   *   *

Joseph didn't say anything for a long time. His face flushed red, and he blurted out, "Goddamn it, Nick, I can't understand how you can stand up for dad, considering how he disgraced our family."

"Christ, it's no disgrace that he lost his job in the Depression, and couldn't pay for mother's hospital care, and take care of eight kids!"

"Damn it, Nick, you know the reason our family broke up, is because dad was arrested, and convicted on moral charges. The Whaley Orphanage took you in when he was sent to prison. That's why I haven't had anything to do with dad."

"I can't believe what you just said, Joseph. It's not true! Dad would have told me about it years ago."

Joseph calmed down. "You never knew, all these years, the real reason our family broke up?"

"If what you are saying is true, I never knew. When I was in the Whaley Orphanage, I was told that dad and mother were dead. Later when dad did show up, I just assumed that he couldn't keep our family together because he lost his job, and mother was put in the State Asylum. God, I don't know what to say."

Joseph went on, "Sonya, Hedy and I agreed years ago not to say anything to you younger boys about the real reason our family broke up. I just assumed when you were older you would know. Mother was physically, and mentally ill after Alfred was born. When she became violent, she was committed to the Asylum.

"Times were tough during the Depression, and dad had

very little work. He managed to keep the family together for three years without mother.

"I was shocked when dad was arrested, and sent to prison. I couldn't have supported, or kept the family together. I was sixteen years old, and had trouble taking care of myself."

"Joseph, what were the moral charges?"

"I don't want to talk about it anymore."

He left without seeing Annie or Zora.

What a lot to learn about your family in such a short time. It would take a while to absorb what I had just heard.

*   *   *

I took a trip to the Flint Journal after Joseph left. I wanted to see it in black and white. I checked through old issues of the paper, from the Depression years.

Joseph didn't lie about dad. I found it; Ziv Sabitch sentenced to five years in prison, for the statutory rape of his fourteen year old daughter.

I was stunned! I read it again. It couldn't be true, but there it was. All those years, and I didn't have a clue. I continued reading the news article. The Whaley Orphanage took over the responsibility, and care of the eight Sabitch children.

I left the Flint Journal in a daze. Driving back, I thought to myself, was it Hedy? She was frequently unhappy, and sometimes quite bitter toward dad. Then I realized, his fourteen year old daughter, had to be my sister Sonya!

I had a lot to tell Annie when she came home. She would be disappointed that Joseph came for a visit, and didn't stay long enough to meet her.

THIRTY NINE

Annie cried when I told her about Ziv.

"Nick, how could that have happened? His own daughter! Poor Sonya, what an ordeal to go through, and have to live with."

"Dad's gone, and Sonya has done a remarkable job of living her life, in spite of what happened to her when she was a young girl. We will manage, too. It will be an awkward situation when we see Sonya, knowing what we know now."

"Yes, it will, and soon, because Sonya called to say that her husband suffered a heart attack."

I tried to think back to the last time I had seen my sister. Sonya sent us a letter once in awhile, but it had been several years ago that we were together.

We drove up to see them. I said little on the way. I was thinking about dad, Sonya, and what our family had been through.

Annie spoke up, "Are you going to say anything to Sonya?"

"No, I'm not. If she had wanted to talk about it, she would have years ago. I understand now why Sonya didn't want to have anything to do with dad, but not her lack of concern about mother."

*   *   *

Sonya's husband was out of the hospital and at home, very weak but improving. Now in his fifties, with hair more white than gray, he walked stooped over. His disposition hadn't improved over the years.

"I've got to retire. I won't get the big pension, and benefits you will working for a big company like GM, but we will manage somehow."

Sonya, at sixty, had white hair, and her blue eyes sparkled when she smiled. She was cheerful and pleasant.

"I do appreciate you taking care of Zora. God knows what would have happened to her if you hadn't stepped in."

It was difficult for me to converse with Sonya. I couldn't get the past out of my mind, even if she had managed to.

As we left to go home, Sonya said, "It's too bad we haven't been a closer family."

*   *   *

Sarah was not happy living so far away from home. California people were not friendly and lived life at a fast pace. Sarah worked part time for a Photo Drive-in Company. Annie and I flew out to visit her during Christmas vacation. We enjoyed the warm California weather. Sarah was doing well at college, but didn't know how much longer she could stay away from home.

When the second term ended, I flew to California and helped Sarah pack. I rented a U-Haul trailer and drove back to Michigan with her. Sarah went back to Michigan State at the start of the spring term.

Sarah soon had enough of the noisy coed dorm life and she settled into an apartment off campus. Ginger, our Brittany spaniel, went to live with her. Sarah exercised Ginger in the big open fields around the apartment. AC didn't hire any people during the summer, so Sarah stayed at Michigan State and took classes.

*   *   *

Annie's boss became ill and was hospitalized with cancer.

It was terminal. She never returned to work and died a short time later. During the time her boss was ill, Annie did the payroll and took over the Office Manager responsibilities. Annie was promoted to Office Manager, Secretary to the Superintendent and supervisor of the other school secretaries.

*　　*　　*

My job wasn't challenging and I didn't feel well. I didn't have any energy, was listless and did very little work around the house.

The lawsuit against Ben Hooper would be scheduled for a hearing soon. I could hardly wait.

*　　*　　*

Annie and I drove to Fenton to visit Maggie Wilton. She was sick with the flu. We couldn't leave her alone, so we asked Maggie if she wanted us to take her to stay with Bert or Watt.

"No, I want to stay with you."

When we arrived home, I called Watt and Bert, and told them that Maggie was going to stay at our place for a few days.

She went from bad to worse. We took her to the hospital, from there she spent some time at Watt's, then to a Nursing Home in Fenton. Bert made up a will, and had Maggie sign it, leaving everything to him. Maggie died a short time later.

Watt didn't get a dime. Maggie left a diamond ring to Annie, that she received from a man friend after Ringo died.

*　　*　　*

Sarah met, and fell in love with a young man at college. Frank Getto was a dark complexioned, nice looking Italian, with black curly hair, a mustache, dark brown eyes, and a white, toothy smile. They would both graduate the following spring.

280

Adam and Syna came to visit us, on his first trip back to Michigan since returning from Vietnam ten years ago. In his early thirties, he still didn't know what he wanted out of life. Syna, a small, pretty girl, with dark hair, was in her late twenties. They were working for the Tampa Tribune, and taking college classes at night. Both of them would graduate the following spring, and planned to leave Florida, and journey to a big city, where they could pursue a career in the publishing business.

*　　*　　*

Annie had matured over the years, but still in good shape for her age. Her hair was thick, and still blonde. She had a clear, creamy complexion, with all the curves in the right places. She had a hearty laugh, the patience of Job, and the personality of a saint. It was January, 1980, Annie's fiftieth birthday.

*　　*　　*

Alpine Nursing Home called. Zora needed surgery on her colon. Annie and I took her to a hospital in Flint, Michigan. The doctor said it was critical that she have an operation, but he didn't think, at the age of 80, she would pull through. The doctor told me I would have to sign papers stating he would not be held responsible should Zora not live through the operation.

Over the years Zora had become a beloved member of our family. We looked forward to visiting her at the nursing home and taking her for a drive in the country. For all her ailments, she was always in good spirits and liked to joke and laugh. She had never been bedridden. I reluctantly signed the necessary medical release.

Zora surprised everyone. The third day after the operation she pulled out her tubes and needles and was up and around.

The doctors couldn't believe it. What a constitution Zora had. Annie and I took her back to the nursing home the following week.

*   *   *

Annie and Sarah were concerned about my continued loss of pep and energy. I made an appointment with Dr. Maltor, who scheduled me for a check up at the hospital. The doctor thought my ulcers were the underlying problem. I remained in the hospital for three weeks undergoing tests. Nothing abnormal showed up. I suggested to Dr. Maltor that I have a treadmill test before being released from the hospital.

I didn't pass the test. Dr. Maltor scheduled an angiogram for the following Monday. I went home from the hospital, with instructions from the doctor, to report to the hospital emergency at once if I experienced any chest pains.

That night I jokingly told Annie we better 'take one,' it might be our last.

"If it's the last, let's make it a good one."

"They're all great, some are just more energetic."

I was so-so in my lovemaking. Later I asked Annie, "Is my flame burning out?"

"No, Nick," laughingly she said, "You need to get away from work and Ben Hooper. A weekend at the Mature Adult Motel will shape you up."

"Goodnight, Annie, I love you."

*   *   *

I had difficulty falling asleep. My chest hurt, so I decided to get up, and sit in my easy chair for awhile. I faintly heard the sound of music outside, and looking out the window I saw Marcus walking down the road singing "Red River Valley." I tried to run after him, but my legs wouldn't move. I was drowning, and couldn't keep my head up out of the water. A hand reached down, and pulled me out of the murky deep. Marcus said, "Nick, you can't go yet." I wouldn't let go of his hand, and blurted out, "I've been searching all over for you, Marcus. We have so much to talk about."

Someone was chanting, and praying. I couldn't make out what a man in a black robe was saying to me. He was mumbling something about God in Heaven. A voice said, "Wake up." Slowly things came into focus. I was in a hospital room. Dr. Maltor held my wrist, taking my pulse. Annie sat in a chair next to the bed, crying.

Dr. Maltor said, "He made it, Annie. Don't stay too long, he isn't out of the woods yet."

I asked Annie, "Where's Marcus?"

"Marcus? Don't you remember, he was killed in the war, a long time ago."

"What am I doing in the hospital?"

"It's probably a good thing you can't remember. You had a heart attack. I rushed you to the hospital, and you underwent emergency heart surgery."

"I'm so confused. It's probably the medication. I must have been dreaming. We're so fortunate to have each other."

"Yes, we are. Rest awhile, and I'll come back tonight." Annie gave me a kiss, and left the room.

*   *   *

I was hospitalized for a month. When Dr. Maltor gave me a release, he said, "You've been to hell and back, I want you to stay home, and take it easy for awhile, maybe think about retiring. A Priest gave you last rites before your operation. We didn't think you were going to live. Not many people are lucky enough to get a second chance at life as you have."

*   *   *

Sarah was still in college. She came home every week to check on and visit with me. She was in the middle of exams at Michigan State when I had my heart attack and surgery. Sarah was with Annie at the hospital most of the time while I was there. She had to make up the exams. Her grades suffered a little, but she was a good student and could still graduate with honors.

* * *

Annie continued to work. Her office was just a short distance from our house. She came home every day during her lunch break to check on me. Annie worried about me constantly. She had a lot of time to think while I was in the hospital.

"If you retire, I will, too. Let's enjoy whatever time we have left together."

I had been home for two weeks and most of the drugs and medicine had been purged from my system. I was feeling good and becoming restless. When Annie came home at noon to check on me, I said, "You will not believe what I have for you."

"You are getting better."

That night in bed my desires continued.

Annie said, "We can't even think about it, can we?"

I persisted, "Turn around and back slowly against me."

She was burning up, but didn't want to hurt me. I slowly entered her soft warm body. Annie relaxed, gave a low moan and sighed with relief as she released pent up emotions and passion when the tension and temper flowed from me to her. It was November, 1982.

FORTY

I was slow recovering from the by-pass surgery. Dr. Maltor told me my ulcers would never cure permanently, they could flare up anytime, it was something I had to live with. None of the AC Managers, or my boss made any attempt to see me.

My medical retirement had been approved. I had a lot of time to think while staying home recovering. Thinking of what Ben Hooper had done to me, kept eating at me, and aggravated my ulcer problems.

I received a call from my attorney. The trial date for the lawsuit was on the docket. My attorney told me he would have to prove that my ulcers, and heart problems were caused by work related conditions, and Ben Hooper. AC would try to keep the lawsuit low key, but would spend a lot of money to keep from losing the suit.

I expected a big attendance at the trial. The only people in the court room were the Judge, court reporter, a GM attorney, Ben Hooper, me and my attorney. Annie sat by herself in the back row.

The Judge, a little man, could hardly be seen behind the high oak bench. The top of his head was bald, with dark hair fringing the back of his head, and down the sides of his face into a long, thick beard. His booming voice made up for his small stature.

The Judge called both attorneys to his bench, and briefed them on how he would conduct the trial. Most of the day was taken up by the attorneys presenting briefs, depositions, and position papers. The Judge announced that court was adjourned.

He wanted to look over the information presented to him. The hearing would reconvene at 9:00 A.M. the next day.

As Annie and I were leaving the courthouse, Ben Hooper stopped me, and said, "You're really stupid to think you can win this suit against, GM, Nick. It's going to cost you a lot of money to pay your attorney, and court expenses."

Annie commented on the way home, "What if Ben Hooper is right?"

*　　*　　*

The next day when the Judge called the court to order, GM's attorney requested that the suit be dropped. "The whole case is a matter of credibility, your Honor, Mr. Wilton's word against Mr. Hooper's."

The Judge said he wanted to question the plaintiff. "Mr. Wilton, approach the bench, take the oath, and sit in the witness chair." The Judge asked, "What do you have to say on your behalf?"

"Your honor, it's not my word against Ben Hooper's as his attorney stated, or that a personality conflict exists between Ben Hooper and myself. I have proof in this notebook that Ben Hooper was unscrupulous, and demeaning in the handling of employees under his supervision, and caused not only my health problems, but others as well."

GM's attorney jumped up, and started objecting. The Judge told him, "Objections overruled; sit down. I want to hear the rest of Mr. Wilton's testimony."

I went on, "I have appraisals regarding my performance, medical records pertaining to my health, and inter-office memos sent by Ben Hooper, regarding all the employees he demoted or fired, while working under his supervision. I have a list of the names of all Ben Hooper's victims. They are willing to testify on my behalf, should the need arise."

The Judge then asked Dr. Maltor to take the stand. He was

impressive as he stated, "Mr. Wilton has been a patient of mine for over twenty years. I have a copy of all his medical history, sick leaves, and hospital stays. I'm sure you will find them accurate and in order."

Dr. Maltor continued, "On one medical leave in particular, I have noted for your review, that the first time I hospitalized Mr. Wilton for bleeding ulcers, he stated on his medical form that his ulcer condition was work related. I agreed, signed the form, and sent a copy to the AC Medical Department. Mr. Wilton later told me that the plant doctor called him at home, and said as a member of management, he couldn't state his ulcer condition was work related. The AC doctor changed Mr. Wilton's medical form to read cause of his ulcer condition was unknown. He acted improperly in making changes on Mr. Wilton's medical papers."

The Judge thanked Dr. Maltor, and said, "I'll review the information, and records you have presented to this court."

*   *   *

The Judge then asked the GM attorney to give him copies of Mr. Wilton's personnel, and medical records to compare with the information, and records that Dr. Maltor presented to the court.

The GM attorney said, "Your Honor, all of Mr. Wilton's medical, and personnel records have somehow been misplaced, or lost. We do, however, request a copy of Dr. Maltor's, and Mr. Wilton's records for review."

The Judge sarcastically said, "I find it hard to believe that all of Mr. Wilton's AC records have accidentally been misplaced. Court is adjourned until 9:00 A.M. tomorrow."

Ben Hooper glared at me as I left the court room.

The next day, after the judge opened the court for arguments, he stated he found my testimony, and records most articulate, and interesting, and asked, "Does the attorney for GM have any written documents to refute Mr. Wilton's testimony?"

The attorney for GM stated, "Your Honor, after reviewing Mr. Wilton's documents, I feel a recess is in order so I may talk to the plaintiff's attorney."

The Judge agreed, and adjourned the court, to reconvene at 1:00 P.M.

Annie and I went to a nearby restaurant for lunch. "What is going on, Nick?"

"The GM attorney thought the trial would be dismissed due to lack of evidence. They didn't plan on me having any documentation of any kind. Personnel threw out my record file at work, not knowing that throughout the years I had accumulated my own file."

At 1:00 P.M. the Judge announced he would review the arguments presented to him, and send his decision to both parties in a few days. Court dismissed.

As we were leaving, I asked my attorney what chance we had of winning the suit. He replied, "Fifty/fifty."

A week later I received a phone call. My attorney said, "We won, Nick, we won! The award money will be paid over a period of years."

Annie and I toasted, and talked long into the night.

*   *   *

After winning the suit against AC, I made rapid progress recovering from my surgery. I scheduled an office visit to have a check up. Dr. Maltor complimented me on how well I was recovering.

"You recently had a very serious operation. Maybe you are feeling okay now, but your heart condition is never going to get better, it will only deteriorate. It's not a pleasant thing to talk about, but I've got to tell you that the heart attack caused the bottom half of your heart to quit functioning. It can never be repaired; the muscle is dead. Only the top part of your heart is working. Any strain caused by lifting, pushing, pulling, mental frustration, or stressful excitement, will cause another attack, that you might not survive. Do you understand, Nick?" I nodded. "Now I'm going to tell you about the surgery that saved your life.

"After you were put to sleep, an incision was made in your stomach to insert a tube that was hooked up to a blood pumping machine. Your rib cage was cut open with a saw, your heart removed from your body, and put on a table. Veins from your leg were removed, and stitched to the heart, by-passing clogged arteries. Two hours later your heart was put back in your body, stitched to the main arteries, jump started, and your ribs stapled and wired together. The operation took about four hours."

Dr. Maltor asked, "Are you all right, Nick?"

I was pale, and felt faint. "I'm okay, Doc, just a little weak."

"I'm not trying to frighten you, I just want you to know it can't be business as usual. You've got to make a drastic change in your lifestyle. I suggest you move to a warm, dry climate."

"How long do you think I've got?"

"Get your house in order, Nick. Most severely damaged heart patients live from three to five years."

It was early spring, my fifty eighth birthday.

FORTY ONE

I left the Doctor's office in deep thought. What would become of Annie if I had a fatal heart attack? An attractive woman in her early fifties, she could live another thirty years, and make a new life for herself. Maybe I shouldn't tell her what Dr. Maltor told me about my life expectancy. No, we had always been honest with each other, I would tell Annie the truth.

I procrastinated for nothing, she already knew.

"Dr. Maltor told me all that information after your operation, when you were still out of it, Nick. With your constitution, you will probably outlive me. Let's get on with our lives. We never planned on living in this big house when we retired, and certainly one of us would never live here alone. Let's sell the house, and go to a warm, dry climate as Dr. Maltor suggested."

"But, Annie, everything is happening so much sooner than we planned. We can't leave Zora, and what will Sarah do?"

Sarah answered part of the question that weekend. She came home to celebrate my birthday. Frank Getto was with her.

She announced, "Frank and I are engaged. We're getting married as soon as I graduate."

That night we toasted Sarah's engagement, and the decision to sell the house. We reflected on our happy marriage of thirty three years. The future looked uncertain, but we would live it one day at a time.

*   *   *

I had the house appraised and listed with a real estate agent. The appraisal value was four times the original cost of the house.

Due to the slow economy, the agent said it might be some time before the house sold.

Annie said, "I hope so, I have a lot of things to do before we can move."

We would both retire at the end of the summer.

"Nick, we have a lot of decisions to make soon. We can't leave Zora."

*   *   *

We decided to take a vacation, and fly to Arizona to visit the little town of Wickenburg, where Annie's brother and sister-in-law spent the winters. I was quite taken with the town, rich in Spanish and Western culture. The clean air, and warm, dry climate was ideal for heart patients.

We had stayed at a motel for a few days, when I received an urgent phone call from the Alpine Nursing Home. Zora had suffered a heart attack and died. We flew back to Michigan the next day.

That evening, at home, Annie and I sat quietly on the couch in the family room thinking about Zora, and the confined, solitary existence she had lived.

"Nick, Zora has found peace in death that she never had in life."

"I hope so, Annie."

The next day while I was at the Funeral Home making arrangements for her service, Annie phoned both our families to tell them about Zora's death. The Funeral Director told me they had no record of the pre-arranged funeral plans I had made with them years ago. I showed him the savings account book and the pre-arranged agreement I had kept in the lock box for thirteen years.

The Funeral Director stammered, sputtered and said, "I wonder what happened to our copy?"

The savings account, plus interest, was now a total of $1000.

The Funeral Director said he couldn't begin to put on a funeral for that amount, but he would have to honor the agreement.

When I arrived home I asked Annie what Joseph's reaction was to Zora's death?

"You know, as usual he is out of state, and can't make connections to be here, but he will drop us a line."

"I'm sure he will!"

* * *

A small group of people attended Zora's funeral; the nurses from Alpine, some of Annie's family, and a few of mine. Most of my brothers and sisters were noticeably absent. Annie wasn't surprised. "They seldom visited her when she was alive, Nick. I don't know why they would show up now."

It was a closed casket service. On a crisp, sunny day we laid Zora to rest in the grave next to Ziv's. She lived fifty-five of her eighty-five years in confinement. That evening we gave a toast in honor of Zora; a woman, the mother of eight children, who was denied the right to love, and know them.

"I hope God makes up for that injustice to Zora in heaven."

"I hope so, too."

* * *

The next morning, going through some of Zora's papers, I came across the letter from the State for her care over the years.

Annie said, "The balance of Zora's bill is almost $47,000. That's a lot of money. Let's talk to Judge Mackey, and see what he thinks our responsibility is for paying the bill."

Judge Mackey laughed, "Nick, why give all that money to the State politicians to piss away on some pet pork project. You're not obligated, and don't personally owe the state that money. You paid your dues by taking care of Zora the last twenty years."

He went on, "I'm retiring, Nick, and stepping down from the bench. I've spent as many years in this court room as Zora was institutionalized. The advice I just gave you is my last official court business. Take it. Zora will never know what a fine son she had, but I do."

I congratulated the Judge on his retirement, and thanked him for helping me throughout the years.

*　　*　　*

Adam and Syna came for a visit. They were anxious to get settled, start working, and earning some money.

I asked Adam, "When are you going to marry Syna?"

"We've been living together over ten years, Dad, a piece of paper won't make things any different now."

*　　*　　*

Annie and I told Sarah, that rather than spend a lot of money for a big wedding, we would give them some money, and have a small wedding at home. They could use the money to make a down payment on a home. No, they both insisted on a formal wedding. Frank had a large family, and wanted to invite their many friends and neighbors.

The wedding was held in the Catholic Church and the reception at the Fenton Yacht Club. Sarah and Frank left on their honeymoon trip the next day. Sarah cried as she kissed us goodbye.

Annie was tearful around the house all that weekend after Frank and Sarah left. Things were moving much too fast. "Nick, you always planned to retire when you were sixty two, not fifty eight years old. We still have a lot of things to do." It was March 24, 1984.

*　　*　　*

ILS

Byron High School was having an alumni banquet. We thought it would be fun to visit with our old school friends, some we had not seen since high school.

We were deep in thought as we drove to Byron to the reunion. It brought back fond memories of school days and the good times we both had attending Byron High. I wondered who would be there from my class. Most of them had married and left Byron a long time ago. Some had passed away. Would Finn Rider and Cassie be there?

The high school auditorium was full when we walked in. Jock waved to me and pointed to the chairs alongside theirs. We reminisced about the good times in grade school, high school, the Navy and our college years.

Jock asked me if I ever found out anything about my brother Marcus' death.

"No, it's bothered me all these years. I still don't know where or how he died."

"Nick, why don't you contact the Veterans organization. If you have some way of verifying Marcus' Army service, they should be able to find out something for you."

"The only records I have of Marcus is the postcard I received when he was taken prisoner by the Japanese, and the letter I received with the one hundred and sixty three dollar check for my share of his back pay."

*   *   *

During the meal and business meeting, I looked over the audience, there were not very many familiar faces. Annie chatted with Ginger. Their girls were all grown up, married and had children of their own.

Social hour, after the business meeting, was a time to mingle and renew acquaintances with old friends. The crowded auditorium made it difficult to see who was in attendance.

Jock said, "Nick, remember when you lived with the Perrys

and a certain girl you used to go with? She's here and asking about you."

I hadn't seen Dora Simpson since my marriage to Annie.

Suddenly a voice said, "There you are."

I looked at the face, "Dora?"

"You really haven't changed much, Nick."

I stammered, "You're looking well, Dora."

"I'm living in Atlanta, Georgia." She chatted awhile and as she left said, "I don't know about you and Annie, but I've been married to a wonderful man for over thirty years. We have three grown children. It's been good seeing you again."

Annie said, "I think Dora is telling you she recovered from her broken heart."

As we were leaving, I looked up and there stood Cassie.

"Annie, this is Cassie Cole-er-Rider. Cassie, this my wife, Annie. Where is Finn?"

"He didn't come with me. I can't get him to go anywhere. It hasn't been easy being married to a military man, but it's all I know."

Driving back home, I commented, "Dora looks good. I am glad she found happiness in her marriage. Cassie's years show. The military life has been hard on her, but it's what she wanted. Annie, I'm glad you came into my life when you did. I couldn't be happier."

FORTY TWO

Zora gone, and Sarah married, we had one more thing to take care of before we could enjoy our retirement. Brother Jay! We had to find him.

We took a ride to the little town where Jay used to live. Stopping at a roadside park just outside of town, to eat the lunch Annie packed, we were approached by a ragged, dirty old man. He asked if he could have something to eat. Annie gave him a sandwich and an apple.

As he left, I said, "Annie, that's the man we talked to the last time we were looking for Jay."

"Hey mister, do you know Jay Lewis?"

The old man turned around, and said, "Yeah, I know Jay, I ran into him last week. Let's see, I guess it was near Fenton. He's staying at the Senior Citizens apartment complex."

On the way to Fenton, I tried to think back to the last time I saw Jay. It had been at least twenty years ago, when I accidentally ran into him one day in Flint, after he came back from lumbering in the west. Annie had never met Jay, but through the pictures Mrs. Lewis gave us, and the conversations we had about him, she felt she knew him.

"You know, Nick, Jay must be at least fifty five years old if he's in a Senior Citizens complex."

*   *   *

I checked the list of names in the hallway of the seniors apartment. Jay Lewis was not on the listing. I went back to the car. "It looks like another dead end."

"Did you check with the building manager?"

"No, I guess it won't hurt, we're this far."

I turned around to go back. A construction worker asked if he could help with anything.

"I'm looking for a man who's supposed to live here. Jay Lewis, do you know him?"

The man said, "Jay Lewis, let's see, no he doesn't live in the apartment building. He stays out behind the apartments."

We walked around the back to a building under construction. The area was a mess, construction material littered the ground. A truck with a camper shell on the back was parked nearby. As I approached the truck, two dogs in the cab of the truck started growling and barking. "Annie, get back, those dogs are vicious." I opened the door of the building. It was dark inside.

"Anybody here?" A voice in the back said, "Who's there? You got my dogs all stirred up."

"I'm looking for Jay Lewis, is he here?" The voice answered back, "Yeah, I'm Jay Lewis."

A light came on, and a tall, thin, bald headed, white bearded man, with piercing blue eyes, stepped out.

"Jay, it's me, your brother."

He squinted at me, and said, "Alfred, is that you?"

"No, I'm not Alfred, I'm Nick, and this is my wife, Annie."

"Well, I'll be damned."

*   *   *

Jay took us to a back room. In the corner was an unmade daybed, an old wooden table, and dirty dishes piled high in the sink. An old wooden rocker, and a floor lamp without a shade, stood in the corner. He smoothed out the blankets on the daybed, and told us to sit down, stay awhile, we had a lot of catching up to do.

Jay started, "You know, Nick, I was a wild, mixed up kid

the last time you saw me. I'm okay now, a loner, I don't mix with other people much. Since we last met, I worked at GM Warehousing for quite awhile, then I drove a gravel truck for a long time."

Annie asked, "Jay, don't you get tired of staying here all alone?"

"No, I like it here, I have my dogs to keep me company. I drive my truck around the countryside, picking up cans and bottles to recycle. Sometimes I make forty or fifty dollars a week doing that."

"Jay, Mr. and Mrs. Lewis are dead."

"You know something funny, Nick? It still sticks in my mind. Mrs. Lewis once told me she wanted to adopt you, but the lady at the Whaley Orphanage wouldn't let you go. I never did know if it would have been you instead of me, or both of us. I guess it doesn't matter now, does it?"

*　　*　　*

I briefly brought him up to date on the doings, and where-abouts of the rest of our family. "Do you want me to let them know where you are, so they can contact you?"

"No, when I'm ready I'll find them. I don't want to go through the trauma again that I did the first time I met all you guys."

I asked Jay what I could do to help him.

"Nick, I don't need any help, and I wouldn't know how to live any other way. I get a pension from GM, and the Teamsters Union, and soon I will get Social Security. It doesn't cost me anything to live in my truck, and I get two hundred dollars a week as night watchman for this building complex. It is a temporary job, but not bad for an old bum, huh, Nick? To keep my mind active, I've got a hobby."

He reached under the bed, and pulled out a small black computer. "With this here gismo I can make stock market transactions twenty four hours a day. I'm doing okay. You are lucky to have a wife and your own family, Nick. I've never been married, or ever had a girlfriend. I've lived in a truck most of my adult years, it's the only life I've known."

Annie looked at Jay, and then the squalor in which he lived, "If you ever get sick, or need help of any kind, Jay, let us know. We can, and will help you."

I told Annie it was time to go. I gave Jay a handshake, and a hug. "We never were family, Jay, but we will always be brothers."

"Let's keep in touch, Nick."

*   *   *

We were deep in thought driving home. "I can't believe we finally found Jay. Your family is something else."

Annie and I talked long into the night about Jay.

I said, "It's hard to believe that he left the comforts of Lewis' home to live in the back of a truck. Scrounging around dumpsters, looking for cans, is no way to live. He isn't interested in getting with his family at all. At least we found him, and will be able to help him if he needs it. I'll let the family know about us finding Jay. I won't give details about how he's living." It was August, 1991.

FORTY THREE

Joseph's letter finally came. To my surprise the letter was short, and to the point, saying that had I delayed Zora's funeral, he would have been there to pay his last respects, but as with Ziv's funeral, he didn't have any say in the matter. Joseph didn't mention my heart surgery or pending retirement.

*　　*　　*

I decided the time had come. I had put off long enough cleaning out the safety deposit box at the bank. I took a brief-case with me, and dumped the contents of the box in it. I was a saver, and had kept all of the important papers we had accumulated over the years.

Annie helped me sort. She came across a reference letter that Mrs. Hardy sent me when I tried to enlist in the Air Force forty years ago.

"This is a trip back in time. Nick, you are a pack rat, I can't believe all the things you have saved over the years."

"If I hadn't been a saver, I would never have won the suit against Ben Hooper and GM."

The memories were thrown out, just the valuable papers kept. Zora's papers were next. I had all the receipts, and canceled checks over the years from her account. Everything went out except Zora and Ziv's wedding certificate, letters of guardianship, and the itemized bill from the State for Zora's care.

*　　*　　*

I opened the folder of dad's papers. His will, death certificate, Social Security, and Citizenship papers were all that needed to be saved. I gathered up the bills and receipts. No need to keep them any longer. I asked Annie to dump them in the wastebasket with the other throwaways. As she stuffed them in the basket, a small yellowed envelope fell on the floor. She picked it up to throw it back in the basket.

"Nick, look at this, it's a letter to you, and never been opened."

"It must have been stuck somewhere in that batch of papers I found in dad's house. There's no return address on it."

I opened the letter. It was dated January, 1965. It was from dad. I read aloud to Annie:

*   *   *

Neeck, I hav wanta talk a long time, So ashamed, couldn't. I go prison, lose famaly, respect. Bad time. I sorry what I put Sonya and famaly thru. Can't change life. You good sun, wife and gran kids only happy I know. Tanks Dad.

"Your dad wrote that letter before he died, I wonder why he didn't mail it?"

"He probably didn't want me to read it while he was alive."

I picked up the letter, and read it again. Dad spent five years in prison, and lived a lifetime of shame. This letter was his apology for what happened years ago.

*   *   *

We decided to pay a visit to my brothers and sisters, before we relocated to the West, and tell them about finding Jay.

We packed a few things, and the next day drove to Iowa, where Joseph had settled temporarily.

He was surprised, and delighted to have us honor him with a personal visit. Now in his middle sixties, bald and paunchy, his age was showing. Pearl, slim and trim, had slightly graying hair. Their married daughter lived in San Francisco. The oldest son and his wife lived in Kentucky. The youngest son was in the Navy.

*   *   *

"Nick, why don't you get all our brothers and sisters together for a family reunion? I tried, but nobody pays any attention. Me, being the eldest, I should get some respect."

I told Joseph that we had located Jay. He asked, "Jay who?"

"Your brother who was adopted."

"Well, I'll be, where did you find him? How is he?"

"Jay is retired, and living alone, and prefers to keep it that way."

"If that's the way he wants it, fine with me."

Joseph was quiet, thinking about the past. "Ziv sure ruined our family, didn't he, Nick?"

"That was a long time ago."

I thought about what Joseph had told me about dad a while back. All those years I didn't know the truth. I decided not to tell him about dad's letter. It wouldn't change anything now.

Joseph was still mumbling to himself, when Annie and I left to go home.

*   *   *

As we walked in the door, we could hear the phone ringing. Pearl had been busy talking to the family about Jay. They all wanted to know more. I promised we would visit soon. We decided to see Sonya next. Annie called to make arrangements.

Sonya had invited Hedy to be at her house when we arrived. Her husband was retired, but still puttered around the farm. Sonya painted as a hobby.

Hedy had retired on a small pension, and Social Security.

Her daughter never married, and visited her mother often. Her two sons, both married, lived nearby. She never talked about her oldest son, who died in an automobile accident.

Over the years we had little contact with Sonya, and Hedy quit corresponding with us after the reading of Ziv's will.

They wanted to know about Jay. I told them that he was in good health, lived alone, and never married. I didn't go into details about his lifestyle.

Hedy had never told her children about the family situation.

Sonya said, "Anytime Jay wants to see us, we will be here. He'll always be welcome."

I had to admire Sonya for managing to overcome the obstacles of her youth, and make a good life for herself.

Sonya and Hedy were teary eyed as Annie and I drove away.

*   *   *

We still had more travel time ahead of us. Brother Alfred and his wife, Reba, were the next to be visited. Alfred, in his middle fifties, had enough years to retire, but decided to wait until Reba could, too. Their son was married, worked at AC, and lived near Flint.

Alfred was most interested in the whereabouts and happenings of Jay Lewis. He had left his adopted family as Jay had, but didn't go through the trauma when meeting his brothers and sisters that Jay did.

I knew Alfred wouldn't be too disturbed by the way Jay lived, so I told him. He laughed to think that Jay could afford a home to live in, but preferred a truck. I gave him Jay's address, a mail box number in Grand Blanc, and the apartment complex, where he could be located. Alfred said he would check in on him soon.

Annie and I left, telling Alfred to go slowly with his contacts with Jay, give him time to sort things out.

*   *   *

Watt and his wife, Amy, had recently purchased a cottage near Lake Superior. They invited us to spend a weekend with them. Watt and I were the only brothers who had lived together as family, and throughout the years maintained a relationship. Whenever we got together, we talked about the past, when we three brothers lived with the Coopers in Fenton.

"We had a lot of good times, Nick, but also some sad ones. I have never forgotten about the Davis' getting murdered, and the time we found Juno, the tramp, in the barn."

I mentioned to Watt about finding Jay. I knew he wouldn't look him up. I was the only family member he had anything to do with. Watt did say that he always thought Jay was a weird guy, and best be left alone. I knew Watt wouldn't be interested in dad's letter. He thought it best to forget the past.

He remarked, "Think how things could have been, Nick. It's too late in life to ever be a family. The Wiltons are my adopted family."

FORTY FOUR

Help came unexpectedly about Marcus' death when a good friend and neighbor of mine came over to see me. He was carrying a computer print out sheet. "Nick, I thought you might be interested in this information. I know you have been trying for years to find out where and how your brother died. I think this will help you."

The print out was from the Internet. It was about a book titled "P.O.W. 83." The story was about American prisoners of war during World War II. The telephone number of the author of the book was on the printout. I placed a call to New York and talked to him. I told him about Marcus being a prisoner during the war.

He said, "I'll send you a copy of the book. I'm sure you will find some answers to what you are looking for."

*   *   *

In a few days the book, "P.O.W. 83" arrived. My excitement turned to dismay and sorrow as I read through the book. It was an actual account of a prisoner of war interned in the Japanese Prison Camp No.2 in the Philippine Islands during World War II.

One of the rescued prisoners from Camp No.2 was still alive and lived in Phoenix, Arizona.

My conversation with him, information from the book and contacts with a group of ex-prisoners of war and defenders of Bataan and Corregidor, helped answer my questions.

With bits and pieces of this information I managed to document Marcus' service records from the time he joined the United States Army until his death.

*   *   *

It is as follows:

Marcus joined the U.S. Army at Los Angeles on July 31, 1941. The S.S. President Cleveland took him to Manila in the Philippines. He was assigned to the 31st Infantry Regiment Company "G", located in Intramuros, Manila.

The Japanese bombed Pearl Harbor, Hawaii December 7th, 1941 and started a war with the United States.

On December 10th, the Japanese started the invasion of the Philippine Islands. Marcus fought the Japanese, with American and Filipino soldiers. The lack of food, potable water and medical supplies to treat the sick and wounded soldiers for beriberi, malaria, dysentery and dengue fever caused the collapse of Bataan. On April 9, 1942 General King surrendered Bataan and his troops to the Japanese.

Some of the defenders of Bataan refused to surrender and 2,000 of them escaped to Corregidor to continue the battle against the Japanese.

The Japanese forced 10,000 Americans and 62,000 Filipino soldiers who surrendered at Bataan, to walk a sixty mile death march from Mariveles to San Fernando. The weak and diseased were shot, bayoneted or beheaded as they fell. 16,000 died along the way. Then the POW's were crammed into box cars and taken by train to Camp O'Donnell.

The defenders of Bataan and Corregidor fought the Japanese on the island fortress of Corregidor until May 6th, 1942, when General Wainwright surrendered his troops to the Japanese. For the defenders of Bataan and Corregidor the war was over. It was the start of the life and death struggle for survival as prisoners of war in the Japanese prison camps.

*   *   *

Marcus was taken prisoner in a field hospital. He had dengue fever and was moved with other sick prisoners to Manila's Bilibid prison. The prison had twenty foot high walls, cement cell blocks and covered a city block.

The Japanese used Bilibid as a clearing house for a continuous movement of prisoners. Built to hold 500, at times there were as many as 6,000 prisoners quartered there.

The POW's were transported by train to Camp O'Donnell and Camp Cabanatuan in steel box cars with 150 men packed in each. The sliding door was locked with a chain, allowing an inch of slack for ventilation. Standing shoulder-to-shoulder in the heat and foul air without water to drink, many got motion sickness and lost consciousness.

Camp O'Donnell lacked nourishing food, had little water and no medical supplies. Some 9,000 American and 50,000 Filipinos were interned there. The living conditions were deplorable and unsanitary. Men lay in their own waste with flies circling around them. Through July, 1942, 1,508 Americans and over 20,000 Filipinos died by starvation, dehydration, disease and brutality from the Japanese guards.

Camp Cabanatuan was located about a 100 miles north of Manila. It consisted of camp sites #1, #2 and #3, several miles apart.

*   *   *

Marcus was located with other prisoners at Camp #2, housing 7,500 American Prisoners of War. There was an eight foot high barbed wire fence surrounding a 600 X 800 yard area. At even intervals were twenty foot high sentry towers.

Three American Prisoners of War tried to escape and were caught. Japanese guards pounded the three with their fists and guns, then hung them on fence posts. At the end of three days, one was buried alive, one had his head cut off and one was shot.

The POW's were divided in groups of ten and told that if one of the men escaped, the other nine would be shot.

Heavy rains made the camp a guagmire. Sanitary conditions were deplorable. Soon everyone had dysentery and many had malaria. Dead men lay on the streets. There weren't enough able men to carry the bodies to the cemetery and dig graves. From June through October, 1942, 2,339 Prisoners of War died.

*　　*　　*

Marcus survived the disease and death in camp #2. In November, 1942 he was put on the torturous train ride back to Bilibid prison, with 1,000 other prisoners, then by ship to be interned at Davao, Mindona, a Federal Philippine Prison that the Japanese had turned into a Prison of War Camp. The Davao penal colony was a barbed-wire enclosure surrounded by swamp and impenetrable jungle.

The Prisoners of War were forced to work as slave laborers under the scorching tropical sun. Some toiled in the fields and orchards, growing vegetables, bananas, papayas and corn. Others labored in the swamp paddies, growing rice and breaking up coral for the Lasang Airfield. A few helped raising chickens and gathering eggs. The Japanese officers and guards had vegetables, fruit, chicken and eggs to eat. The prisoners diet consisted of rice, fish and seaweed. Sickness, malnutrition and the lack of medical supplies caused the death of many prisoners daily.

*　　*　　*

General MacArthur returned to the Philippine Islands in the summer of 1944 with an army of over 200,000 men. The Japanese soldiers guarding the American prisoners at Camp Davao were soon isolated and cut off from their main army.

*　　*　　*

Marcus was hastily loaded aboard a Japanese hell ship, the Shinyo Maru, with other Prisoners of War to be shipped to Japan, after being in prison two years at Davao. The Japanese crammed the prisoners in the bottom hold of the ship, putting their troops, equipment and supplies on the top deck. The ship was not marked to identify her as carrying American Prisoners of War.

The prisoners were packed so tight in the ship's cargo hold, that they had to take turns sitting. There was no room to lay down. The intense tropical sun shining on the steel deck caused the heat in the cargo hold to be unbearable and suffocating. Once a day they were given eight spoonfuls of water and a dab of rice. With no ventilation, dehydration soon took its toll. As the prisoners passed out and died, they were hauled out of the hold by rope and thrown overboard.

*   *   *

The USS Paddle (SS-263), an American submarine on patrol, Captained by Lt. Commander Byron H. Nowell, torpedoed the Shinyo Maru, not knowing that below decks it carried a human cargo of 750 American Prisoners of War.

The Shinyo Maru exploded, and the ship slowly started to sink. Water rose in the hold. There were no life preservers for the prisoners. The ones that could swim treaded water. Those who couldn't went under and drowned. They panicked and tried to climb to the upper deck. Japanese guards threw hand grenades and fired machine guns at the prisoners, driving them back into the hold.

Life boats were lowered for the Japanese and they abandoned the ship. The prisoners that were still alive climbed out of the hold and jumped overboard into the oil covered water.

Lt. Hashimoto, the Commander of the Lasang Airfield, and Lt. Hosida, another Japanese officer, in the lifeboats with

Japanese soldiers, ordered American war prisoners shot as they struggled in the water.

*   *   *

A total of 667 American prisoners suffocated in the cargo hold, drowned, or were killed by Japanese gun fire. Philippine Guerrilla Forces helped the eighty-three American prisoners who managed to escape and swim to shore, contact the U.S. Navy. One died four days later. On September 29th, eighty two survivors were rescued and evacuated by the U.S. Submarine Narwahl, Captained by Lt. Commander Jack C. Tites. This rescue operation took place off Lily Point, Shindangan, Mindanao, Philippine Islands.

Of the thousands of American soldiers who surrendered, defenders of Bataan and Corregidor, few survived to return home at the end of the war.

*   *   *

Marcus was an eighteen year old boy when he was captured and imprisoned by the Japanese. After three years of torturous inhuman treatment he was killed at the age of twenty one, when the Shinyo Maru sank. It was September 7, 1944.

*   *   *

This brought to closure the nagging questions of Marcus' death almost 60 years ago. Now that I knew where and how Marcus died, it wasn't the memory of him I wanted to live with the rest of my life. I wrote a poem about him.

*   *   *

MARCUS SABITCH

It's been many years since last we met
    My big brother Marcus I'll never forget
We were separated at first, it was by fate
    Then briefly we lived together at a later date
It was during the Depression when living was rough
    We were just kids and the times made us tough
To Marcus living was fun, he did it a day at a time
    It didn't bother him that we didn't have a dime
I was the kid brother, he was older by three
    I tagged along with him, he looked after me
He taught me how to survive when I was seven
    And the next four years until I was eleven
Marcus had a way about him when things were sad
    Nick, he'd say, it's not really all that bad
On a bright clear night, with his head held high
    He howled like a dog at the moon in the sky
A cowboy he wanted to be and live in the West
    Red River Valley was the song he sang best
We said goodbye when he left years ago
    To join the United States Army, he was all aglow
He fought the Japs until the Philippines fell
    Then he was taken prisoner and lived through hell
Fate dealt him a hand, the worst that could be
    He was killed on a Japanese prison ship out to sea
The war was almost over, most of the fighting done
    Why did he have to die at the age of twenty one?
It's too late now and I'm sorry as can be
    Because I never told him how much he meant to me
His memory will always live in my mind
    My big brother Marcus truly was one of a kind

*   *   *

I wrote a letter to the Military Personnel Records Department in St. Louis, Missouri, along with a copy of this information, requesting that Marcus' Military Medals and a memorial headstone be sent to me.

*　　*　　*

It was some time before I received an answer to my letter. It came in the form of a bulging manila envelope. A letter inside addressed to me stated that a memorial headstone was being sent to the local funeral home. Also enclosed were many small boxes containing meals and ribbons, awarded posthumously to Private Marcus Sabitch. They included:

Bronze Star Medal, Purple Heart with two Oak Leaf Clusters, Prisoner of War Medal, Good Conduct Medal, Philippines Presidential Unit Citation, American Defense Service Medal, Asiatic-Pacific Campaign Medal with one Star, World War II Victory Medal, Philippine Defense Medal, Honorable Service World War II Button.

*　　*　　*

I received a phone call from the Village of Fenton, inviting Annie and me to attend a Memorial Day service honoring the boys from Fenton who were killed during World War II.

A small group of family members, the Fenton Council and Officers from the VFW Post were present for the service. A plaque had been mounted on a large stone with all the boys' names on it. It was surrounded by a stand of pine trees. One for each young man killed.

The Commander of the Post read a brief passage from the Bible, followed by a rifle salute and the playing of Taps. My eyes moistened as I thought of Marcus. His remains were not here, but memories of him would never be forgotten.

*   *   *

Annie and I lay in bed talking about my family and what the future had in store for us.

I dozed off to sleep. "Nick, Nick." It was Marcus calling me. I looked out the window, he was standing in the moonlit road waving to me. I ran outside, "Marcus, don't leave, we have to talk."

"It's time to let go of the past Nick, Ziv and Zora have sown the seeds of the future. Their children and grandchildren, will carry on for them. The Sabitch name may be gone, but will never be forgotten. Goodbye, Nick, I have to go."

Marcus turned and slowly walked away. I tried to run after him, but my legs would not move. I tried to whistle but could only mumble.

"Nick, Nick, wake up." It was Annie. "You were kicking and making strange noises. Are you all right?"

"Yes, Annie, everything is going to be fine now."

*   *   *

YES, THAT'S THE WAY IT WAS

EPILOGUE

It is time to update the Sabitch family and bring closure to Nick's story.

*   *   *

Annie and I still live happily in the Southwest. We are fortunate that our children and grandchildren are close enough to maintain regular contacts with them. We have many friends, old and new, that we share the past and present with.

Our son Adam is now 50 years old. He and Syna have been together over twenty five years. They have no children. Adam is writing a novel he hopes to have published soon.

Our daughter, Sarah, 40 years old, has a 15 year old son and a 14 year old daughter. Her husband died eight years ago of heart failure at the age of thirty three. Sarah has never re-married.

*   *   *

Joseph, 84 years old, lives with his wife Pearl. They have two sons, a daughter and two grandchildren. Joseph lives in the past with his military memories.

Sonya, 81 years old, twice divorced, has no children. She has a happy life with her husband Pitt.

Hedy, 80 years old, twice divorced, lives alone. She has two sons and one daughter. She is renewing contact with her sister and brothers.

Watt passed away at the age of 70, after having heart by-pass surgery. Surviving him are two daughters and three grand-children. His wife Amy, 74, is remarried.

Jay, 72, still lives the life of a recluse and homeless person. Never married, he remains a stranger to his sisters and brothers.

Alfred, 71, divorced once, is married to Reba. He has one son and one grandson. Alfred is interested in inventions and patents.

*   *   *

Clark and Ella Phipps are in their eighties. They still live in the same house in Fenton, Michigan, where Marcus, Watt and I lived with them back in the Depression years of the thirties.

*   *   *

Annie and I had lost contact with Bert Wilton many years ago. We finally located him in a Veteran's Hospital, being kept alive hooked up to an oxygen tank. His many years of heavy smoking and hard drinking caught up with Bert. He died a destitute man at the age of sixty nine. Surviving him are two sons.

*   *   *

Jock and I keep in contact with each other. Our friendship has lasted over fifty years.

*   *   *

It's March 25, 2001, my seventy fifth birthday.

IN RETROSPECT

I have no regrets, guilt, or owe apologies to anyone. Life has been good to me. I've been blessed with two fine children, and two special grandchildren, the best wife, friend and lover any man could ever ask for.

I couldn't just sit down and write this story, without delving into and reliving the past. Some memories were painful, some sad, most were happy ones. Life is lived day by day without much thought, it just happens. Years later, as I revisited my past, I had time to ponder, and think about it. I have a better understanding why and how my life happened as it did.

I feel fortunate to have lived with the many different families who took me into their homes. I learned something from each one, that helped shape and strengthen my character, so that I could cope with the challenges that life seems to offer.

I am thankful to my father and mother, who immigrated from Serbia and Albania, to this country, with little education, unable to speak English. They endured the hardships that confronted them, as young people in a strange new world, so their children could have a better life and world to live in. Tragically they were denied the right to raise their children, and enjoy their grandchildren.

I think about their sad, bleak, empty life, and wish that I could have helped them live a more fulfilling one. I grieve over the injustices that my mother endured throughout her lifetime. I hope she found peace in Heaven that she never had on earth.

I forgive my father for what he did that caused our family to break up. Did God forgive him?

I feel remorse to think I have lived such a long life, my brother Marcus, such a short one.

I am grateful that my sister Sonya managed to make a good life for herself, in spite of the physical and emotional suffering she endured at an early age.

I doubt that if I had my life to live over, I would change it much. I only wish that I had the patience and time to spend with my son and daughter, that in my retirement, I have with my grandchildren.

ABOUT THE AUTHOR

Ted grew up around the Flint, Michigan area. He served a two year hitch in the Navy during World War II. Ted is a graduate of Central Michigan University, with Bachelor and Masters Degrees. He retired from General Motors and lives with his wife, Jean, in Wickenburg, Arizona. They have two children and two grandchildren.

The people who immigrated to America in the eighteen and early nineteen hundreds were mostly from the European Countries.

Now a new generation of immigrants come from all over the world, Mexico, South America, Southeast Asia, China, Cambodia and Vietnam. They all share the same goal as my parents Ziv and Zora did. They want to live in America and make a better life for themselves and their children.